INNOCENTS IN THE ARCTIC

That which is bitter to endure
may be sweet to remember.

Thomas Fuller (1654–1734), *Gnomologia*

For Robert & Janet Forrest,

I hope you enjoy reading this little book as much as I enjoyed writing it.

With all very best wishes,

Colin Bull

30 July '05

INNOCENTS IN THE ARCTIC
THE 1951 SPITSBERGEN EXPEDITION

Colin Bull

Graphics by
Lionel Weiss

University of Alaska Press
Fairbanks

University of Alaska Press
P.O. Box 756240
Fairbanks, AK 99775-6240
fypress@uaf.edu
888-252-6657
www.uaf.edu/uapress

Library of Congress Cataloging-in-Publication Data
Bull, Colin.
Innocents in the Arctic : the 1951 Spitsbergen Expedition / Colin Bull.
   p. cm.
ISBN-10: 1-889963-73-9 (isbn 10: hardback : alk. paper)
ISBN-13: 978-1-889963-73-0 (isbn 13: hardback : alk. paper)
1. Bull, Colin—Travel—Norway—Spitsbergen Island. 2. Bull, Colin—
Travel—Arctic regions. 3. Spitsbergen Expedition (1951) 4. Spitsbergen
Island (Norway)—Discovery and exploration. I. Title.
   G780.B85 2005
   919.8'1—dc22
                            2004029229

Printed in the United States of America
∞ This paper meets the requirements of ANSI/NISO Z39.48–1992
(Permanence of Paper).

Cover design by Mike Kirk; oil painting of Colin Bull by Gillian Bull,
   March 2005
Cover photo by Lionel Weiss
Interior design and layout by Sue Mitchell

Dedicated to the memory of Ted Hitchcock

*Our fearless leader, who volunteered for the job
when we needed him most.*

*And who, by his boundless energy and profound
medical ability, became a foremost explorer
of the human brain.*

CONTENTS

DRAMATIS PERSONAE

Members

Box, Michael. B.Sc. (Civil Engineering), Birmingham, 1949. Civil engineer, surveyor, sled designer, tent tidier, and rock carrier. Twenty-three years old when expedition began.

Brace, Gordon. B.Sc. (Geology), Birmingham, 1951. Undergraduate student, geologist, letter-writer, and raconteur. Twenty-three years old.

Bull, Colin. B.Sc. (Physics), Birmingham, 1948; M.Sc. (Physics), Birmingham, 1950. Graduate student, geophysicist, cook, sleeping bag squeezer, and rock carrier. Twenty-three years old.

Cloke, Stan. B.A. (History), Birmingham, 1950; B.A. (History), Oxon, 1951. Unemployed boat driver, tenor, and wit. Twenty-three years old.

Dineley, Dave. B.Sc. (Geology), Birmingham, 1948; Ph.D. (Geology), Birmingham, 1951. Assistant lecturer, University College, Exeter. Geologist, cartoonist, and sandcastle builder. Twenty-three years old.

Garrett, Phil. B.Sc. (Geology), Birmingham, 1943. Lecturer, University of Birmingham, geologist, money counter, and tent tidier. Twenty-eight years old. The Old Man.

Gossage, David "Goss." B.Sc. (Geology), Birmingham, 1950. Graduate student, geologist, cook, poet, and tent untidier. Twenty-two years old.

Gray, Dennis. B.Sc. (Mining Engineering), Birmingham, 1949. Graduate student, surveyor, and rock carrier. Twenty-four years old.

Hitchcock, Ted. Penultimate-year medical student, Birmingham. Leader, medical officer, scrawler, and rock carrier. Twenty-two years old.

Weiss, Lionel. B.Sc. (Geology), Birmingham, 1949. Graduate student, geologist, slave driver, book writer, and duck shooter. Twenty-three years old.

Crew of *Miss Mabel*

Pirie, Roger. Lieutenant, Royal Navy (Retired). D.S.C. Skipper, tolerant, lovable martinet, pink gin aficionado.

Evans, Alan. Mate, yachtsman, spirit-raiser.

Firth, Alan. Engineer, hard-work model setter.

FOREWORD

The Svalbard Archipelago is a group of islands north of mainland Norway that cover altogether more than sixty thousand square kilometers, approximately one quarter the size of the United Kingdom. The islands extend to nearly 81 degrees north latitude, that is, to within one thousand kilometers of the North Pole. But an extended branch of the Gulf Stream causes the climate to be relatively mild for so far north. Many aspects of this mild climate are brought out in the present account!

The unresolved issue of sovereignty over Svalbard, or Spitsbergen as it was commonly called then, was a minor aspect of the Versailles peace negotiations after the First World War. Before that war several countries felt they had basis for claims, but it was still politically a no-man's-land. In 1920 it was agreed that Norway, which was the closest country and which had been neutral during the war, should have sovereignty. One important aspect of the Svalbard Treaty was the prohibition of military installations. Another was that citizens and companies of countries that are signatories to the Svalbard Treaty should all be treated equally, that they should have the same rights as Norwegians, both for access and to carry out businesses such as resource exploration and mining. Thus the Svalbard Treaty opened the area for many adventurous expeditions, including the one you can read about here.

The geology of Svalbard is magnificent and unique. The largest island alone, Spitsbergen, contains rocks from nearly all geologic periods and has therefore been studied by expeditions for more than a century. About three hundred million years ago, Svalbard was geologically connected to the landmasses of Norway, Scotland, and Greenland, it being the geological northward continuation of the Caledonide mountain belt. Since that time geological processes including polar migration, tectonic plate movements, renewed uplift, and tilting have led to the preservation and exposure of very long geologic sequences. Lack of vegetation also allows easy access to bedrock.

Svalbard explorations have been made by British university expeditions since the 1920s. British studies after the Second World War started in 1948 with a University of Cambridge party led by Brian Harland and the Birmingham University Expedition, the forerunner of the expedition described here.

The British expeditions could generally be characterized by fine academic work, great enthusiasm, high self-reliance, and very often a lack of funds! Sometimes they also lacked practical knowledge of how to behave most efficiently and comfortably under polar conditions. This probably led to many more exciting episodes than those experienced by the expeditions of seasoned veterans and consequently to better tales of (mis)adventure.

This particular expedition of 1951 was one that avoided serious mishaps, and it achieved much, considering its resources. It would not be fair to compare it with modern expeditions, which instead of backpacking have efficient transport, with helicopters and boats. But for its time, and together with the 1948 and 1954 expeditions to the area, it brought much new knowledge of a previously little-studied section of Spitsbergen. Stratigraphic sections studied and described by Dineley, Garrett, and Gossage (and by Weiss in 1948) still stand and are referred to in the modern geological literature.

The Svalbard Treaty led the Norwegian government to establish the forerunner of the Norsk Polarinstitutt (the Norwegian Polar Institute, NPI) in 1928. NPI was given the responsibility for mapping the archipelago and for organizing scientific investigations. In the early years the main research thrust was in geology, which was then the biggest science section in the institute. Today the institute is mainly concerned with research on climate, biodiversity, and environmental pollution. However, NPI still produces the topographic maps of Svalbard and has the responsibility for assigning official names. It is therefore a pleasure to note that NPI awarded two names on the west coast of Spitsbergen in recognition of the expedition described here, Dineleyelva (D. River) and Piriepynten (P. Point).

I have been the director of NPI since 1993, and my polar career in many ways has been shaped by the author of this book. I met Colin Bull in McMurdo in Antarctica in 1967, and a year later he enticed me to become a Ph.D. student at what was then called the Institute of Polar Studies (now Byrd Polar Research Center) at The Ohio State University in Columbus, Ohio, where he was director. From that base I studied the glaciers on Deception Island in the South Shetland Islands. Here volcanic eruptions had split two glaciers so that we could read the climate history by walking (and sometimes climbing) the freshly exposed ice surfaces. By comparing this record with others it was possible to get a grasp of global changes in glacier mass and of the relationship between climate changes in northern and southern hemispheres.

Colin and I had our most memorable expedition there in the Antarctic summer of 1971–1972, together with Valter Schytt, an eminent Swedish glaciologist who incidentally had also done much work on Svalbard. I believe it is entirely in keeping with the spirit of this book that I mention one paper from that cooperation which is still sometimes quoted, perhaps especially late in the evening, though rarely because of its scientific content. Because I was the principal investigator of the project, and Colin was my Ph.D. advisor, the sequence of authors naturally became myself, Colin, and Valter, so that the publication is widely known as the Orheim-Bull-Schytt paper.

Olav Orheim, Director
Norsk Polarinstitutt
Tromsø, Norway

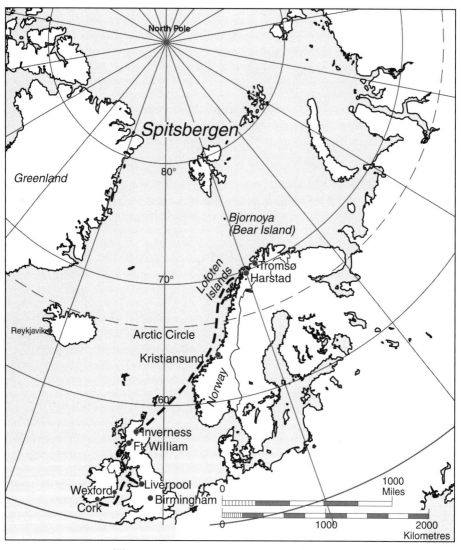

The arctic region around Spitsbergen (Svalbard).
Route of the Miss Mabel *is shown by the dashed line.*

PREFACE

*"For many are called, but few are chosen" (Matthew 22:14).
Or, as Stan said, "For many are cold, but few are frozen."*

*M*ore than fifty years ago, in 1951, ten young men from the University of Birmingham went on an expedition to Vestspitsbergen, an island in the archipelago of Svalbard, a glaciated and almost uninhabited land in the high Arctic. For nine of us it was our first experience in such a desolate place. We had some excellent scientific reasons for going and, by and large, we eventually accomplished much of what we set out to do. However, in our inexperience we made a large number of mistakes, which limited our time on that northern island and made the living conditions of some of us very miserable indeed. Two of the ten of us have since died, but the remaining members have kept in touch with each other over the years. I think that we have all realized how large an influence that first harsh experience has had on each of us.

In September 2001, five of the original ten, along with their spouses, met for a lengthy lunch and for a further set of conversations, which all started with either "Do you remember when…?" or "What do you think would have happened if…?" Then someone, I think it was Dave, suggested that we make a collection of our memories and try to convert them into a book. I was called on to be the compiler. Two of our members, Goss and Dave (you'll meet them soon), generated from their diaries excellent accounts of their parts in our adventures. Mike sent me not only a lengthy summary of his part but also a copy of his excellent diary of our time together. Jill Hitchcock, widow of Ted, our fearless leader, was kind enough to send me his diary. When we went to Sunny Svalbard, Ted had not yet qualified for his medical degrees, but it seems that he had already passed, with highest honors I imagine, all of his required courses in "Doctors' Handwriting," hence much of the diary is almost illegible. This is a great advantage to a compiler: when I wished the diary entry to read *"Porridge for breakfast. Sun shining,"* I could easily read that from the scrawl, even if Ted imagined that he had written *"Pemmican for breakfast. Raining hard."* Much later Jill told me of an event in Ted's final year as a medical student. He had written a very long paper, of which he was quite proud. He handed it to his instructor and a few days later it came back with a small scrawled note at the end, which Ted couldn't read. None of his colleagues could either, so Ted took the paper back to his instructor who, after close examination, said "Mr. Hitchcock, the note says 'I can't read your blasted handwriting.'" Obviously Ted was being trained very well indeed to be a successful physician.

Lionel, Stan, and Gordon all sent me valuable contributions. I've kept fairly closely to these written accounts; although, as you will see, I've taken some liberties. I hope they are all obvious: there never was a Number 8 (Birmingham, Inner Circle) bus plying along the south shore of St. Jonsfjorden.

I know I'm guilty of the sin of plagiarism in this compilation, when I've forgotten to put quotation marks around another person's utterances or writings. However, I'm also guilty of antiplagiarism, when for the sake of clarity in the story I have attributed to someone else some of my own thoughts or words.

When I was a young scientist a wise old friend said to me: "Take your work very seriously, but yourself not seriously at all." It does seem to me that even if one's work is extraordinarily important, like finding the elixir of world peace, one may quite rightly take the matter very seriously and still treat it rather light-heartedly. Our science wasn't that momentous, but it has helped to push back the frontiers of knowledge—or is it the frontiers of ignorance? It was serious work; however, it is difficult to be wholly serious when one is wringing cold rainwater from the sleeping bag in which one intends to spend the night or when one is wondering if one's marine transport will break in half and dump one in the North Sea.

Lionel, who is married to a fine Norwegian lady, Liv, chided me for the improper use of the English versions of the names of many of the features and places in this Norwegian land. I've used the Norwegian names wherever possible, but I have difficulty in calling Norway *Norge* or *Noreg* (the Nynorsk version of the same name). So, if I have offended Norwegians or anyone else in this way, please forgive me. It's all quite simple: *-fjell* means mountain, *-fjellet* indicates 'the mountain,' *-fjella* means 'the mountains'; *-breen* means 'the glacier'; *-neset* indicates 'the cape,' and so does *kapp*; *bukta* is 'the bay,' and you'll never guess *fjord*! Most of the other place names are quite obvious. The only place name I know where we haven't followed the rules is with *strandflat*, which really should be *strandflaten*.

I need to add another word, following the custom in many books: all of the people in this book are real and any resemblance to fictional characters (except Goss and Tweedledee, or was it Tweedledum?) is completely accidental. No, that's not entirely correct: Sven Larsen and Lars Svensen were real enough people, goodness knows, but their names are the product of Dave's fertile brain. And I'm responsible for naming Saul Yorn, the shopkeeper in Longyearbyen who would not let us pay for anything but would always brush away our attempts at payment with "It's all yours," or "S'all your'n." Fred Sæther, the proconsul in Tromsø, was a wonderful character and a great friend. We were distressed to hear, shortly afterwards, that he was no longer proconsul. In fact we, like Tromsø, were disconsolate.

I sent first drafts to the other expedition participants for their additions, corrections, and so on. Shortly after distributing the copies for corrections I accompanied my wife to Italy, where she participated in a painting workshop and I sat in the sun, drinking Chianti and editing the first draft. By good luck one of the painters, Kate Ely, is also a geologist and an editor. Her comments have been most useful. One of the copies of the first draft reached Anne Jones, a professional editor and reviewer. Her criticisms have proven to be very valuable. In particular I appreciated her very positive remarks on the "Aftermath" chapter, in which I had started to consider the role of the expedition in the development of our careers and why the adventure has remained so powerfully present with all of us. Anne's remarks stimulated me to go back to my colleagues with the repeated request for their contributions.

I handed copies of the first draft to some of my American friends and to my family to determine whether they would be able to understand my version, which I had tried to write in British English. The comments from Rick, Wayne, Ken, Marc, and Mirek and those from my wife, Gillian; offspring, Nick and Rebecca; their spouses, Janet and Brian; and from Gillian's (and Phil's) sister Sheila have all been very valuable. Several of them suggested that I change "flat" to "apartment" and so on. I refused to do so, feeling that they should make some attempt to become bilingual. However, as a concession, I should note that paraffin in English is kerosene in American.

Scads of people have been most kind, supportive, and cooperative in every way, so that what might have been a chore has been a genuine pleasure. Four people I delight in mentioning in particular. Firstly, there's Gillian, my wife, ever helpful and tolerant, even when I erupt into inexplicable laughter at the dinner table at the recollection of Commander Everitt being "tied down for the night" or Goss, sitting cross-legged in the leaking tent, generating soul-searching poetry! It was obvious from her brother Phil's generosity with the bar of chocolate that the family had good genes. Why, she has even painted the portrait of me, for the back flap of the dust-jacket, without charge! Then there are two ladies at the University of Alaska Press: Jennifer Collier, the executive editor, and Sue Mitchell, the copy editor and layout person. Both have been understanding, extremely competent—and good fun to work with. Through them I've learned all about the dreaded serial comma and what people do in Fairbanks when it is −50° F.

Thanks to the Norsk Polar Institutt for honoring members of the expedition with placenames and for permission to use the maps.

Most of all I am pleased to acknowledge the many contributions from Lionel. Fifty years ago I thought he was a prince of a fellow. I still do! He's taken all of the photographs from the expedition that any of us can find and cleaned them up, both physically and digitally, whatever that means. He has read meticulously through sundry versions of the manuscript, correcting many of my inexactitudes, altering Chapter Twelve to chapter 12, nineteen forty-eight to 1948, deleting commas, adding a few bon mots, and suggesting that I change many of the "whiches" to "thats," known in the trade as "which hunting." I've accepted about half of these suggestions—and that's a whole lot more than I would have done in nineteen fifty-one. I mean 1951.

GREAT EXPECTATIONS

*Y*ou just wait till we get to Svalbard. Then you'll see!" If Lionel had said this once it would have been fine, but he must have said it several times a day for more than six months. The other nine of us who were members of the Birmingham University Spitsbergen (Svalbard) Expedition of 1951 consequently became pretty desperate to reach Spitsbergen, if only so that we "could see," and have Lionel talk about something else.

In 1950 I shared a sordid flat at 56 Beaufort Road, just off the Hagley Road, with Lionel Weiss, who was a graduate student in the Department of Geology at the University of Birmingham. I was a graduate student in the physics department, working on my Ph.D. in solid-state physics: *The Nature of Electron Trapping States in Solid, Inorganic Phosphors*. That work kept me in a darkroom most of the time, even on nice sunny days. Lionel, in contrast, could do much of his work in the open air. I was envious. The university was and is one of the "red-brick" universities (in contrast with the ancient "Oxbridge" universities). It was established in 1900 and, when we were students, there were about five thousand students altogether. Nowadays there are nearly twenty-five thousand!

Our apartment was on the second floor of a 1920s house, about three miles west of the middle of Birmingham. Even when we had cleaned up from the farewell party for Derek, my predecessor in the apartment—replacing the broken toilet seat and recovering thirteen shillings and four pence on the empty beer bottles (two pence for each)—the hovel was still a seedy, grimy dump. The main room held two narrow beds, a gas fire into which we fed shillings at a great rate, and a naked light bulb hanging from the middle of the flaking ceiling. Also in the room were a wobbly paper-littered table, a bookshelf over the fireplace, with geology and physics textbooks as well as Gromich's *History of Art* and *A Treasury of Modern Verse*, a few pieces of Salvation Army furniture, a radio, a corner cupboard, and a clothes box. This box was unusual: it opened at the top and had a drawer at the bottom. Lionel and I were much the same in size. Our system was to throw all our dirty clothes into the top of the box and pull out the drawer at the bottom to find replacements. Thus the first one up in the morning was the better dressed. An article of clothing usually took about four months to pass from top to bottom, by which time it was comparatively odor free, if not clean. The system was known as the "fallow" system. A few bits of Derek's clothing turned up from time to time.

We shared a kitchen with Gwyn and Gwen, two young, vivacious Welsh ladies (we were never quite certain which was which), who lived in the next room. The landlady, Mrs. Tooms, and her detestable child lived somewhere downstairs. The child endeared himself to us by shaving Lionel's shaving brush; we fixed him by lacing the sausage roll I had made, and which he stole (we guessed he would), with phenolphthalein, a strong purgative...or did we just chat about doing that? Except at weekends, we spent very little time in the kitchen, and not much then, for we were both occupied for as many hours as we could stay awake with the research for our advanced degrees, and anyway, even six years after the end of the war, many foods were still very severely rationed, including bacon, cheese, butter, margarine, meat, sugar, eggs, and tea. One of my acquaintances was a butcher, with a shop a mile away, near Five Ways, and on some Saturday afternoons, in response to a postcard (we had no telephone), I walked or cycled there to collect half a pound of liver, which wasn't rationed but was difficult to find. Our chief protein source was fish, either as tinned fish (taken off rationing in May 1950) or in the form of fish and chips, which we ate perhaps four nights a week at the café on the

Colin Bull in north Wales, 1949.

Hagley Road that stayed open till 11 PM, half an hour after our usual time of quitting work at the university. Six months later some of us, but not all, were required to surrender our ration books when we left Britain to go to Spitsbergen. (I also had to give mine up when I left Britain again in July 1952 as a member of the two-year long British North Greenland Expedition, but food rationing had finally ended before I returned in July 1954).

Lionel had a 1928 vintage Austin Swallow seven-horsepower car, which managed fifty miles to the gallon. That was for petrol; it managed about the same fifty miles to the gallon for both oil and water. When we could afford the petrol we drove the three miles to the university. Otherwise I cycled or went on the Number One bus, the Moseley bus, which was distinguished from all the other city buses by the parlance of the bus conductresses. Whereas all the others said, "Hold tight!" the Moseley bus ladies said, "Hold tightly!" Lionel also had a .410 shotgun, which he fired only once in my presence. He hit the mouse scrabbling about among the shoes at the bottom of the cupboard, and my shoes didn't suffer too much. More interestingly, Lionel had been to Spitsbergen. While an undergraduate student in geology, he had been a member of the four-man Birmingham

University Spitsbergen Expedition of 1948. The other members were two other geology undergraduates, Brian Baker and Michael Holland (the leader), and a very newly qualified medical doctor, John Nunn.

Before the Second World War, small parties from many British universities, usually with a scientific bent, traveled to places in and around the Arctic, such as Labrador, West and East Greenland, Iceland, northern Norway, Sweden, and elsewhere. The archipelago of Svalbard (we often called it simply by its Dutch name, Spitsbergen or Spitzbergen, given to it by whalers in the seventeenth century) was a favored destination. One can reach a higher latitude there than anywhere else on Earth with comparative ease: the Gulf Stream and the North Atlantic Drift, carrying warmer water from the Caribbean, keep the shores of Svalbard relatively free of sea ice during the summer months. The Birmingham University Spitsbergen Expedition of 1948 was one of the first university expeditions to venture north after the Second World War.

The archipelago of Svalbard is centered at about 78 degrees north latitude, about midway between the northern tip of Norway and the North Pole. The biggest islands are Vestspitsbergen and the almost completely ice-covered Nordaustlandet (North East Land). Altogether the islands cover close to twenty-four thousand square miles, about three times the area of Wales or New Jersey; more than half of this is ice covered. The mountainous inland areas are mostly draped with glaciers and ice fields; towards the sea, especially on the west coast, there is a coastal plain (the *strandflat*) a few miles wide.

It seems likely that the Svalbard (meaning "Cold Coasts") mentioned in the Icelandic sagas from the late twelfth century was in fact Spitsbergen, but the more recent history of the area really starts with the islands' discovery, or rediscovery, by the Dutchmen Barents and van Heemskerck in 1596. Shortly after that, in 1610, the Muscovy Company started whaling—an industry that continued until about 1800, by which time the Greenland whales had been virtually exterminated. A few English whalers wintered ashore on Vestspitsbergen in 1630, and sometime in the late eighteenth century there were perhaps a thousand Dutchmen working in their processing plants during the summer. There is an account that in the hundred years from 1669, the Dutch caught more than fifty thousand whales west of Spitsbergen. No wonder that the whales were exterminated!

The archipelago of Svalbard. Base map courtesy Norsk Polar Institutt, licence 01/2005.

Russians started wintering ashore around 1715, hunting walrus, seal, fox, reindeer, and polar bear, but wintering did not become common until the end of the nineteenth century. Lionel thinks that the remnants of a hut, just a few rotting timbers, that they found on the coast south of Müllerneset (Cape Müller), may well have been a trappers' hut dating from an early time. The Norwegians even built a small hotel on the shores of Adventfjorden, or Advent Bay, in 1896, and for a few years a steamer took visitors to it from Norway.

Because of the islands' northern situation, they have long been used as a base for explorations towards the North Pole. Phipps in 1773, Franklin in 1818, and Sabine in 1823 all tried to sail northwards but were soon stopped by sea ice. Parry in 1827 tried sledging over the ice and with a great effort got as far as 82 degrees, 45 minutes north, a "farthest north" but still a long way from the pole. The Swedish balloonist Andrée started his brave but unsuccessful and fatal attempt to reach the North Pole by air, in 1896, from the northern part of Vestspitsbergen, as did Amundsen in 1925 in the first attempt to fly an aircraft there. That year he reached 88 degrees north, but two years later, with Nobile in the airship *Norge,* he made the first undisputed trip to the North Pole—although that was above the surface! A few days before Amundsen set out, Byrd claimed that he had flown his plane to the pole from the same spot in Spitsbergen, but that claim has been hotly contested.

Some of the earliest visitors must have been intrigued with what they could see inland from the coasts, because the first geologist, a Norwegian named Keilhau, went there quite early, in 1823. There were a dozen other expeditions, from Sweden, Norway, Britain, and Germany before 1896, when Sir Martin Conway and his party made the first crossing of West Spitsbergen. He wrote up his adventures in an excellent book, appropriately called *The First Crossing of Spitsbergen* (what else?), which I read sometime in the spring of 1951 and which made me anticipate our forthcoming adventure even more.

After Conway's effort the pace of exploration increased, especially the scientific, mainly geological, exploration. In 1906 and 1907, the Scottish explorer W. S. Bruce, supported by funds from the prince of Monaco, worked on Prins Karls Forlund, and the Norwegian Gunnar Isachsen and the geologist Adolph Hoel started their excellent mapping of the northern part of the coast of Vestspitsbergen, some of which we profited from in 1951.

British university expeditions to Svalbard started in the 1920s. George Binney from Oxford University organized the first three in 1921, 1923, and 1924, of increasing complexity, so that the third one, to North East Land, had two ships and a seaplane. Other expeditions followed in 1933 to Vestspitsbergen. In 1935–36, a ten-man team from Oxford wintered over in North East Land, and did first-rate work mapping the ice cap, maintaining a small station on the ice cap for ten months and doing some of the early ionospheric research at their main base. Richard Hamilton was one of the members and when, in 1952, he became the chief scientist of the British North Greenland Expedition, of which I was a member, I learned much more about the North East Land expedition than ever appeared in the written accounts.

However, most of the mapping and exploratory work in Vestspitsbergen has been done by members of the Norsk Polarinstitutt and its forerunner. Following from Isachsen's work early in the century were studies by Adolph Hoel, A. Staxrud, and many others. In 1929, Anders Orvin worked in the area around Kongsfjorden (King's Bay) and produced the first detailed paper on the stratigraphy and structure of the rocks, mainly Carboniferous, there. In 1936 he worked with Hoel in areas south of Isfjorden. In 1940, Orvin published his *Outline of the Geological History of Spitsbergen* (*Skrifter Svalbard og Ishavet* Nr. 78, 57 pages). He described the large lateral variations in the Carboniferous and Permian rocks in these two widely separated areas; when the two Birmingham expeditions of 1948 and 1951 went to Spitsbergen, Orvin's account was the fullest that we had.

Much of the exploration work in Vestspitsbergen over the years has been in coal geology, for coal mining was the only substantial industry until recently, when perhaps tourism has taken a more prominent place. Coal had been discovered first in 1610 but wasn't exploited till 1904, when Charles Longyear from Boston, Massachusetts, formed the Arctic Coal Company and started mining on the south side of Isfjorden, at the place that became known as Longyearbyen. Other countries—the English, Russians, Swedish, and Dutch—had mining operations for a few years but by the time we reached Spitsbergen, only the Norwegian and Russian operations still remained.

The annual production of coal by the Norwegians since 1916 has been as high as four hundred thousand tons, very valuable to Norway, which has no coal on its mainland. The Russians have probably produced about the same amount; they can take Spitsbergen coal to Murmansk and northern Russia more cheaply than they can transport it from the Ural Mountains. Much of the coal is from the Tertiary period, less than sixty-five million years old. Obviously the climate was very different then! During the Second World War the importance of the coal and of the location was keenly appreciated. In September 1941, the Allies evacuated all the Norwegians and Russians and destroyed all the power stations, radio stations, and all the stocks of coal to prevent their being used by the Germans, and they set fire to some of the mines. Secret meteorological stations were later set up by both sides, and in 1943 a large German fleet, with the battleships *Scharnhorst* and *Tirpitz*, destroyed Longyearbyen and the Russian bases and set fire to the mines again. The towns were all rebuilt after the war and all of the fires in the mines, except one, had been extinguished or had burned themselves out by the time we reached there. Interestingly, we met *Tirpitz* in 1951, in Tromsøfjorden, where she had been sunk in 1944.

Currently coal production is much reduced, largely because Norway can now use North Sea oil and gas for power, but the Norwegian government has a plan to triple its former coal production from Spitsbergen to 1.2 million tons annually, a plan that is being questioned by lots of environmental groups. The plan argues that that amount of Spitsbergen coal, which is hard and "clean," would satisfy the needs of much of northern Europe, so that they would no longer have to use the "dirtier" local coal.

The four-man party of 1948 worked near the mouth on the north side of Isfjorden, the longest fjord on the west coast. Their base, an old trapper's hut, was not far from the spot where George Wilkins landed in April 1928, after his record-breaking flight from Alaska. Around the fjord, mountains rise to three thousand feet or more and are heavily glaciated with numerous cirque*s, arêtes,* and valley glaciers. The coastal plain (probably a raised wave-cut platform) is up to four miles wide at the mouth of the fjord, on the north side. On the south side of the fjord are the main permanently inhabited parts of the Svalbard Archipelago. At the time of our expedition, in 1951, there were several operating coal-mining settlements, both Norwegian and Russian. The biggest was Longyearbyen, the "capital" of Svalbard. Since 1925, Svalbard has been administered as part of the Kingdom of Norway. As we found it, the population of Longyear City—as it is usually called in English—was about one thousand, nearly all men occupied with mining coal. Most of the mines are now closed.

The geology of much of Svalbard was known in outline, even before the First World War. Some of the best early work was done in 1909 and 1910 by the Norwegian expedition led by Gunnar Isachsen, mentioned above, which also named many of the topographic features. The oldest rocks, called the Hecla Hoek (or Hook) formation, crop out in the west of Vestspitsbergen and on the island called Prins Karls Forland off the coast; there are rocks in North East Land of about the same age. The formation consists of ancient sedimentary and igneous rocks then believed to be of Cambrian to Ordovician age, say 550 to 450 million years old. It is quite probable that the formation also includes older rocks of Precambrian age. All the Hecla Hoek rocks are metamorphosed, that is, they have been greatly changed by heat and pressure during strong earth movements, and no fossils have been found. Therefore, there was no paleontological evidence for their real age.

To the east the Hecla Hoek formation is overlain by sedimentary rocks of Carboniferous (say, 300 million years) age and younger, Permian. These rocks are not metamorphosed and contain abundant well-preserved fossils. These were the rocks on which work had been carried out in the 1930s by the Norwegians, in the areas near Kongsfjorden and south of Isfjorden. However, no one had looked at those between St. Jonsfjorden to the north and Isfjorden to the south.

In 1948, near Kapp Scania in the middle of an area that was considered to consist entirely of Hecla Hoek rocks, Brian Baker and the others were very excited to find fossils, which were later identified as Carboniferous. This discovery promised to shed new light on the structure and geological history of Vestspitsbergen. The expedition didn't have time to do much with the sedimentary rocks inland, but Lionel did work out an interpretation of the structure of the Carboniferous rocks in the area and their relationship to the Hecla Hoek (Weiss, 1958). The main work on the stratigraphy would have to wait for another expedition—which turned out to be ours of 1951. But they had found those fossils in the metamorphic rocks—perhaps!

You know how these geologists are—they can grow excited about almost any bit of rock—and Brian and Lionel had found something they thought very important. After graduating from the University of Birmingham in 1949, Brian joined the British Overseas Geological Survey to work in Kenya; Lionel stayed on at the university for graduate studies. Anyway, Lionel spent quite a lot of the limited time we were together at the flat telling me all about Spitsbergen.

∞

When I was a ten-year-old, I can remember reading *South With Scott* by Teddy Evans, second-in-command of Scott's last expedition in 1910–1913. I was most impressed with it and, with the usual unconstrained enthusiasm of a ten-year-old, I decided that when I grew up

Geologic time chart (simplified)

Era	Period	Events	Age
CENOZOIC (Mammals)	Quaternary	Recent deposits, including Dave's beach deposits. Periods of glaciation	0 to 1.6 million years
	Tertiary	Earth movements disturb all underlying rocks, including Hecla Hoek. Age of the Spitsbergen coal deposits	66 million
MESOZOIC (Reptiles)	Cretaceous Jurassic Triassic	Marine sediments deposited	245 million
PALEOZOIC (Invertebrates)	Permian Carboniferous Devonian Silurian Ordovician Cambrian	Phil, Goss, and Dave in 1954 mapped rocks of these ages. Caledonian Orogeny: Earth movements deform the Hecla Hoek. The Dreaded Hecla Hoek, Lionel's main worry. How did Carboniferous fossils get here?	570 million
PRECAMBRIAN			4 billion

I would try to become a polar explorer. Thirteen years later I still had the same ambition, and Spitsbergen sounded a good place to start.

Lionel wished to return to the area, for a whole bunch of geological reasons. Most simply he wanted to find out about those Carboniferous fossils at Kapp Scania: how and when they got to be apparently embedded among much older rocks. His first task was to find out the extent of the inlier of Carboniferous rocks by tracing the outcrop to the north. He also needed to establish the tectonic (structural) relations between the fossiliferous beds and the Hecla Hoek: were the fossiliferous beds an unconformable outlier of the main Carboniferous-Permian sequence exposed to the east, or were they a tectonic inlier faulted and folded into the older formation? Whichever of these possibilities turned out to be true, the fossils were clearly of no help in determining the age of the Hecla Hoek. On the other hand, tectonic inclusion of these younger rocks in the older Hecla Hoek revealed intense deformation of the region in post-Carboniferous times. When did this occur and how widespread were its effects? In addition, the evolution of the Hecla Hoek was important in understanding the geological evolution of countries bordering the North Atlantic. It was clearly, in part at least, of similar age to the very thick, often metamorphosed Lower Paleozoic rocks of Norway, Western Britain, Ireland, East Greenland, and even Newfoundland. All these formations were involved in the great mountain building episode of 400 to 450 million years ago known as the Caledonian Orogeny. In addition, we could do some valuable work on the sedimentary rocks inland, filling in the gap between the work that had been done on them to the north and to the south.

Obviously, the possible scientific returns from just one little geological discovery in 1948 could be very significant. Lionel was therefore working hard to put together another expedition, for the summer of 1951. I wanted to go too, but wondered what I could do to justify my inclusion. I couldn't even pretend to be a geologist. And I didn't want to be just a geologist's assistant: I pictured such people carrying great weights of food for the geologists up incredible slopes and then, as the food was eaten, replacing the weight with rock samples to be carried down. Initially, I volunteered to be "in charge of the weather," intending to set up a little meteorological station. However, as often happens, the unexpected changed this plan. While experimenting on the luminescence of silicates (the most abundant component of the earth's mantle), I'd had some ideas about the origin of the earth's magnetic field. There might be convection currents in the fluid metallic core of the earth, making "hot" and "less hot" spots at the boundary between the core and the nearly solid mantle of the earth. Then, if the mantle were a semiconductor, like the silicate phosphors I was working with, thermoelectric currents might be generated in the mantle by the voltage differences between the hot and cold spots. These currents would produce a magnetic field, observable at the surface of the earth. At a student meeting in 1950 I gave a little talk on the subject and, some time later, received an unexpected visit from Keith Runcorn, a senior member of the Department of Geophysics at the University of Cambridge. He also was interested in the origin of the earth's magnetic field. When he learned I was expecting to complete my Ph.D. degree in the next few months, he offered me a position in his laboratory in Cambridge. He forgot to mention (and I forgot to ask) whether there was any money attached to the job until long after I had accepted. None was. I also mentioned that I hoped to go to Spitsbergen for the summer of 1951 but except for the possible meteorological studies, I hadn't yet developed a work plan. Keith mentioned, very helpfully, that the Royal Society was contemplating establishing a scientific station somewhere "up there," perhaps as part of the International Geophysical Year (1957 and 1958). Keith suggested I might do something useful for them by recording the variations in the earth's magnetic field for a month or two.

That sounded just fine to me. Over the next month or so Keith and I arranged for me to borrow from the Greenwich Observatory a La Cour three-component magnetic recording apparatus, very delicate but not very sophisticated. I spent some time at the observatory Herstmonceux, learning how to operate the apparatus, thereby disrupting my plans to complete my dissertation before leaving for Spitsbergen. After this break-in period, I concluded I could indeed set up the apparatus in the field and gain some useful results. Partway through my training it occurred to me that there was just nothing to be gained by taking the apparatus to a spot on a remote shore of Svalbard and building a laboratory there. It would be much easier and more sensible to set up the apparatus in an unused shed in Longyearbyen, where someone could "hold the other end" when

I needed help. However, that didn't sound as interesting a scenario as the possibility of working in the field, so I kept the Longyearbyen thought to myself. In the end it made no difference: I had no opportunity to do any of the work.

Although I was not aware of it then, our venture to the Arctic was occurring during the beginning of the most significant period in the development of the earth sciences, the "earth sciences revolution." Keith Runcorn and his students were doing the first experiments on paleomagnetism, examining the fossil magnetic properties of sedimentary and igneous rocks. From the direction of the residual magnetic field in the rock they could determine the latitude of the rock when it acquired that magnetism. When I went to Cambridge after returning from Spitsbergen, I saw Keith's first map of the movement of the North Pole relative to the rocks of Britain and, shortly afterwards, his map of the movement of North America relative to northwest Europe and the opening of the North Atlantic Ocean. One of us calculated that the opening was continuing at about the same rate as a person's fingernails grow. Maurice Hill, another member of the Department of Geophysics at Cambridge, was just starting his oceanographic work that showed a significant rift along the middle of the North Atlantic Ridge, one of the first pointers towards the existence of "convection currents of material" in the earth's mantle that cause the movements of sections (plates) of the earth's crust: plate tectonics as the process soon came to be called. It was an exciting time, and I am pleased to have been able to see quite a lot of the developments over the next fifty years—and to make tiny contributions here and there.

The revolution has been a rapid one. In 1952, before I left on my next expedition, Maurice Hill asked me to give a lecture to his final year class in geology. I asked the class, about twenty students, how many of them believed in continental drift. One hand went up. In 1960 in Canberra, I asked a dozen of Dr. John Jaeger's students the same question, and this time all the hands were raised.

I can't recall that I ever officially signed on to the expedition, but when I did join, around Christmas of 1950, most of the other members had already done so. Lionel intended to take up a prestigious scholarship at the University of California, Berkeley, immediately after returning from Spitsbergen, so because most of a leader's responsibilities lie in clearing up everything afterwards, he declined that position. Phil didn't want the job; Dave and I would be leaving Birmingham. Fortunately Ted Hitchcock, a penultimate-year medical student, volunteered to be leader, and a very good one he turned out to be. Like everyone else, he was already saturated with work, studying for his exams and also, in his case, working the night shift at Cadbury's Bourneville factory, putting the chocolate on finger biscuits. Ted was a very keen mountain man, an avid and well-known member of Stoats, the university mountaineering club, and he liked organizing things. In the event of arguments among the geologists over the strategy of the expedition, his total lack of geological knowledge perhaps made him the ideal person to make wise and impartial decisions!

For Christmas 1950, I cycled the fifty-four miles to Kingsland, Herefordshire, where my parents lived and where I had grown up. Over the holidays Lionel, staying with his parents near London, produced a written plan that we later used mainly to help raise funds. He finished the text of *Proposed Birmingham University Expedition to West Spitsbergen in the Summer of Nineteen Fifty-One* on the third of January of 1951. I was allowed to proofread it in the apartment, after promising Lionel not to get ketchup on it. The core of the work in Spitsbergen was obviously the two parts of the geological exploration, the fossils in the Hecla Hoek and the stratigraphy of the sedimentary rocks inland. For that Lionel had already recruited three other geologists. One was another research student, David Gossage, always known as Goss, soft-spoken and full of fun. "Lugubrious" was the word I sometimes applied to Goss, although he always had a quiet grin, which reminded me of Tweedledum (or was it Tweedledee?). The second geologist was Phil Garrett, a lecturer in the geology department. Phil was then twenty-eight, a few years older than the rest of us, married, and with a young son. As he proudly pointed out, his presence added a little respectability to the group. Phil had begun his undergraduate work in oil engineering and mining geology at Birmingham early in the Second World War. After graduating he had served in the British Army in the U.K. and in Palestine, ending his service with the rank of captain in the Royal Engineers. Now he's my brother-in-law. The third geologist was David Dineley, called Dave to distinguish him from Goss! He had been a graduate student

David Gossage, always known as Goss, in Swanage in 1950.

David Dineley, Dave, on Miss Mabel, *1951.*

at Birmingham and after gaining his Ph.D. had accepted a position as assistant lecturer in geology at University College, Exeter. He joined us in early January but had teaching duties in Exeter until June. As well as being a very good scientist, he was, and is, an absolutely all-round great guy, with a wonderful sense of humor and appreciation of the ridiculous, which we were to encounter not infrequently.

Another recruit to Lionel's cause was Gordon Brace. He was, and is, an old friend of Lionel's since earliest secondary-school days. They had started their geology studies together, but Gordon's undergraduate work had been disrupted by two years of military service, so that he didn't gain his degree until 1951. After the expedition he changed direction and went into industry for a few years, later completing a master's degree in production engineering. He signed on to the expedition as assistant geologist and surveyor. He would have gone with the 1948 party, but couldn't afford it. He provided much amusement to us all, with his sometimes sardonic humor—and he could always be relied upon to help. I was listed as physicist and meteorologist.

Lionel had also written down in the plans: "Two surveyors, graduates from Civil Engineering or Mining Engineering Departments" but they, Michael Box and Dennis Gray, didn't come along until very much later and I didn't meet them until we were ready to leave. Their task in Spitsbergen was to make a broad plane-table survey of part of the west coastal region between the Eidembreen (Eidem Glacier) and St. Jonsfjorden, on which to plot the geology. Mike had graduated in civil engineering from Birmingham University in 1949. In 1951 he was a fully employed civil engineer, but he felt he was in a dead-end job and was happy to accept Gordon's invitation to join us. Dennis was a graduate student in mining engineering and had attended one of Phil's classes. He had been Ted's roommate in a student hall of residence and was also Gordon's friend. He too was a keen Stoat and, as we discovered to our pleasure, a very good engine mechanic. That brought our numbers up to nine.

Finally, Stan Cloke joined us. He was a friend of both Lionel and Gordon, a student of history, and a graduate of Birmingham University. At that time he was just completing a second degree in history at Oxford University. Previously he had been the informal harbormaster of the little fishing village of Mevagissey in Cornwall, and was a great hand with an outboard motor. Because our plans in the work area in Spitsbergen included exploring the coast by small boat, we thought Stan's expertise would be valuable. We invited him to join us just when he had "endured one of the worst experiences ever devised by man—taking Oxford history finals in five days. I jumped at the chance." Even without the boat and outboard engine he turned out to be a great member of the party. Not least of his assets was a fine repertoire of Cornish songs, several of which could even be sung in polite company.

The site for most of our planning was the large cluttered room in which the geology research students worked in crowded and convivial chaos. Sharing the research room floor were numerous mice, and from Goss I learned a new way to catch them. We needed only a long map tube—a cylindrical cardboard container an inch or two in diameter—into which any self-respecting but frightened mouse was happy to scamper. Hands clapped over the two ends and *voila*! I deny that I ever emptied the mouse-occupied tubes into the secretaries' room, just down the hall, occupied by Mrs. Mary Darley and Miss Iris Haynes.

These ladies were nice friendly people, always ready to help with typing, but as our lists grew longer we found our office chores becoming excessive even for lightning-fingered Iris. Owning a typewriter of my own, I became one of the expedition's scribes. Gordon was another: he maintained that he wrote 216 begging letters too. Most of the letters were similar in content. Our stereotype form letter ran something like this:

Dear Sir [if I could not discover the name of the managing director]:
I write on behalf of the Birmingham University Spitsbergen Expedition, 1951. This expedition intends to leave this country for Spitsbergen on about July 1 and to spend the following ten weeks conducting geological, geophysical, and topographic surveying in an area of Spitsbergen south of St. John's Fjord, as outlined in the accompanying brochure.

This expedition, like most other university enterprises of these days, finds itself greatly in need of public support. We find that for our work we shall need the following of your products:

Then followed a list that might be one item, such as an outboard motor, or, to Smedley's or Chivers, innumerable items, such as all the canned food we needed. The letter ended with some plaintive plea, such as:

> We hope you find yourself in a position to supply these items free, or at a greatly reduced charge. If you can, we assure you that not only will you be supporting a most worthwhile scientific activity, but also you will be helping ten young and irresponsible people to have a good time in an interesting place.
> I look forward to your reply,
> Yours sincerely,

Not really! The others in the room made me change that last paragraph to something reflecting credit on the company as well as on the expedition and the university.

I don't ever remember putting stamps on the envelopes. I expect Mrs. Darley took pity on us and sent them all through the university mail. The explanation for such generosity was the man who in spirit was the eleventh member of the expedition, our vice-chancellor (president, in U.S. terms), Sir Raymond Priestley. While still an undergraduate student in geology he had been a member of two famous Antarctic expeditions, those of Shackleton, 1907–1909, and of Scott, 1910–1913. He'd been the head of our university since 1938 and had been very helpful with the earlier expedition in 1948. Early in our preparations, Ted and Lionel had asked him if he would be our patron. Of course he had agreed. He not only gave us general encouragement but he was a most valuable asset as we approached potential donors. Over the years Sir Raymond made many profound remarks on polar exploration, of which three remain most clearly in my memory. Before we set off for Spitsbergen he offered us the consoling thought that if we had the misfortune to fall into a crevasse and be unable to escape, after a few years we would be much better preserved than those who had not fallen in. From his unique perspective, he compared Scott and Shackleton as leaders. For the control of a scientific enterprise Scott was the better man; for straightforward morale building and bonhomie he preferred Shackleton. Another time he described the winter of 1912, when he, two naval officers, and three petty officers were forced to live in an ice cave, with completely inadequate clothing and food (mainly seals). I'd read his account of this savage time in his book, *Antarctic Adventure*, and knew of the arrangement they had made in the cave. Sir Raymond was made an "honorary officer" and he and the other two officers occupied one side of the cave, with the three petty officers on the other side. They drew an imaginary wall down the center of the cave, with the rule that what was said on one side "could not be heard on the other." He explained the great value of the "wall" in allowing free and open discussion. I'd wondered how he felt in 1951 about this apparent class distinction and inequality.

Following Sir Raymond's patronage we gained other assistance from the university. The university finance officer, Mr. Summers, and his office staff were also very helpful, although they were somewhat suspicious of us at the beginning. Sir Raymond asked Phil, as the "established" member of the party, to keep an eye on financial matters.

The letters asking for goods met with a wonderful response. Obviously we concentrated on local companies. Typhoo Tea, HP Sauce, Cadbury's chocolate, Kunzle's, Masons, Quaker Oats, Harris Bacon, and Palethorpes (who made delicious canned sausages) all gave us goodies galore. We were given excellent boots, two pairs each, by Timpsons, all but Stan, our last recruit, who signed on too late for the Timpsons boots but came with a stout pair of hob-nailed boots, which served him well. Jaegers gave us socks and sweaters, and Horlicks gave us malted milk tablets galore. (A photo of Goss, standing on a Spitsbergen glacier, handing them out, appeared in the Horlicks house magazine, *The Gossiper*, along with a short account of the expedition.) They also gave us Milo, a delicious milky-malty hot drink ("a cup of Milo brings a Smilo!"). A well-known industrial manufacturer offered us all of the heavy-duty electrical switching equipment we needed. As hard as we tried, we were unable to think of any problems the offer could solve. Smedley's, bless them, offered us free all the fruit, jam, spaghetti, and everything else that we needed that came in cans. The one slight drawback, which we regarded as yet another challenge, was that none of the cans had a label.

Ted was in charge of medical supplies and the food rations for our fieldwork. He based the rations on those used by the Falkland Islands Dependencies Survey in Antarctica and the experience of the 1948 expedition. The basic daily ration was pemmican, four ounces; MacVita biscuits, five ounces; porridge (oatmeal), four ounces; chocolate, two ounces; cheese, one ounce; dried milk, one ounce; dried egg, one half ounce; margarine, two ounces; dried fruit, two ounces;

sugar, three ounces; barley sugars, one ounce; and tea and cocoa. The field ration was supposed to provide us with 5,500 calories each per day. Of course at the base camps we could also feast on sausages, Chivers' jam, and the contents of those Smedley's unmarked cans. As I mentioned earlier, many of these food items were still rationed in Britain at that time. We had to gain permission from the Ministry of Food to collect it and to promise to export all of it—no sampling!

Perhaps I should explain that pemmican is man's best attempt to stuff a whole cow into a one-pound can. Cooked beef is dehydrated and powdered, mixed with something like forty percent fat, and crammed into a can. When one is working hard and the weather is cold, pemmican, made into thick soup—usually called "hoosh"—is a marvelously satisfying and indeed delicious food, absolutely loaded with calories. However, I admit in civilized haunts it lacks something. Gordon and I once took pemmican to a meeting of the Stoats in North Wales, and it just didn't compare in smell with the bacon being cooked in the next tent. Some of this basic food we had to buy, including the pemmican. However, Bovril, who made it, gave us a favorable price. One company gave us an almost endless supply of toilet paper; another gave us pounds and pounds of Capstan pipe tobacco.

Ted received just as courteous and helpful responses from the medical and pharmaceutical people as we had from the general food and field equipment suppliers. Smith & Nephew gave us stacks of first-aid bandages, plasters, elastic bandages, forceps, scissors, even a set of Thomas splints and a first-aid booklet. Herts Pharmaceuticals gave us enough Nivea Shaving Cream to have allowed us all to shave daily; most of us didn't. Dr. Audrey Baker, of Vitamin Ltd., analyzed our proposed rations, suggested supplements, and gave us 1,000 tablets of Ribovel and 3,600 tablets of Pregnavite vitamin tablets, to our amusement and undoubtedly the benefit of our bodies. We were given bottles of Xylocaine, Uniprin (a kind of aspirin), Metaphen, and even a few bottles of the antibacterial liquid Dettol. The response to our begging letters was most gratifying. Ted developed a set of physiological experiments to test how our bodies reacted to hard work, low temperatures, and standard food rations; perhaps, for our comfort, it is fortunate he was unable to carry out many of them.

Money was our biggest problem. Early on Dave, Phil, and Ted had made a budget and reckoned our expenses would total something like twelve hundred pounds. Each of the members contributed fifty pounds initially—hard going, because all except three of us were students (and Phil and Dave didn't have much in the way of salary). My total income was 260 pounds a year! Later, when our costs had risen to sixteen hundred pounds, we each put in another twenty-five. We appealed to many organizations for funds: the Royal Society, the British Association, the Scott Polar Research Institute, and Shell Petroleum among them. The Charles Henry Foyle Trust gave us two hundred pounds through the good offices of Sir Raymond. The university also helped us balance the books at the end of the expedition, when our expenditures, including the bills for repairs and spare parts for our vessel and trivial sums for salary, had reached at least four thousand pounds (in those days, a formidably large sum). They ended up shelling out quite a lot of money. The Royal Geographical Society asked for more information on our scientific plans, and then responded to Dave's proposal to map the raised beaches and work on the littoral fauna with a grant of seventy-five pounds. That added a third geological purpose to our expedition's proposed work. Ted and Dave persuaded the lord mayor of Birmingham to open a public appeal for us, which produced twenty-five pounds, of which five came from his worship's own pocket.

We even placed a few advertisements in newspapers, including the London *Times*, offering any adventurous and well-heeled person inclusion in the expedition in return for a large contribution. The most memorable response came from an aging actor who went so far as to take Lionel to lunch at his London club.

By early June, just a few weeks before we were due to leave, we had still collected only a small part of what we believed to be minimum funding. The future looked dismal. At that time of year the classic English horse race, the Derby, is run. Well, none of us had ever had anything to do with horse racing or gambling, but we noticed that two of the horses running were named Expeditious and Arctic Prince—a good omen, we wondered? Hence I suggested we take all available funds, and bet on these two horses to win and to place. My companions were more cautious than I, even cowardly I thought, and wouldn't agree to my plan. However, after much argument, a compromise was reached: I was allowed to bet one pound each way on both horses. As far as I know Expeditious is still running around the track but to our great surprise the other horse, Arctic Prince, romped in at odds of forty to one. After I had said, "I told you so" many times to anyone who would listen, we collected the money from Mr. Bloggs, the bookmaker in Selly Oak, near the university. The most interesting part of this story came after the expedition was over when Phil was reviewing our accounts with Mr. Summers, the university finance officer. He was horrified to see in the receipts column an entry reading: "Winnings on horse race, £36 12s. 6d." He reprimanded Phil for such irresponsible behavior with public funds and cleared his conscience by changing the entry to "Contribution from Mr. Bloggs, Selly Oak, £36 12s. 6d."

After that several more small bundles of money arrived, so that it really did look as though we might afford to go. Several of us had much of the climbing gear we needed. We borrowed the rest. The vice-chancellor gave us his pair of skis from the Antarctic (he'd lent his Antarctic camera to the 1948 expedition). The skis were heavy and robust and were later converted into a sled. We made a big mistake (among many others) by believing a statement we read somewhere (perhaps in *Hints to Travelers*, the compendium produced by the Royal Geographical Society): "…it never rains inland in Spitsbergen." Therefore we decided to conserve funds by not buying flysheets for the Meade tents to be used by the inland people, but only for the coastal workers. Later, as we wrung the rainwater from our sleeping bags, a plaintive voice could often be heard, *sotto voce*, across the glacier, lamenting: "It never rains inland in Spitsbergen." We acquired a spare geology hammer or two, a couple of theodolites, plane tables, a surveyor's tape to measure a baseline, and a notebook. For me, we accumulated meteorological instruments from the Air Ministry, the magnetic recording gear, some quick-setting concrete to make a base on which to mount it, photographic chemicals to develop the records, and the wherewithal to make a tiny light-proof shelter to go around it.

Time was rushing by. It was already June and the stores and equipment for the expedition were being gathered by the diligent pursuit of discount schemes and by direct donations from that long list of friendly and supportive suppliers. But our transportation to Spitsbergen had stood for several months as a vital yet unsolved problem. The 1948 quartet had traveled as passengers on one of the coal ships that plied between the Norwegian ports and Longyearbyen. The governor, or *sysselmann*, of Svalbard had generously transported them from Longyearbyen to and from their field area in his cutter, the *Ole Ø. Lian*. From Longyearbyen they returned to Tromsø on a Norwegian navy corvette, *Nordkyn*, which, on reaching Tromsøfjorden, promptly ran aground and sank. But that's another story! With our much larger and heavier party in 1951, the colliers did not seem a viable option. A passenger, freight, and mail ship named *Lyngen* made an annual visit to Spitsbergen from Tromsø, but it sailed too late in the year to be of any use to us. A dozen other ideas came and went until it became clear to us that the only way we could reach Spitsbergen in time was to charter our own vessel.

We dithered with the idea of chartering a Scottish drifter, but couldn't afford it. Then we thought a Sunderland flying boat would fill our needs, but costs and leasing conditions proved impossibly expensive. The skipper of an aged schooner named *Nelly Bywater* offered her for charter with himself and his daughter as crew. An inspection of the vessel failed to raise any enthusiasm for acceptance of the offer, which was just as well: a year or so later she broke up in a gale in the English Channel and sank with all hands. And then, just as time was running out for us, someone spotted an advertisement announcing that a vessel named *Miss Mabel* was available for charter at a price we could afford.

ENTER *MISS MABEL*

*M*iss Mabel belonged to Commander Gordon Everitt, ex-Royal Navy, and was berthed in Cork, Eire. On June 19 Commander Everitt sent us a cable saying that she would be ready for charter in two or three weeks, for a fee of eight hundred pounds. We argued about the price but eventually reached an agreement. Without delay we invested in an air ticket for Lionel, who flew from Birmingham to Cork to talk with the owner and inspect the vessel. In retrospect we should have also sent along someone a little more experienced with seagoing craft, but when Lionel returned his report was favorable, though he did point out some of the disadvantages in her design.

Miss Mabel was a converted Second World War Fairmile motor launch, Type E, if you please, with a hard chine, though I doubt whether many of us knew what that meant or its implications for a seagoing boat. In fact it meant that the vessel had no real keel, and as we found out to our discomfort, she rolled like a telephone pole, even in a calm sea. Originally she had been fitted with high-powered aircraft engines and was used in the war to chase German U-boats and E-boats 'round the North Sea at speeds exceeding forty knots. By the time we chartered her, the high-performance engines had been replaced with three prosaic AEC (Associated Equipment

Company) diesel engines of the kind used in Centurion tanks and in metropolitan buses. In the advertisement it said that these gave the vessel a top speed of fifteen knots. She was about 115 tons displacement, 112 feet long, drawing six feet or so, fully laden. Her bow was strengthened with steel and concrete, for ramming German E-boats and submarines. We thought the bow might be useful in dealing with floating lumps of sea ice, but in the end its greatest boon to us was to prevent serious damage to the vessel when we hit lock gates and other obstacles, sometimes quite hard. With the hard chine I expect she would have ridden quite comfortably, planing on the surface at thirty knots or more. At ten knots or less she was a very poor sea boat. As one of us said after a few hours of very uncomfortable wallowing, "this damned thing would roll on wet grass." However, she could accommodate sixteen people and seemed to be just fine for taking ten enthusiastic but nautically challenged young people to Spitsbergen.

Even *we* were not so naive as to imagine that we could man the vessel by ourselves: we needed professional help. A few volunteers surfaced. Fortunately, from them we selected Roger Pirie. He was a laughing, heavy-set man in his late thirties with a firm hand, an ex-Royal Navy lieutenant and ideally suited to take charge of the vessel and all of us (he actually *owned* a sister ship of *Miss Mabel*). Alan Evans, an enthusiastic amateur yachtsman, joined him as mate. Alan lived on the Hebridean island of Raasay, where his telephone number was Raasay 1. When we assembled in Liverpool to load ourselves and all the food and equipment on board, we were able to persuade another Alan, Alan Firth, an engineer at AEC—the factory where *Miss Mabel's* replacement engines were made—to join us for a summer holiday. As Lionel commented afterwards: "That Alan knew his engines backwards. Without him we would have gone nowhere." Very soon they were known as Alan the Mate or Alan the Ropes, and Alan the Engines. Then, at the last minute, we acquired a passenger. Alf Roknes, a Norwegian engineering student at Birmingham University, asked if we could take him home for the summer, and since home for him was near Tromsø, in northern Norway, and since he was a good sailor who offered us twenty pounds, we agreed. He became known as Alf the Stowaway. We were way behind schedule but, somewhat to our surprise, we began to think that we might after

Alan "the Ropes" Evans and Roger "the Skipper" Pirie.

all be ready and able to set out on this extraordinarily foolhardy and character-forming adventure.

∞

June was filled, day and night, with lists, heaps of tents, stores, equipment, financial calculations (including some imaginative accounting of the kind nowadays in vogue among some CEOs of great corporations), typewriters, geological literature, and overflowing enthusiasm. In the case of Lionel and me it was filled also with last-minute efforts to complete our doctoral dissertations. I had missed the deadline to graduate in July; but if I ran all the way, I could submit the dissertation before we left. I could hold my defense of it sometime in the autumn and, if it were accepted, I could graduate at Christmas. And I could catch up on sleep when we got on board *Miss Mabel*. I made it, but Lionel missed his deadline and did not submit his dissertation until after he returned from the United States in 1953.

The advance guard (Goss and, a day later, Lionel) was to travel to Cork to collect *Miss Mabel* and sail her, with the help of Skipper Roger, to Liverpool, where the rest of us would meet her and embark all the stores, equipment, and personnel. On June 29, Goss, overloaded with a stuffed rucksack, map cases, and assorted hand luggage, took the train to Fishguard. At the quayside he met the Skipper, who carried even more paraphernalia, including impressive-looking nautical essentials such as a sextant, a chronometer, coast pilots, charts, navigation tables, binoculars, and sea boots.

Roger had been a submariner during the Second World War and had been decorated with a Distinguished Service Cross for bravery in his work. He had been very disappointed at having his prospects for a continuing career in the Navy cut short by what appeared to him to be a trivial defect in his eyesight, which forced his retirement. He and his wife were considering moving to Kenya to take up farming. He'd seen in our Arctic expedition an opportunity to go back for a few more months to the place he liked most to be, at sea.

Tight economy governed everything Goss and Roger did. So, as Goss reported afterwards: "We eschewed any sleeping accommodation" on the Fishguard-Cork ferry, *Innisfallen*. They slept in the saloon. Goss thought it a mild, calm, and beautiful night, as the ship whispered across the sea, leaving in its wake a long straight track of wonderfully bright greenish fluorescence. From the bar down below rose the sound of familiar Irish songs, sung by Irish men who worked in Britain, returning home for the holidays with their families.

Early the next day, a Saturday, they traveled up the winding estuary towards Cork harbor. The low hills, farms, fields, and cottages looked peaceful and welcoming in the sunshine. Soon the ferry tied up and they disembarked into a busy mass of people, motor vehicles, and horse-drawn traffic. Squeezing themselves and their copious baggage into a taxi, Goss and Roger reached the quay where lay *Miss Mabel*.

Goss wrote later:

> All seemed very informal: barriers, fences, and checkpoints were not in evidence. Someone had been sent by the owner to meet us, but he soon left and we were free to devise our own program. Once we were on board Roger penciled out a list of comestibles and sent me off to do the shopping. At that time, in the U.K., most meats and groceries were still rationed. I found it hard to believe that the shopkeepers here were going to part with such items as a pound of bacon, two pounds of sugar, a pound of butter and a couple of beef steaks for money alone. The shops were generously stocked; the foodstuffs were of good quality and the shopkeepers most helpful. Ration books were nowhere to be seen.

The anthracite-fired Aga stove in the galley of *Miss Mabel* was full of spent ashes, so they unearthed a Primus stove and were soon enjoying their first breakfast of bacon and eggs in the saloon, immediately aft of the galley, followed by coffee and cigarettes. Then came the preparation of lists of work that lay ahead.

> On looking round we soon saw the enormous amount of work needed to make the vessel habitable, let alone convincingly seaworthy. Since her conversion [changing the high-performance engines for three 100-horsepower AEC diesels, which now drove three screws] she had only been used for leisure purposes, in the Cork estuary and elsewhere close to shore. Her engines and vital systems such as bilge pumps, electricity, fuelling, and freshwater supply all needed to be thoroughly checked and repaired or upgraded where deficient. Rubbish had to be cleared out, small carpentry jobs to be done; some of the

woodwork had to be cleaned off and repaired, loose items to be made secure and so on. Most important, some sorts of sea-trials were going to be necessary before *Miss Mabel* could be realistically assessed and committed to the journey.

By mid-morning Roger and Goss were fully occupied, although delayed by curious passers by.

On July 1, Lionel arrived from Birmingham. He'd expected a very cold night on the ferry, sleeping on deck, but had roasted in the outer bag of his brand-new double sleeping bag. He woke at about 5 AM to find himself surrounded by envious, shivering, economy-conscious passengers who had spent the night crouching in various corners of the crowded deck.

Soon after his arrival Lionel found *Miss Mabel* tied up in the Innisfallen dock. After he had eaten a delicious breakfast of bacon and eggs, cooked by Goss, they cast off and, accompanied by Commander Everitt and two or three dozen assorted citizens of Cork, motored in the bright sunshine down the estuary. Roger tried a few bursts of speed, maybe reaching thirteen knots. Goss and Lionel, as the new

Miss Mabel *at the Victoria Docks, Liverpool.*

boys, tried to be unobtrusive but Goss couldn't resist the temptation to inspect the engine room. He found the noise and heat to be unbelievable and the atmosphere acrid, smoky, and oily. The center engine was not running. Roger, Commander Everitt, and a few others were working with the machinery and circuitry in the hot, stinking, lurching hell-hole, and Goss was disconcerted by the many frowns and head-shakings he saw during his few minutes down there.

For several days they all worked like Trojans on *Miss Mabel,* punctuated by a half day of lavish entertainment in Commander Everitt's substantial home. As an antisubmarine patrol craft, *Miss Mabel* was designed for high speed and maneuverability. Apart from the steel bow, the hull was built almost entirely of wood so that she was light, and her hard chine shape allowed her, when travelling at speed, to plane over the water surface. On the main deck only the wheelhouse remained as originally built. Immediately aft of that came the galley, perhaps eight by ten feet. Since I spent a lot of time there, almost as much as in my bunk, I'll tell you more about that place later. Then came the saloon, which had upholstered wall seating and a gimbal-mounted dining table seating six or eight people. Some of us found this table optically troublesome: tables are supposed to stay in the same place, even when they are on a pitching vessel. An inexperienced nautical diner amongst us found it disconcerting to see a plate

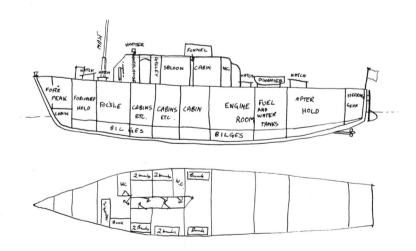

Lionel's sketch plan of Miss Mabel.

of soup accelerating towards him only to stop and accelerate away, without spilling a drop.

A door astern of the saloon led to a large cabin, with beds and a dressing table, known as the bridal suite. The Skipper appropriated that. Below decks, from stem to stern, were the forepeak, with the anchor chain locker and the forward hold. Aft of this lay the fo'c'sle, with three bunks and a "head." Aft of that, off a central companionway, were eight cabins, each with two bunks, four to port and four to starboard. Then came another head, which many of us insisted on calling a toilet to the amusement or annoyance of Roger, which one depending on how well our vessel, also called a boat, was progressing. Then came the main cabin, across the full width of the vessel, with bunks for three. The aft partition of this cabin was built around the exhaust ducts from the diesel engines, which rose vertically from the engine room below, through the bridal suite above, and into the structure that some of us called the funnel and others called the chimney.

Aft of the cabin, and reached through a hatch from the deck, lay the engine room, the fuel and water tanks (fully loaded she carried three thousand gallons of diesel fuel), and then the after-hold and the steering gear. Underneath were the bilges, which I never inspected.

The usual safety and small-craft marine equipment was minimal or nonexistent. There were two small dinghies, one of which sank when we launched it in Tromsø harbor, a Carey float, and a few buoys. There was no marine band radio transceiver, VHF ship-to-ship radiotelephone, or depth sounder. Loran, satellite navigation, and small craft radar did not exist at the time or was unavailable to us. Our piloting depended solely on binoculars, a compass, and a trailing log for dead reckoning—assisted by several pairs of sharp eyes. For celestial navigation we had Roger's sextant, a chronometer, and navigation tables.

On July 4, Roger declared that all was ready enough to sail for Liverpool. That evening *Miss Mabel*, with Roger, Lionel, Goss, and Commander Everitt on board, passed down the estuary towards St. George's Channel into a moderate swell, with a following wind. At an early stage, as soon as they decided they had left Irish territorial waters, a sealed case of John Jameson's very best ten-year-old Irish whisky was brought up from the bonded locker and enthusiastically broken open with a short crowbar. They duly spliced the main brace (whatever that means), ate some sort of evening meal, and allocated the forthcoming watches among the Skipper, Lionel, and Goss.

Goss's account of his first watch is a gem. He wrote:

I was faced with another completely unfamiliar task. Alone at the wheel, I was steering our vessel, mostly by compass, into the gathering darkness. The Skipper looked into the wheelhouse at intervals, usually with practical advice but once or twice with choice naval expletives when he sensed that my attention was wandering and we had moved off heading.

Some hours into the night I was relieved from watch by the Skipper and retired to the saloon for refreshment. Inside, the Commander had fallen asleep on one of the upholstered wall seats, no doubt benefiting from the soporific properties of a few shots of John Jameson's finest. The swell and spray were increasing and as Lionel and I watched the recumbent figure, we feared that he might soon be precipitated onto the deck. After some tentative but unsuccessful attempts to wake him up, we solved the difficulty by gently tying him down onto the seat, full length, using a few feet of line.

Of the departure, Lionel wrote:

The sea during the first part of the journey was quite rough. Goss and I staved off seasickness and stood watch, turn and turn about, almost continuously. Everitt entered a state of mild intoxication soon after passing the three-mile limit and opening of the duty free gin and whisky. He remained in much the same state until we reached Liverpool. Unfortunately he had set our course.

He was right: earlier, before Mr. Jameson had joined them, the Commander had charted the course to Liverpool. During the night they were able to work out their position from identifiable lighthouses on the Irish and, later, the Welsh coasts; but by first light a shift in the wind, haziness and cloud cover caused some uncertainty in their position. Undaunted they kept on the prescribed course, knowing that South Stack, the Holyhead lighthouse on Anglesey, would sooner or later appear to starboard. What could be simpler? Both Ireland and Wales were visible as distant bluish hills. All they had to do was drive on and turn right just after Holyhead.

About the voyage, Lionel wrote, "The center engine (one of three) had given up the ghost soon after leaving Cork; the port engine lost its cooling water soon afterwards. We ran for a while on one engine, only starting the port engine again when it had cooled sufficiently to introduce more water."

The Commander rose for breakfast, not too disturbed to find that he had been securely lashed down for his night's sleep. By dawn's early light, they enjoyed bacon and eggs and a pot of powerful coffee. After a round of Craven A cigarettes, they settled down to the serious task of establishing their position. Roger scanned the eastern horizon with binoculars but could not be certain that any of the distant buildings matched the guidebook's illustration of South Stack lighthouse. He read the ship's log, did some arithmetic to allow for tidal current, and concluded that South Stack would appear in an hour or two.

Again directly from Goss:

It was some time after midday when hazy bluish mountains were sighted ahead and another attempt was made with the guidebook and chart to identify them: Lleyn Peninsula of North Wales? Holyhead Mountain? Neither interpretation was convincing. But at that moment a medium-sized passenger ship traveling westwards would shortly cross our path, and someone had the bright idea of hailing this ship and simply asking where we were. A loudhailer was produced from a dirty locker below; the engines were revved down as we waited for the ship to draw close. Several times Roger yelled through the hailer, "Where do we lie?" No one appeared to answer the plaintive cry. The ship kept straight on course with its crew either oblivious to our presence, or possibly just too disdainful to react to anyone so inept as to be lost in such a simple situation. At any rate we gained no new knowledge and had not much choice but to carry on towards the high blue mountainous land straight ahead.

Some of Lionel's geological fieldwork for his dissertation had been done in Anglesey. He knew South Stack lighthouse. As *Miss Mabel* approached the land it became obvious to him that the approaching lighthouse was not South Stack. Instead it was a perfect match for the guidebook illustration of Chicken Rock light on the Isle of Man. They'd missed Anglesey completely and were fast approaching Castletown on the Isle of Man. Embarrassment all round! The owner had been aboard the whole time, had set the course and had only himself to blame. But the experience may have started him wondering how Roger would ever succeed in navigating his vessel into the Arctic and back.

They edged close in to Castletown, taking soundings until they found a good spot to drop anchor. They weighed anchor at 3:45 AM the next morning and set course for Liverpool in good weather. Low tide caused further delay, but early in the afternoon of July 5 they tied up in their allotted berth in South Victoria Dock.

Meanwhile, back in Birmingham, I spent Tuesday, July 2, sticking the last diagrams into the copies of my dissertation, which just *had* to be in the Registrar's Office by 5 PM. The next day I went to Liverpool. My usual mode of transportation in those days was by thumb, hitchhiking, but I had so much junk with me that I admitted defeat, caught a bus to the railway station, the train to Lime Street Station, Liverpool, and finally another bus to the docks.

But *Miss Mabel* wasn't there and no one knew anything about her. After many hours of frustratedly traipsing around and around unsavory docks, I gave up, had some fish and chips, and found myself accommodation in one of the university's halls of residence, Derby Hall. There I had a bath, in case I didn't have the chance of another in the next couple of months.

Dave and Ted had had a different sort of trip to Liverpool. Dave's dad was the regional manager of United Dairies and hence Dave had access to lorries. That morning he went on the bus to the university, where Ted had slept the night on Phil's camp bed in the geology lab, alongside our tons of cases and tents. The lorries arrived there at 9 AM along with Bill, the dairy carpenter, who nailed up, screwed down, and otherwise sealed the many cases that were still open. Alf, our passenger, arrived in a natty suit and with a huge suitcase. Among them all they completely loaded everything onto the two lorries. Alf declined to travel on top of the cases and opted to go by train.

Just as they were about to set off, Ted received a letter from Lionel (phoning was too expensive!) saying that they expected to sail from Cork late on Tuesday (it was then Tuesday morning) and hence would be a day late at least in reaching Liverpool. Dave had been able to borrow the lorries for one day only. They were already loaded and there were no arrangements to store their loads at the docks. What a mess!

Through the Mersey Tunnel, they drove down to the docks and phoned Bahr Behrend, the agents through whom we had booked *Miss Mabel* into the docks. They claimed to know nothing about us! Then followed a chaotic conversation, leading to a succession of visits to little cobwebby offices, to meet other people who'd never heard of us. Eventually the dock master, a Captain Woods (who also hadn't heard of us), arranged with Bahr Behrend for Dave and Ted to leave all the boxes in a shed belonging to British Coastal Seaways. With the help of Joe, the night watchman, Mr. Jones, the shed clerk, and the drivers, they unloaded everything. The lorries drove off back to Birmingham and at 5 PM Joe locked the shed. Phew—another disaster averted!

By chance Ted and Dave had also booked into Derby Hall. Before we left Derby Hall in the morning we booked in again for the next night in case *Miss Mabel* still hadn't turned up. The morning papers didn't say anything about a motor launch being lost at sea. Where was she? Ted and Dave went to the university where Ted took blood from them both, for blood cell counts, and then visited the geology department. I was nominally looking after the gear; in fact I was just talking to Joe. He asked me why we were going so far away, and I tried to tell him something of our aims, without too much success. He asked: "Couldn't you do all of that nearer 'ere?" He had a point. I don't know how it happened but in the early afternoon someone brought me a telegram that read "Weiss, Birmingham. Ship will arrive Wednesday evening or Thursday morning." Why Birmingham? Mike turned up. He'd come with his parents, by car.

The ship was certain to come the next day, wasn't she? Ted took Gordon and me off for blood tests; then we went down to the docks, where Alf and Dennis, looking very neat and tidy, were waiting. Dennis had spent the night aboard an Irish vessel. After lunchtime over at Bahr Behrend's office we learned *Miss Mabel* was in, and we rushed over to the dock to greet her and see our fate. *Miss Mabel* looked a very small untidy ship. Lionel and Goss looked very nautical in plimsolls (they've been turned first into "tennis shoes" and later into "sneakers" over the passing years), dirty trousers, sweaters, and a few days' growth of beard. They and the Skipper welcomed all the rest of us most warmly. Commander Everitt, still half-tight, disappeared into the mists.

CRUISING IN
HOME WATERS

iss Mabel, tucked into berth thirty-one of Victoria Docks,
did look a small and fragile ship. One of us confided to
another that he was sure the ship would never get us to Spitsbergen
and that he loathed it already. I thought about those huge icebergs
in Ponting's photographs from *Scott's Last Expedition.* Gordon was
much more enthusiastic. He wrote: "She is wonderful, 112 feet long
and 104 tons, tidy lines and a remarkable amount of accommodation.
I telephoned Stan Cloke to tell him there was room for him."

Our reunions on the dockside and in the saloon, accompanied
by the remnants of the opened whisky bottle, consisted of hearing
the amusing but ominous reminiscences of the voyage from Cork to
Liverpool—via the Isle of Man. However, those talking sessions were
very short, for there was so much to do. Nonetheless, we did have
the opportunity to make the acquaintance of another crew member,
Alan Evans. Alan was our mate, a nonscientist, as he said, but a key
member of the group. About forty years of age, he was the oldest of
us. He was a small, fit, and wiry dark-haired man with an outdoor
background—mountaineering, sailing, scouting, canoeing, and the
like. He had recently retired from a job in Edinburgh, in charge of
the apprentices at the Ferranti works. He was a bachelor and had
set up home on the Isle of Raasay, east of Skye. His attachment to

sea and mountains, and his considerable knowledge of both, were obvious. He took pride in telling us that a letter addressed simply as *Evans, Raasay* and posted anywhere in the U.K. would be certain to reach him.

Dave and several others cleared out the dirt and rubbish from the aft hold and then he had to ask Joe, the night watchman, for something, whereupon the following conversation ensued:

Joe: "Where are you going with all this stuff?"(indicating our pile of crates and boxes).

Dave: "We're going to Spitsbergen."

Joe: "Where's that?"

Dave: "Oh, it's in the Arctic, about six hundred miles from the North Pole."

Joe: "What do you want to go there for? Won't it be cold? It's bad enough here. I hope that thing (pointing his smoking Woodbine at *Miss Mabel*) will get you there. Anyway, what sort of tub is it?"

Dave: "It's a Fairmile oceangoing launch. Used to chase German E-boats."

Joe: "It doesn't look much to go that far in. Anyway it's Irish. Didn't know they chased E-boats."

Dave: "No, Joe. It *used* to be a Royal Navy vessel, but its owner lives in Cork, hence the ensign. We think it'll do us nicely, and we'll be back before the summer is out."

Joe: "Oh yerss. Going for one of them Festival of Britain larks are you? I thought you was all up to something nutty. Charity is it? A bet? Odds is you'll all come back with chilblains and frostbite, or one of them Eskimo diseases or the like."

Dave (anxious to put our case properly): "No, no. We're going to do some geology. We're from the University of Birmingham. Nothing to do with the Festival of Britain. It's scientific work."

Joe sniffed and flicked his fag end into the dock. "What good'll it do? I reckon you lot are just out for a bit of a lark. Who's payin', anyway?"

Dave was just about to tell him, but Joe wandered off in search of a liquid lunch. That seemed a good idea, so Dave retreated to the saloon.

Goss and I cooked dinner and I inspected the kitchen, I mean, galley. There was a sink, with hot and cold running water, a draining board, two small cupboards, lots of hooks for unused pots and mugs, and a hatch through which food could be passed into the saloon and dirty dishes the other way. The Aga stove still needed another cleaning, maybe two or three. There were a couple of small tables on which Goss and I, as volunteer cooks, might be expected to produce a continuing stream of delicacies, but only after we had scrubbed them down a few more times. The whole galley seemed awfully hot and smelly—squalid was the word that sprang to mind. And there was barely room for the two of us to work.

The Skipper needed a lot of spares and nautical gear for the ship. Dave's first trip to the ships' chandlers to borrow items was unsuccessful, but later we did better. The people who were competent with engines, the Skipper, Dennis, Alf, Dave, Lionel, and a few others, worked in semidarkness on the engines, taking the cylinder heads off two of them, to replace broken valve springs and guides—a sweltering job. According to Lionel, "the worst mishap occurred when Roger dropped one of the oil injectors into the bilge, to be lost for all time. Phil and I spent several fruitless hours scouring Liverpool for a replacement. We were unsuccessful and eventually had to sail without it."

Our charter agreement said that we must engage an engineer for the voyage. We desperately needed one! Ted had made contact with the Liverpool Marine Engineering College, and one prospective engineer came to see us on Friday evening and turned us down next morning. Now what? However, all was not lost: the dock policeman stood guard while we pinched coke for the galley stove.

On Saturday we took on fresh water and diesel fuel. Mr. Firth, the representative from Esso, arrived to see what other help he could offer. Mr. Firth produced his brother, Alan, an AEC-trained engineer, a pleasant young man of twenty-two, who agreed to come with us for the princely wage of thirty pounds per month. He needed a passport, but agreed to obtain one and to meet *Miss Mabel* in Ft. William on the coming Tuesday. Another panic over!

Some visitors arrived. Roger explained to them that Spitsbergen was in the Mediterranean and that we were Spanish gunrunners. At one stage Stan, on the dock, was pushing *Miss Mabel* away from the dock's side with a boat hook. Dave asked him: "Shouldn't you be on the boat when you are pushing off?" Gordon, showing the visitors how to climb aboard, fell with a sickening crash onto the deck and subsequently was on light duties, like shopping for bread, booze, and the like. Gordon indeed did quite a lot of shopping. He telephoned an order for anthracite. He bought nails (one shilling and two pence, that is 1s. 2d.), a mop for us in the galley (11d.), an enamel bowl (2s. 3d.), milk, bread, and spuds (8s. 5d.), and plugs (£1), a V-belt (£2 8s.), and a feeler gauge (3s. 10d.) for the engine room. Other items included rhubarb (1s. 3d.) and a chain (11s. 6d.). Later the anthracite arrived. We loaded it into the ski box, emptied of its skis, which Ted, Gordon, and I then lashed to the deck forward of the wheelhouse.

Phil; his wife, Joy; and Goss's fiancée, Chris, turned up on Saturday, along with some of Phil's electrical engineering friends, including a chap named Henry Giffin, who lived in Liverpool and had been Phil's fellow officer in Palestine. He promptly sent the dynamo for overhaul. Stan Cloke, the last expedition member, arrived with very little gear, not even a passport (he had arranged for it to be sent to the harbormaster at Inverness). Meanwhile Joy and Chris were busy in the kitchen. No, I mean galley. I was concerned that they might set a precedent for good food that would produce heightened expectations, which Goss and I might have trouble in meeting. The press, including the *Sunday Dispatch*, came and insisted on photographing the raising of the expedition flag, a geology hammer rampant on a field of the colors of the university, made for us at Fentham Road School in Erdington, Birmingham. At her stern *Miss Mabel* flew the

The expedition flag, a geology hammer on the colors of Birmingham University, at Miss Mabel's *masthead.*

Irish Republic ensign. Stan made a politically incorrect dire prediction that, sailing under that flag, "We would all Come to No Good." Joe, the watchman, had been hovering around, so Dave gave him a present of several bottles and ten shillings. Before turning in for the night, a few of us put all our empty bottles in a long line on the quay, brown and white bottles alternating, with a note to Joe telling him to keep the considerable deposit from their return.

Some of us were in our bunks from about 1 until 3:30 AM, when the roar of engines and gentle movement of the ship woke us. Roger, Dennis, and Alf had finished "fixing" the engines; only the port engine still smoked like a volcano. It took us half an hour to leave the lock and to move into the river. Lionel, Stan, and Dave were handling ropes and heaving lines. There was rope all over the place. Dawn broke with a fantastic translucent purple, which slowly changed into a brilliant pink, over Liverpool. Everyone was on deck, excited. We were off at last! Lionel wrote, "Finally, we are underway at 3:30 AM on Sunday morning, July 7. As dawn broke enthusiastically beautiful over Liverpool, we left Joy Garrett waving farewell from the quay."

Heading down the Mersey estuary, we were delighted to see Liverpool's skyline silhouetted against the reddening sunrise. Our departure was many days later than we had planned, but spirits were high as, for the first time, the expedition began to move as a single unit.

∞

Goss and I fired up the galley stove with paper, firewood, and anthracite. We opened three of the Smedley's unmarked cans. Two were spaghetti in tomato sauce and one was strawberry jam, so for breakfast we had tea and coffee, porridge, spaghetti-on-toast (a first for everyone who dared to eat it) and more toast, with the strawberry jam. Ted and Roger set the watches: Red Watch: Lionel, Dave, and Stan; Blue Watch: Phil, Mike, and Gordon; White watch: Ted (medical officer or Kwell anti-seasickness tablet dispenser), Colin and Goss (cooks), and Dennis and Alf (engineers).

Goss noted in his diary:

By mid-day we were by the Isle of Man, putting up clouds of seabirds as we rounded the southern tip, the Calf of Man, and by midafternoon both Ireland and Scotland were clearly visible. There was work to do for everybody for most of the day, sorting out equipment, personal clothing, maps, literature, and finding suitable lockers, shelves, and boxes into which all this gear could be stowed. The demands on the galley staff were incessant, although there were fleeting moments when a cook could enjoy a cigarette or a cup of strong tea, laced with a splash of rum. Refuse disposal from the galley was extremely simple: the doorway to starboard looked out straight over the sea, with only two feet of deck and a skimpy-looking handrail between. All empty cans, bottles, and other rubbish could be tossed out directly from the sink, stovetop, or work surface. This made for a degree of cleanliness, and the sea birds were usually close by and ready to pick up any edible items. I will add that although on one or two occasions one or another of our colleagues managed to pass through our line of fire at an inauspicious moment, we never deliberately targeted anyone, not even the Skipper.

Reading Goss's commentary again, fifty-plus years after the event, I am horrified at how environmentally irresponsible we were!

We passed quite close to the Isle of Man, with clouds hanging over the island. The sea roughed up a bit and Gordon, the helmsman, found that the wheel kicked and bucked. He and Mike decided that Ailsa Craig appeared like a gigantic bun drifting in the sea.

Gordon wrote: "By mid-day some were seasick. I was mercifully spared. Mike and I were on the wheel from 1200 to 1600 and from 2000 to 2400 hours. We also prepared the evening meal—a cheese omelet that didn't [turn out to be edible], and boiled potatoes. Ugh!" Phil was the worst affected by *mal de mer*. The swell was slight, moderate, or appreciable, depending on the recorder. Phil took to his bunk and stayed there until we reached Ft. William and the peace of the Caledonian Canal. Nevertheless, as we settled into the watch system most people had a chance for a few hours at the wheel to find out how *Miss Mabel* handled. For most of us this was a new and very pleasing experience, far more impressive than any test ride in a vehicle on land. Mike took to his bunk with the after-effects of a smallpox vaccination. When a visiting Ted asked what ailed him, Mike murmured, "smallpox," whereupon "Ted shot out of the cabin so fast that it was a wonder he did not fall overboard."

The Caledonian Canal.

The voyage to Ft. William was uneventful. Lionel wrote: "The beauty of the scenery from the Mull of Kintyre to Ft. William was the most memorable part." The engines ran well and the weather was fine so the first day and night at sea went smoothly. Phil had his dinner in his bunk and we reckoned he could not have had better service on a luxury liner. There was a short period of special interest as *Miss Mabel* passed through the narrow straits between Islay and Jura, where tidal currents can be hazardous. Two lights, one steady and one flashing, marked the entrance to the narrows. At one point the Coast Guard saw us moving towards dangerously shallow rocks and fired a red flare for our benefit. Tidal disturbances at the northern tip of Jura are sometimes spectacular and dangerous. These are the Whirlpools of Corryvreckan, which we did well to avoid.

In the early morning we sighted Oban and at about 9 AM Ft. William appeared against the impressive backdrop of Ben Nevis. Layers of mist lay at several levels and patches of snow were visible close to the summit. Just beyond Ft. William we came to the sea-lock of Corpach, the beginning of the Caledonian Canal. A basin follows this, and a mile or so further on, a flight of ten locks, known as Neptune's Staircase. Moving up the flight took time and a good deal of hard physical labor by the deck hands, assisting the lock keepers, all of whom seemed to own Cairn terriers. Nowadays people only have to press buttons to open or close the electrically operated gates; but in 1951 the gates were old and stiff, and they and the sluices all had to be operated by hand. Ted and Gordon took a bus into Ft. William, as they said, "to forage," and then walked back the three miles or so in time for lunch.

At the top of Neptune's Staircase Alan Firth joined us. Our expedition was now complete. *Miss Mabel* made steady progress along the canal and through Loch Lochy, always through beautiful scenery. Over the measured mile the Skipper decided we should see what *Miss Mabel* could do, so he revved up the engines. He seemed to be satisfied with the results. We tied up for the night at a lock not far from Laggan. Ted spent some time sketching the scene. Over drinks in the evening there was much praise for the great engineer Thomas Telford, who designed the canal and its twenty-seven locks and supervised its construction, 130 years earlier. There was also nearly as much praise for Skipper Roger Pirie, who had shown appropriate appreciation of the potential of his crew to bring us through the canal, rather than the cheaper way, through the tumultuous seas around Cape Wrath.

Unfortunately, our sprint over the measured mile had overheated the exhaust ducts from the engines. During our evening meal a small fire broke out in the ornamental woodwork around the funnel. Reaction was rapid and effective. A bucket was dropped over the side on a line and several gallons of water were poured down the chimney, I mean funnel. After the hissing, smoke, and smell had died down, Mike displaced that incident in our immediate thoughts: while fixing the gangplank, he fell overboard, wearing a heavy duffel jacket. Stan, in a most solicitous fashion, asked Mike if he could swim. "Yes," Mike said. "Fair enough," said Stan, going about his business. Mike swam easily to the canal bank and was soon back aboard, wet and cold but unhurt. He looked like a drowned sheep, but laughed it off. Both incidents made us all a little more careful. We knew that in the weeks ahead conditions would be much more hazardous and such events could become extremely serious.

Earlier, we had seen rabbits playing on the banks of the canal so, notwithstanding the serious diversion of the fire, Lionel, Phil, and Dave, armed with shotguns and cartridges, made up an evening shooting party. In less than an hour they returned with six good-sized rabbits, which Alan Evans and I skinned and gutted. Lunchtime rabbit stew the next day was delicious, in fact one of the best meals I ever made.

Goss wrote:

Roger ordered an early start for the next morning to give us a chance of reaching Inverness before the close of business hours. Breakfast was to be served before casting off, so just before first light I found myself busy with the galley stove, which was soon up to full working heat. Before rousing the deck hands Roger thought that a shot of Spey Royal whisky would do wonders for both himself and the cook. To the singing of the kettle and the first whiff of frying bacon we enjoyed our glass of scotch with an incomparable dawn scene emerging around us: heather-covered hills and mountains, copses of pines and wisps of gray mist becoming clearer in the growing silent dawn. I have never since that time found better circumstances in which to enjoy a glass of Scotland's most famous product.

Loch Oich was followed by another section of Telford's canal and then, after passing Ft. Augustus, *Miss Mabel* entered Loch Ness. The town appeared like a typical alpine village, with a square-towered church and thickly wooded hills beyond—a wonderful, sleepy little town. In addition to the rabbit stew, Goss and I had made an experimental dish that we called "cheesey-eggy-oatey," which we cooked in a hand basin. Unfortunately the unsophisticated deck hands declined more than one helping each and the remainder went over the side to feed the Loch Ness Monster. She didn't appear and has not been seen since. There are some who attribute the disappearance of Nessy to our cheesey-eggy-oatey. More serious was the lively discussion among the geologists, including a now-vertical Phil, of the geological setting of the whole long, straight furrow of the Great Glen. It is one of the great dislocations of the earth's crust in Britain, with strong evidence of lateral movements of at least sixty miles over hundreds of millions of years.

We had to tie up to allow a small merchantman, *Marshlea* of Cardiff, to overtake us and then we descended the four locks in the late afternoon and tied up at the Inverness quay. A lovely Scottish voice called out: "Is that *Miss Mabel*? Have you a Mr. Cloke aboard?" Stan's passport had arrived. In the evening a few people went into the town to phone home.

Approaching Inverness.

For most of the next day we remained tied up at the same spot. There was refuelling to be done, restocking of comestibles (I found it quite exciting, ordering food for fourteen people) and a host of spare parts to be found. Alf and a couple of others dismantled the cupboard that had been the scene of the fire on the previous day and stuffed it with asbestos wool. Sheets of asbestos were fitted between the exhaust ducts and all the adjacent fire-prone woodwork.

These operations took much longer than planned and we weren't ready to put to sea again until the early evening of July 12. The Skipper and Alan the Mate settled our canal fees with the local office. *Miss Mabel* had to anchor in the Firth while the bilges were being pumped. Dennis, Lionel, and Dave took the dinghy and outboard motor to collect the mail, some more spare parts, including oil injectors from Esso, and, at the Skipper's insistence, a heavier anchor, five hundred pounds or so. This anchor later proved to be a good investment. On their way back the outboard motor died, the dinghy leaked abominably, and it rained. They rowed all the way back, arriving tired, wet, and cross. When the Skipper investigated the stuff that the boys had brought back from the Esso store he found that instead of oil injectors and filters they had been given two packs of Esso notepaper. Dave was the hero who volunteered to empty the bilges and clean the bilge pumps—a filthy job, as they were full of rubbish and foul, rusty, and oily water (but the oil injector, dropped there in Liverpool, didn't turn up). Since we had to have the injectors replaced, Roger returned *Miss Mabel* to the quay and Dennis walked up to the Esso store to return the notepaper and collect the injectors.

Goss said he felt better now that the bilge pumps were clean (I did not feel any emotion at all about them) and the asbestos sheeting was in place, but the breakdown of the outboard motor didn't bode well. Lionel was becoming concerned, very concerned, at the length of time we were taking. We were treating this all as a holiday, he thought, while there were scads of work to be done in Spitsbergen. Nevertheless we were now ready for the next leg, across the North Sea to Norway. Roger and a few of us plotted our course to Kristiansund. Enthusiasm in all of us reached a new high. Except for Mike, who was unwell with a chill from his unscheduled dip in the canal, or maybe the smallpox inoculation, we were all fit and eager to go.

To Tromsø,
Paris of the North

*W*e sailed from Inverness into the Moray Firth in improving
weather, at 5 PM on July 12. It had taken us nearly a week to
get this far from Liverpool—the easy part of the trip. A seal surfaced
to make sure we really did leave; shortly after, swells began to roll in
under *Miss Mabel*, followed by the gradual disappearance below of
expedition members. Phil was the first to succumb, not to reappear
until we reached Norway. Others followed him, including me. Dave
and Gordon volunteered to take my place in the galley, and for a
couple of days the meals were unadventurous. Asked by Goss to collect the wherewithal to make supper, Gordon reported:

> The small dinghy, in which we stow sacks of vegetables, under the
> tarpaulin, was full of water. The Skipper and I lifted the sacks to
> the deck to dry and bored a hole in the bottom of the dinghy to let
> the water out. We must remember to stop up the hole with a cork
> before the dinghy is required for its legitimate purpose. I had the
> most severe seasickness test yet, when I helped Goss prepare the meat
> for the evening stew.

Goss wrote, "Galley work was light although much more difficult
and hazardous when our vessel was rolling violently, as she had been
since leaving the Moray Firth. In a way the work was self-regulating,

from the cook's viewpoint; rough seas meant tricky and dangerous galley operations, but the same rough seas ensured there would be fewer mouths to feed." Ted, ever the medical scientist, managed to write a few words in his diary during these two days: "Kept to my bed with seasickness. Fo'c'sle up and down; roll and dip; water gushing down the ventilators and waves banging hard on the hull. The heavy crates on deck are slapping up and down and there is no peace." On July 14, he wrote: "Lay abed of the seasickness. Weather a little easier. Got up at 11 PM for the seasickness drill (dispensing Kwells). Corned beef, leathery onions (they do not go down well), fruit juices, biscuits, and apples. Back to bed."

For our hard-chine vessel the sea really was rough. The wind was only force four but from *Miss Mabel*'s low freeboard the waves were impressive. The vessel tried every known gymnastic move except somersaults, pitching and rolling vigorously as she moved obliquely across the swells and through the spray, slamming violently down from each wave onto her hard-chine bottom. Stan noted: "We were not very good at concentrating on the course set. Some people would read a book while steering, only to be dragged back to reality by a loud shout from the Skipper. If two of us were on watch and one was making cocoa, the other had to leave the wheel to read the log. Often the boat held a better course with no one at the wheel."

The landlubbers fared poorly and while some merely declined to eat, others would only leave their bunks to attend to recurring personal emergencies. The true sailors—Gordon, Stowaway Alf, Mike, Lionel, and (most of the time) Goss and Dave—tucked in heartily at breakfast, talking loudly and making poor jokes about the antics of the gimbaled table. I resented Alf most of all, when, on my way to the head, I saw him lying on his bunk, with his sea-boots on, smoking his utterly foul pipe, reading *Krydde*, or at least looking at the pictures, and laughing. During the night, with nearly everyone seasick, the Skipper was heard to complain about the boat being "full of flipping pongoes." But he reduced speed a little, to make our lives easier. Gordon noted: "I managed a fairly healthy meal of stew. I hope I keep it. Below deck Phil, Ted, Dennis, Stan, and Colin were staggering about with buckets and haggard faces. They are all very sick."

At that stage, as we sailed parallel to the Scottish coast and past the Orkneys, Fair Isle, and the Shetlands, the two watches had two members each and they took alternate two-hour stints. Each successive wave pushed the bow off course, so the helmsman was constantly adjusting to keep the heading. We passed a few small fishing boats, which seemed to be pitching and rolling even more crazily than we were. Goss was impressed: "One could only admire the toughness, skill, and dedication of those who spend their lives as fishermen in the North Sea." Mike's least favorite job was reading the log on a dark and stormy night. At hourly intervals the log, consisting of a dial mounted on the taffrail and a spinner towed astern to measure the distance traveled, had to be read. Mike commented: "In calm daylight this was a pleasant duty. On a dark night, with the deck bouncing on the swell, that solitary passage along a narrow gangway by the light of a hand-held torch, with only a guard wire set at a level more like that of a trip wire than a handrail between one and the sea, was less attractive. I was always glad to be safely back in the wheelhouse."

Gordon's account of life at sea is illuminating:

Progress has been very slow over an unkind sea. All night long and all day today the ship has been buffeted and pushed, rolled and pitched by short steep rollers coming in from the north-northwest. The longer waves lift the prow right up and the boat then falls back with a sickening thud. I lay in my bunk and wondered whether the next crash would break her in two. She is a wooden craft and Alan has found dry rot in the starboard bow. Doors slammed, bottles fell, water dripped onto my bunk through the deck planks, and my sleeping bag got wet. Every now and then a blow, like that of a pile driver, shook and shivered the whole vessel. I thought of the hole we left in the dinghy last night. Anyway a dinghy could not survive long in this.... At 4 AM I relieved Alf at the wheel. The Skipper came, chatted, and cooked a couple of kippers for us. Then he too went to sleep. I was the only human being awake for perhaps seventy miles. Every hour I had to go to read the log and, as Phil and Stan, my watch companions, were both below, sick, I had to leave *Miss Mabel* to steer herself. I wondered how long it would be before my absence was discovered if I fell overboard.

Sunday, July 15, at 2 AM, the engine exhaust pipes became red-hot and set fire to the deck head of the engine room. Those awake tackled the fire with hatchets, buckets of water, and fire extinguishers, throwing the burning timbers and paneling from the saloon overboard. Many of us were not aware of the problem, except that we awakened to the sound of the engines running with unusual quietness, instead of with the usual noisy throb. The weather was a bit calmer. No, I should say it was slightly less rough; and by the time Gordon woke me up at 4 AM (with a cup of tea, bless him!) to start breakfast, the panic was over. Dave's recollection of the incident was strong: the smell of burning reminded him of frying kippers, and fifty-odd years later, he can still recall it.

∞

By morning, the mountains of Norway were beginning to appear and we were diverted by more wildlife. Flights of little auks scurried over the waves, sometimes diving under for food. Gulls kept a sharp eye for any debris thrown from the galley, and arctic terns kept their distance but complained noisily. As we approached the coast the weather improved. Mist lifted slowly from the steep mountainsides, which, with snow still in the gullies, swept right down to the sea. We—even Phil, on deck at last—were all impressed with the neat little farms dotted about the green fields. We were grateful to Alf for explaining many of the puzzling aspects of the scenery, including racks for drying fish and the various little storage huts or *sæters* near the farmhouses. A flashing lighthouse, Ona Light, enabled Roger to fix our position. We were too far north, but this problem was attributed to failings in the compass and not the inadequacies of the successive helmsmen. After lunch we turned into a stretch of fjords leading to Kristiansund. Alf said he knew the way into the harbor, but no one seemed to take him seriously. Despite his protests, we sailed right past the approach to the port and then had to return to it. We passed under a wonderfully fragile-looking ultra-modern suspension bridge and into the harbor in early afternoon.

The approved technique for a vessel coming alongside a dock is apparently to head towards the up-tide side of the structure, put the engines first into reverse, then into neutral, and let the tide carry you in. The stern clutch failed to hold. We continued forward and removed a length of timber from the quay. Unfazed, the mesmerized harbor-master, who had been watching our antics open-mouthed, fished the wood out of the water, signed it "A Present from Kristiansund" and presented it to the Skipper.

The town, of fifteen thousand or so inhabitants, was built on a series of small islands around the harbor. Parts of it had suffered a devastating fire and had only recently been rebuilt. It now looked very smart and attractive in its bright reds, yellows, and blues. The beautifully kept houses were all of wood, rather box-like, and of an almost uniform design. The harbor was full of ferryboats and other small craft, scurrying around in all directions, narrowly missing one another, with much blowing of klaxons and hooters. A number of Sunday afternoon strollers came to gaze at our unusual vessel and its even more unusual crew, youthful and unkempt. At this stage we were all growing beards, or at least we hadn't shaved, and it was most amusing to hear the comments of the girls as they passed the ship, all quickly translated for us by Alf. Most of our visitors were very well dressed—the men in spotless light-colored raincoats, silk ties, and rather wide-brimmed American-style felt hats; the women were even more ornately and immaculately turned out. Everyone carried umbrellas. Many wanted to know our destination and purpose. Some came to practice their English and others to acquire cigarette papers, which were strictly rationed and very expensive, and alcoholic drinks. The town laws governing alcoholic beverages, we gathered, almost amounted to prohibition. The Skipper added to the attractions of the scene with his "creaking leg stunt," by limping along the deck

A Norwegian town.

53

while creaking a match between matchbox cover and matchbox tray in his pocket—a hilarious effect! The local press came to see us. That evening, the expedition was the subject of a front-page article in the main newspaper. In it our leader, Ted (still fearless), was described as "an engaging young man with a shy moustache."

Customs and passport formalities were soon dealt with. We all set off, clad in our army camouflage anoraks, unshaven and all smoking pipes, to inspect the town. The locals said they thought we were British commandos. As we were now in port, Goss and I decided that he and I, as sea-cooks, could be excused from dinner preparation duties. Ted and Dave were voted cooks. Dave reported, "Meat roast, spuds, broccoli, and a gluey cheese sauce. Ted invented a sweet of fried bread, fruit and condensed milk; it was not a success." Ted was more succinct: "Dave and I spent several fruitless hours, preparing a rotten dinner." After supper we wandered along the waterfront, looking at the ferries and the blondes and then sat in the saloon, writing, drinking, and yarning. Alf decided that we really needed to learn some Norwegian phrases and especially singled out Ted, who might be called on to speak in public. One of the phrases, which Alf contended could be used in any circumstances, turned out to mean "leave your ugly husband and come with us."

Monday was a workday. After breakfast various Norwegian bodies came aboard and made sympathetic noises about the fires, the

Commandos in Kristiansund: Phil, Colin, Stan, Alf, Gordon, and Dave.

engines, and so on. We moved across the harbor to the shipyard where the shipwrights ripped out and replaced the funnel lining with asbestos sheeting and new lengths of wood: we did not fancy a third and perhaps catastrophic fire. We "swung the compass" (I'd always wanted to do that!) and found that it was twelve degrees in error. Lionel and Roger explained very carefully that this was the reason they had missed Anglesey altogether and why we had arrived on the Norway coast too far north. We arranged to recharge the batteries and overhaul the dynamo again. Gordon tackled the unsavory task of stripping the sludge pump in the forward head, which had been leaking fluids and awful smells. Ted and Dave cleaned out the bilges and bilge pumps in the engine room and the fuel hold, collecting

Ted and Goss peeling spuds.

two large buckets of wood shavings, sawdust, and other debris. This seemed to please them. Goss and I did the food shopping, collecting a great ten-pound lump of whale meat. Goss had the temerity to ask the vendor: "May I please have the head for the cat?"

We found among our supplies several strings of bright green sausages, which we, still being environmentally irresponsible, donated to the harbor. One seagull managed to gulp down one great string, sinking lower as it swallowed each sausage. It landed in the harbor so stuffed it couldn't take off again. Ted, Dennis, Mike, and Dave went over the plans for surveying the *strandflat* and inland areas of Spitsbergen.

By the following early evening, July 17, we were ready to refuel at the Esso quay and depart heading north, still full of enthusiasm but shaded with apprehension about the behavior of *Miss Mabel* and reports of worsening weather. After only two or three miles bad news came from the engine room yet again: this time there had been a total failure of the mechanism for putting the propellers into reverse. We returned to harbor for examination and more repairs. These were quickly accomplished, but our second attempt that evening to leave Kristiansund was no more successful than the first, because of yet more engine problems. We felt sorry for ourselves but even more for Alan the Engines, our valiant engineer. He really was having a rough time.

What should we do? The Skipper and several of us had a discussion in the saloon. Roger reported that the starboard clutch was oozing oil and wondered whether he would be forced to head directly back to Ireland. Ted pointed out that transport, other than with *Miss Mabel*, would be very difficult if not impossible to find. We decided to head back to Kristiansund, directly to the jetty of the shipyard, to see what their mechanics could do for us. Next day we sat in dejected heaps around the saloon, "ashamed to go ashore," as Gordon put it, while the engines were repaired. The clutch was fixed somehow. Only a few simple adjustments seemed to be needed on the water pump—or so they thought. Lionel got out the Svalbard maps, as though he actually expected to get there. While all of this was going on, Ted and I spent time in the fore hold getting the crates in some sort of order to be off-loaded at the base camps.

With fingers crossed we once again left the harbor. After the evening meal, in a heavy swell and with a tail wind that made steering very difficult, *Miss Mabel* returned to her usual skittish behavior. Goss did the washing-up; I went to bed. Goss wrote: "During the night we were awakened by the sudden cessation of the roar of the engines. *Miss Mabel* was hove-to, with all three engines silent. We had thoughts of drifting powerless and helpless onto the rocks of the nearby coast." The center engine had slowed and then stopped. Valve springs had broken and needed replacing, a delicate job, quite impossible to do at sea with the engine room a swaying inferno. There wasn't even a guardrail to prevent the engineer from falling against the red-hot exhausts. For good measure, the water pump on the port engine had broken down again and the engine had seized up. However, the Skipper fixed this problem by ingeniously connecting the priming pump to the cooling system. All the while the vessel was rolling like a pig in swill. By 5 AM we had two engines going again, capable of nine knots or so, but the Skipper declined to limp along in the open sea and turned *Miss Mabel* towards the coast, intending to travel along the sound between the Lofoten Islands and the mainland.

Sunshine, a quiet sea, and light winds favored us the next day as we approached the Lofoten Islands, keeping forty to fifty miles from the main Norwegian coast. We were nearing the Arctic Circle,

The Lofoten Islands.

and although it was a month after the summer solstice the hours of darkness were remarkably short. That evening, in gorgeous sunshine, Stan, ever the historian, put down his book and reminded us of the commando raid on the islands during the war, a few years earlier. The Lofotens appear a grim set of islands. They rise very steeply from the sea, in places as vertical cliffs, and ascend to a jagged skyline, clad, at that time, with a good deal of snow on the upper slopes and ridges. It was difficult to imagine how a landing there had been planned and carried out. Through the binoculars Ted could see the fantastic shapes of some brownish yellow rocks and what looked like a diminutive lighthouse. The pilot chart showed it was actually 158 feet high—hardly diminutive! Near the sea, some places were relatively flat areas with little houses, fields, and woods. Some parts reminded us of the Cuillin Hills of Skye, an impression enhanced where patches of cloud trailed skirts of rain over the black and brown rocks and scree slopes. I, as a nongeologist, agreed with the similarities and thought that the two places, the Cuillins and the Lofotens, could be made up of the same kind of rock. It turned out that I was correct: both are composed of gabbro, whatever that is. At that point, being ahead, I gave up making geological pronouncements. And everywhere were birds! Clouds of sea- and land-birds kept us interested all the way up Vestfjorden (West Fjord), which separates the Lofoten Islands from the mainland.

In the fine, calm weather the cooks were very busy, even enjoying their work. Before lunchtime Goss looked in despair at our moldering loaves of bread and had an inspiration, born of wartime shortage years. He simply cut off the affected parts, homogenized the good parts together with beaten egg and dried fruit, and baked the resulting bread pudding in the largest available washing-up bowl. Goss wrote in his diary: "This product found many willing customers, but it was so voluminous that in the end the gulls benefited from the uneaten remains." Dave, on the other hand, wrote: "It was a bit tough, even for Dennis. We ate about half of it and threw the rest to the birds. They pounced on it with gusto but afterwards, I swear, some of them sank!"

After lunch Stan and Gordon were at the wheel. Lionel joined them and the trio sang a number of popular songs "in harmony." It sounded pretty awful and most of the seagulls flew away. I'm involved in the next episode, so I'll let Gordon tell the story:

Colin wandered in from the galley at about 3 PM. His appearance was remarkable but as he now always looks the same, we have ceased to remark on it. He was wearing filthy white windproof trousers, at least five sizes too long, so that although he wears a large flap at the waistband over the top of his belt, like a kind of apron, the crotch still hangs at about the level of his knees. He has to walk with his legs apart. The lower parts of the trouser legs were rolled up, as they have to be if he is not to fall over them, and he was wearing plimsolls and no socks. His ensemble was, and is, completed with a khaki bush shirt tucked into the top of his trousers. Like all of us he has four weeks' growth of beard and his is dark and showy. Like all of us he badly needs a haircut and his hair falls over his eyes in front and stands up like a flue brush in the back. Behind this screen of beard and hair, I could see that Colin was grinning. "Let me congratulate you on the straight course you steer, Gordon," he remarked facetiously. I had just altered course by two degrees, but as he surreptitiously proffered a hand cunningly camouflaged with khaki cuff, I foolishly shook it. The horrid hand that grasped mine was coated in an inch of yummy dough, the cake mixture for Alan Evans' birthday cake. My immediate reaction to Colin's friendly gesture was to wipe his cake mixture on the back of his neck. This brought a somewhat priggish rebuke from Lionel, who apparently would have taken no revenge whatever. Colin, however, did not respond with a brawl, in which he would assuredly have overcome me, but retired, still in good humor, to wash.

It was indeed Alan the Mate's birthday, so for teatime I had made him a cake. It turned out better than the one I had made a couple of days before—that one was burned on the outside and raw in the middle because the oven was much too hot. Alan's was just right. On board we had only one candle, a normal household one, so I sharpened both ends, drilled a hole in its side, supported it on a pencil, lit both ends, took Alan's photo with it, and then we ate the whole thing, except the pencil and the candle. It was really pretty good! Alan made a long speech (for him): he said "Thank you." The rest of that calm day was spent reading, taking photos of the passing scene, and holding learned discussions on many subjects: geology, marine currents, sea birds, the Norwegian language, and the next meal.

By about 6 PM we were some way up West Fjord. The mountains of the mainland, visible since noon, were now much closer and we could make out houses and roads. The cloud-filled sky was most impressive: cumulus clouds, low on the northern horizon, engulfed the mountain tops; above were stratus clouds in long wispy purplish-gray bands, silhouetted against a light blue sky. We were flying Flag G, meaning we wanted a pilot, but although we cruised around outside a small port, no pilot appeared. Maybe the cowards knew we were coming? We carried on, *sans* pilot.

The fjord grew narrower and we could see that the way ahead was a labyrinth of channels, some amazingly narrow: the need for a pilot had become critical. At around 11 PM, a pilot came aboard from the little village of Lodingen, at the extreme east end of one of the Lofoten islands, the headquarters for pilots on this coast. He was youngish and immaculately dressed in a light-colored raincoat, a well-cut suit, and a nautical peaked hat. He was pleasant, spoke excellent English, and was welcomed aboard by Alf. He insisted on shaking hands with everyone. For the final hundred miles or so to the port of Tromsø, our route passed through a complex pattern of narrows, islands, and fjord entrances. We passed through Skanland Narrows, under the high bridge joining the island of Hinnøy with the mainland, past Harstad, one of the coaling ports, through Solbergfjord, Malangen, and into Tromsøsund. All the way the scenery was utterly spectacular, with near-vertical mountainsides plunging into the sea. What a place to live, at least in the summertime! But snow patches extended down to sea level and we wondered what winter might be like. The pilot joined us for breakfast, so Goss and I made an effort to impress him. After all, he impressed us with his English, as well as his ability to guide us. We passed the rusting overturned hulk of the German battleship *Tirpitz*, sunk in Tromsøfjorden by bombers of the Royal Air Force in November 1944. A cluster of grey buildings slid by, followed, at last, by our quay.

For a touch of irony, *Lyngen*, of all ships, was moored there too. We had to tie up beside her, looking and feeling awfully small and inconspicuous alongside her. Although she was only a two-thousand-ton coal-burning steamer, her hull towered over us. *Lyngen* was the vessel that took cargo, mail, and a few passengers to Spitsbergen in the summer. Six months earlier we had rejected the idea of taking passage on her because she would be sailing much too late in the season. Now she was being refitted, due to sail for Svalbard on August 1.

While most of us washed and brushed up for a walk into town, several local authorities came aboard, led by the customs man, the harbormaster, and the *skipskontrollør*. They came for some paperwork formalities and to inspect the vessel. Immediately, disaster struck! First of all the customs fellow—Gordon thought he was probably a Lapp—became upset because we had opened the in-bond store, which had been sealed in Kristiansund. Roger argued that we were within our rights as we had been forty miles outside the three-mile limit. In the end that dispute was settled with a bottle of Irish whisky.

Then came the real disaster: the ship inspector would not hear of *Miss Mabel* sailing to Spitsbergen. She had no ice-skin, no radio, and no motors in the "lifeboats" (in reality, no lifeboats). Also, the sea ice that year extended to within two or three hundred miles of Tromsø, and *Miss Mabel*'s wooden construction would be completely inadequate to withstand any serious impact with sea ice. In rough seas and poor visibility this could easily happen. Of course, we already knew all this—we couldn't even pretend to be astonished. Whatever had induced us to start out in this ridiculous vessel? Nevertheless it was a very despondent crowd of would-be explorers who watched the ship inspector nail his official writ on the mast. It read: "This vessel is unsafe to proceed in any direction"—or something very like that.

DESPAIR AND RELIEF—
TROMSØ AND BEYOND

$\mathcal{I}$ don't know who was the wiseacre who first called Tromsø the "Paris of the North." I guess he was related to Erik the Red, who called Greenland "Greenland." Perhaps "Hull of the Fjords" or "Jersey City of the Arctic" would have been more appropriate. Half a mile along the quay was a huge dump of Spitsbergen coal. Maybe the geologists should collect some of that, I thought, as the closest they would get to Svalbard rocks. The streets were largely unpaved and coated in places with a particularly tenacious muddy goo. It all added to our gloom.

Our initial reaction to the *skipskontrollør's* writ confining us to Tromsø Harbor, perhaps forever, was a mixture of frustration and anxiety, but after our experiences with *Miss Mabel* over the previous weeks, we could understand his point of view. Long and serious discussions followed. We thought of making a run for it, an idea that lasted only a few seconds. In the worst case our expedition would simply abort and we would all go home from Tromsø, a very depressing prospect for members and sponsors alike. Even if we found a substitute means of transport it would mean further delays, resulting in serious curtailment of our working time in Spitsbergen, drastic cuts in our program, and increases in our costs.

Our time in Tromsø was frustrating, confusing and depressing. The first sign of hope was when Fred Sæther, a very friendly Norwegian who also happened to be the British proconsul in Tromsø, came aboard to see what he could do for us. He was a wonderful chap, anxious to help in any way possible—and he did. He also told us that the police were looking for Alf the Stowaway. It turned out that Alf had forgotten to tell his parents how he was travelling to Tromsø—no doubt because, if they had known, they would have refused to allow it. They had been telegraphing up and down the Norwegian coast for news of him. His mother "had not slept for the past ten days." Alf shaved, spruced himself up, said some regretful good-byes, and tried to catch the daily bus to his home, eighty miles away. It had already left. He thumbed a lift half-way home, and we hoped he made it the rest of the way. He'd been an excellent companion and a great help.

For lunch I had made a boiled suet pudding (suet? we couldn't even spell the word cholesterol in those days), which I turned out onto a large plate and poured over it some heated dark treacle. The sight of that treacle running down the sides of the pudding struck me as being a perfect reflection of the way gloom and despair had descended on the ship's company. The Skipper and Alan the Engines announced more engine trouble. Possibly a big end had gone in the center engine. If so, it would take at least three days to fix. So even without the boorish *skipskontrollør*'s writ, we weren't going anywhere for some time.

Phil, Dave, and Lionel went ashore by clambering over the intervening *Lyngen* and down onto the quay. They reported that Tromsø was still very much a frontier town, dusty and unkempt; Dave said he felt like the town looked. They found a statue of Amundsen somewhere and polar bears in several shops, stuffed of course, but real enough for Dave to wonder what would be the outcome of an encounter with a real live one in Spitsbergen—if we ever got there. When they returned to the *Miss Mabel* they found black gloom thick enough to be cut with a flensing knife. Alan the Ropes and Roger the Skipper tried to raise our flagging spirits. Roger wrote out for me a document that I treasured for years and years. He wrote: "This is to certify that Colin B. B. Bull has proved himself to be a competent and imaginative sea-cook, although somewhat unreliable in a heavy sea. [Signed] Roger Pirie, D.S.C. Lieutenant, (retired) Royal Navy."

Its monetary value was slight, in fact zero, but its bragging value was inestimable. He wrote something too, for Goss, who was a much better sailor than I was, but I've no idea what it said.

That evening after dinner, Dennis, Mike, Alan the Engines, Dave, and I went for a stroll into town to find something to cheer us up. It was indeed a grimy little town, with many fur shops, all with polar bears and sealskins galore. The only cinema was full, it being Saturday night, so we eventually went into the Nordcafe for a coffee. It was so full, steamy, and noisy that we gave up and were walking home (I never thought I would regard *Miss Mabel* as "home") when a plump youngish Norwegian chap hailed us. He spoke good English but seemed a bit tight. However, he took us to Kafestruva B.U.L., a kind of Lyons cafeteria, where he bought us coffee and *smørbrød*, raw salted fish on bread, and then sausages in greasy paper. After that, we all repaired to *Miss Mabel* for a drink. Over a couple of tots of the Skipper's gin, J. Hagerup, Jr., told us of his times in Scotland and London during the war, and of life on the Arctic convoys to Murmansk. At 1 AM Tromsø was as open and busy as at midday. Mr. Hagerup wanted us to go with him for a beer and then to a dance, but we packed him off, rolling like a lord, and went to bed.

The next day, July 22, was a soggy and cheerless Sunday. Mr. Sæther, the proconsul, and his boss, the consul, with their wives, were to visit us for drinks and in preparation we spruced up the saloon. The visitors, like most of the people in Tromsø, were very smartly dressed. The Skipper, the two Alans, Ted, and Lionel had a Very Important Discussion with them. The consul felt that he could arrange some sort of transport for some of us, at least, on *Lyngen*. However, she wouldn't be sailing until August 1. Ten more days wasted! Mr. Sæther thought the governor of Svalbard would be able to arrange to take a few people to the geologists' field area, as he had in 1948, and perhaps the chosen few could come back to Norway on a coal boat. All of that seemed a far cry from the glamorous trip we had imagined, cruising serenely through beautiful sunshine and placid fjords in our own vessel. However, it would give some of us six weeks' work time. In all likelihood it would have taken me at least three weeks to set up my magnetic gear. If that went well, I would be left with perhaps two weeks to get results. Clearly it wasn't worth my going just for that and for the meteorological stuff. Obviously

Lionel and Ted should go, as well as Dave, to do his work on the raised beaches, if it could be arranged. All of us except Ted and the Skipper spent the rest of the day and evening reading and playing cards, a noisy and low-grade bridge. Ted and Roger had accepted an invitation to dinner from the consul. Ted shaved off his beard and "shy moustache" and scurried around looking for presentable clothes: a shirt and flannel slacks from Stan, and a tie and sports coat from Gordon. Roger wore a brown suit that he had bought from necessity during the war when, as a survivor from the *Royal Oak*, sunk by a German U-boat in Scapa Flow in October 1939, he had come ashore wearing only dirty overalls. We packed them off at 8 PM, telling them to behave themselves and make a good impression. They both had a good time and arrived back on board at 1:40 AM, when it was still as light as an English summer dawn. Ted reported: "The smoked salmon was great but the vermouth was dreadful." We all hoped that our representatives had made the right impression.

The next day the *skipskontrollør* came on board to confirm that we could not go anywhere until *Miss Mabel* had passed inspection. A policeman-type came to tell us the same thing and to stamp our passports. Ted and Lionel walked up to the proconsul's office. They arrived back elated, with the great news that five people could go on *Lyngen* on August 1. Who? It took a long discussion to decide that it should be Lionel, Dave, Goss, Phil, and Ted—four geologists and a field assistant-cum-leader. At that stage I felt sorry for Ted and even more sorry for myself. Alan the Mate decided to go on the round trip on *Lyngen*, at his own expense. Another policeman came along to

Serious discussion in Miss Mabel's *saloon: Alan the Engines, Alan the Ropes, Dennis, Mike, and Roger.*

find out which of us was going to Spitsbergen and a naval gentleman came to advise us where to anchor *Miss Mabel*. Another naval official came along and tapped the hull of *Miss Mabel*. He shook his head, saying: "No damn good! No damn good!" and walked away. Roger asked Stan to go into town to buy a Jubilee clip (hose clamp), and on the way Stan was very impressed with the massive icebreakers in the harbor. He was delighted with the cooperation of the shopkeeper. Stan spoke Norwegian as well as most people from Mevagissey, but he had the expedition's Norwegian phrase book with him, and using that he gave a very detailed description of the item he wanted. After listening patiently, the storekeeper said: "Oh, you mean a Jubilee clip." Mike and I sat down with a map and started to make plans for a trip to Lapland.

After lunch I watched the little fishing boats, all with single-cylinder diesel engines, going round the harbor, tunk, tunk, tunk. One of them was even entitled on her side *Fisk. Tunk.* The engines sounded so much more reliable than others we knew. Phil and Dave went for a stroll along the quay and spent much time examining a wooden sealer drawn up on a slipway. The massive timbers at her bow and hull were badly scarred—by ice, they presumed—and her keel was ripped to shreds, a very sobering sight; a sight that gave them some idea why the authorities had been so scathing in their lack of regard for *Miss Mabel*. Back on board, they found that Fred Sæther had sent round a pile of *Esquire* magazines, and later the secretary from the consulate brought a stack of English newspapers. I think she mainly wanted to see what we looked like.

Tromsø is on the inshore side of an island, about a mile from the mainland, to which, in those days, little ferries went very frequently. Visible from our quay was a shapely snow-streaked mountain, about six miles away, beyond the head of a forested valley. This was Tromsdaltinden, a peak about four thousand feet high. We decided its ascent would offer a good day of strenuous exercise, which we were all beginning to need. So, as Goss recorded, "in groups of three or four each day, just about everyone found a chance to walk to the summit. Darkness never fell, so the walk was possible any time the weather and duties allowed."

On Tuesday, Goss, the Skipper, and Alan the Mate set off to climb the mountain, while another bunch of folk started packing trekking rations for the lucky people going to Spitsbergen. They now numbered six. Ted agonized over his responsibilities of discrimination at this stage. He decided the sixth one should be Gordon but he also decided not to tell Gordon that he was in or the other four of us that we were out. It really concerned him that his decision—and we had all agreed it should be his alone—would cause someone to be left out. In the end, still worried, he went to see *Annie, Get Your Gun* at the local cinema. Meanwhile I went round with Dennis, Mike, and Gordon to the local museum to see if they had any ideas of what we could profitably do in the area. The assistant geologist was very helpful. He phoned the Norwegian Department of Industrial Research in Oslo, and we were able to make some very tentative arrangements to accompany their Mr. Polsen, a geologist, to one of the Lofoten Islands where we would drill for graphite. What's more, they would pay us, about ten shillings a day! That seemed a very satisfactory arrangement. However, when we returned to the ship, we were told that *nine* of us could go on *Lyngen*, so for a short while we argued about who would be the most useless of us in Svalbard and should therefore stay with *Miss Mabel*. Ted had decided it should be Stan who stayed, partly because he was pretty good with engines, but several people pointed at me. However, I argued that, if I were to stay on *Miss Mabel*, apart from cooking, I would be useless to Roger and the two Alans, a trio who could benefit from having a competent companion.

In retrospect I am still surprised at how well-behaved we all were about these discussions. If the situation had continued I'm sure we would have settled it with a coin toss. However, on July 28, "they" said all ten of us could go. The atmosphere at teatime was downright cheerful. We reorganized the parties yet again. Lionel, Dave, Stan (without his outboard motor), and Gordon would constitute the coastal party and the other six, divided into two trios based on Goss and Phil, the two geologists, would be the inland group. Not being able to do any work on my own behalf, I would be a geologist's assistant after all. As I had feared eight months before, I now seemed doomed to carry incredible loads of food up impossible slopes and equally incredible loads of rock specimens down. Now things looked as though they might be even worse than I had feared then. It turned out that much of the interest of Goss and Phil in the rocks that we would encounter lay in the microscopic fossils they might contain. Since these fossils couldn't be seen by eye, the only possible approach was a statistical one. The more rock the geologists brought back to examine under a microscope, the greater were their chances of finding something interesting or important. Mike, Dennis, and Ted were also destined to be mountain mules, carrying tons and tons of rock. Still, we were *all* going to Spitsbergen!

Stan was perhaps the most concerned at this point. He was due to be called up for his military service at about that time and the Ministry of Defence hadn't a clue where he was. Perhaps he was AWOL! The village policeman in Mevagissey kept asking Stan's father where he was, and his reply "on *Miss Mabel*" was easily misunderstood. In the end, Stan's calling-up papers were waiting for him on *Miss Mabel* when we returned from Svalbard.

Mike and Dennis spent several days making enlargements of the map of St. Jonsfjorden, taken from the nautical chart. We packed food boxes for the two bases and another waterproofed box to be deposited at Farmhamna (Farm Haven), a prominent natural harbor at the southern end of the area to be covered by the coastal party. Ted packed two boxes of medical supplies. The one for the inland group included the Thomas splint, for broken legs. However, he left out nearly all of the equipment and supplies for his proposed blood-cell studies, another casualty of the erosion of our expedition time. He gave to Lionel sundry items like penicillin, morphine, and forty tablets of amphetamine sulfate, "just in case," as he said. I made sure the magnetic recording gear was safe on *Miss Mabel*, together with all the weather instruments. That was a mistake: we arrived in Spitsbergen without even a thermometer! That evening Ted wrote a long illegible letter to our patron, Sir Raymond, detailing all of the disasters that had befallen us in the previous weeks, but letting him know that there would be something that we could call "Birmingham University Spitsbergen Expedition, 1951." The other letter he had planned to write was to Commander Everitt, from whom we had chartered *Miss Mabel*, again giving an account of her failings, and opening the door to renegotiating the charter fee, recovering repair costs, and so on. However, Ted didn't feel up to tackling that one and he put it off for another day.

The ten of us were going off to Spitsbergen, leaving the Skipper and the two Alans to repair and worry about *Miss Mabel* and await our return. Alan the Mate was coming up on *Lyngen* and returning with her to Tromsø, but the other two would not see Sunny Svalbard at all. I'm sorry now that I never asked them how they felt about that.

Tromsø and its environs provided enough of interest to fill the hours not spent cooking, planning, packing rations, and so on. Phil and Dave, and the next day Mike, Dennis, and I, climbed Tromsdalstindet, each group starting immediately after breakfast. Dave was surprised at how unfit he was. He and Phil had to stop frequently for rests, while the three young Norwegians they were with kept steadily on, reappearing at the top, brewing coffee. Phil had with him our little book of Norwegian phrases produced by Esso, but all the Norwegians wanted to speak English. We were entertained, just where the hill grew steeper, by a longhaired, middle-aged poet, declaiming his latest masterpieces. They were in Norwegian of course, but we clapped vigorously all the same. Puffing and blowing, we slowly climbed the hill. The route through the forest was not difficult to follow and was replete with fascinating vistas. There was a wood and stone bridge over a sizeable stream and a substantial wooden hut, with the door open. It was sparsely furnished and no one was there, so we closed the door and continued upwards. There were fine waterfalls and soon we were walking across stony areas, strewn with

The Skipper and friend on the slopes of Tromsdaltinden.

snowbanks. After the first summit, perhaps at two thousand feet, we had lunch at about 1:30 PM. There followed a long, tiring grind to the proper summit, which we reached at 5 PM. The weather was overcast and dull; but we could see that the view would be spectacular on a good day. At the top in a big rock cairn was a wooden box containing a visitor's book, well wrapped in oilskin. Goss had signed it and Dave had added one of his inimitable cartoons. So we signed it too and had a second meal. Despite the clouds, it really was a gorgeous day and we voted to continue down the other side. The snow at the top was quite deep and the going was hard, but conditions eased as we got lower. Mike had his first glissade, at first terrifying then exhilarating. I, with the rucksack, got into difficulties with large unstable rocks and the others had to wait twenty minutes until I caught up. There was still a long way to go round the mountain and we were all absolutely famished and exhausted by the time we reached *Miss Mabel* at 11 PM. Good old Goss had kept us some soup and stew.

While we were away the others had spent a long time going over the work plans. With luck, Lionel could reach the locality with the Carboniferous fossils in the Hecla Hoek (called the Hookla Heck by the always-disrespectful Stan) main outcrop and find out how far they extended north. Dave would have lots of coastal area in which to map the raised beaches. The Royal Geographic Society had shown enough interest in these to give us money. However, it didn't seem likely that he or Goss would find any old red sandstone, their particular geological love, an affection generated by their earlier work in Britain. The work originally proposed by Ted, the surveyors, and me would go by the board.

We entertained ourselves by watching the antics of the sailors from an American destroyer that had tied up one hundred yards away. Their loudspeaker kept shouting weird orders; the sailors, all apparently bow-legged, ignored these while riding their bicycles round and round on the quay and playing baseball. One adventurous party from our group went to inspect the *Tirpitz*, lying hull-up a few miles away, taking the better of our two dinghies and the temperamental outboard motor. The leaks in the dinghy meant almost constant bailing, but they did manage to come alongside *Tirpitz*. They found a group of welders cutting up the hull for scrap steel. Goss thought it was a suitably inglorious end to the pride of Germany's wartime navy. Meanwhile, two of us decided to launch the other dinghy. Fortunately we had tied a line from it to *Miss Mabel*, for the dinghy immediately sank. How can a wooden dinghy sink? *Miss Mabel*'s did, even with a cork stuck into the hole that Gordon had drilled. We slowly recovered it with the line.

While we were moored in the harbor we ate stacks of fish, most of it bought from two fishermen who often hailed us from their boat when they had some to sell. It was inexpensive and first rate, tasting marvelous compared with the usual fare on *Miss Mabel*. Dave asked them where they did their fishing. They pointed out into mid-fjord. "Just there—never fails." Dave incautiously asked further: "Why there?" "That's where the town sewer comes out." The fish was nonetheless delicious.

Ted distributed snow goggles and whistles to all of us, as well as army gas capes, which we had bought instead of better-fitting but much more expensive waterproof coats. Anoraks were a big problem. Being short of money, we had only bought ten of them, one for each of us. Ted's problem was to ensure that each person had one that fitted within acceptable limits. In his diary he remarked: "What false economy it was to buy so few!" Some of us tried to make our anoraks more waterproof by soaking them in a solution of Mesowax. It made them sticky but didn't seem to help weather-wise, as Gordon and Ted discovered when they tried an overnight trip up the mountain and got completely soaked.

Miss Mabel *(center) in Tromsø harbor, dwarfed by the Norwegian Antarctic exploration ship* Norsel *(left)*.

As Dave recalls,

> Then there was our distress one morning on finding that tied up alongside us was a Norwegian fishing smack with a deck cargo of codfish bones and heads. As the sun came out it warmed the place up so the smell grew until it was unbearable. No fisherman was to be seen anywhere. We were gasping by the time we had finished breakfast. Then we noticed that a plague of bluebottles had settled on that boat—and on ours. Several of us managed to haul this hell ship well aft of our own berth and there it lay, gently reeking to heaven.

We wondered if tying up this stink bomb next to us was some sort of gesture from the local populace.

The last two days in Tromsø were frantically busy. On July 31 we assembled the innumerable small items we would need to tackle our reduced fieldwork programs as efficiently as possible. Dennis and Mike worked hard to complete the maps for the geologists. Some of us had a pre-Spitsbergen bath. We packed our personal gear and worried that we might have forgotten some vital item. (We did: I carefully wrapped all the thermometers for recording air temperatures and left them on the shelf over my bunk.) On August 1 after breakfast we moved *Miss Mabel* alongside *Lyngen* while Ted went to see the proconsul to arrange for the customs folk to come to inspect the stuff we were taking north. As Ted wrote: "I really don't know what we would have done without Mr. Sæther." After lunch the customs people gave us the okay on all our crates and the crew of *Lyngen* winched all sixteen from our deck into *Lyngen*'s hold. The Skipper and Alan the Engines came on board *Lyngen* to bid us farewell and then returned to *Miss Mabel* to celebrate our departure with a couple of Roger's pink gins.

Lyngen was a comparatively sedate little old lady of some two thousand tons. We were allocated eight bunks in the fo'c'sle and three, taken by Phil, Mike, and Alan, in a cabin close by with the four other passengers. The vessel was not very well ventilated and smelled of paint. In the eight-bunk cabin there was only one wash stand in the way of furniture but all the sheets were sparkling white, and it seemed a shame to put our grimy bodies between their white smoothness. We sailed at 9 PM. Quickly we passed *Miss Mabel*, which was flying three flag signals: "Please send a ship's inspector aboard,"

"Farewell and good luck," and "Now for some peace." The Skipper made rude gestures.

There had been crowds of people on *Lyngen*'s decks before we sailed, but most of them had now gone ashore and it was clear that, except for ourselves, there were indeed only four passengers. Supper was served in the saloon on two long tables, one of which we completely filled. The food was good—bacon and eggs, assorted pressed meats, *smørbrød* with goat's milk cheese, and tea. No washing up was required! The cheese came in two colors, light brown and dark brown. The light brown stuff was excellent. The dark brown was strong, pungent and, we decided, to be avoided in future. Goss coined the expression, in praise of the light brown cheese: "It puts the ø in smørbrød," a phrase to be repeated at least five thousand times over the following weeks and many more in the years down to the present.

In calm sunny weather we went on deck to watch the scenery as we headed north along the fjord. We glimpsed a wonderful panorama of jagged mountain peaks, with a golden orange sun peeping through the ranges and wisps of cirrus clouds hanging in a blue-green sky. A tall Norwegian-American botanist from the University of Michigan—Yodel by name—wearing a three-pointed Lapp hat (tried on, for size, by Gordon) told us all about his adventures taking photos across the Iron Curtain in Finland. He had the biggest telephoto lens I had ever seen. He was planning to spend a few weeks studying plants in Adventfjorden and gave us a running commentary on the passing vegetation until some time after midnight when we headed into the open sea and I went to bed. Mike had been equally enthralled. He wrote:

> Stayed on deck till 11:30 PM watching the scenery and the sunset. Both were too magnificent to leave. I have felt that superlatives were necessary all the way up this coast from our first landfall, and each stretch has been better than the last, leaving me at a loss for words, but these, tonight, have been the most superlative views we have seen. The sky was cloudless, apart from a few streaks low down, catching the setting sun, and all the world seemed bathed in very pale yellow light, except low on the horizon, where for practically the full circle there was an orange and red glow, everything being in wonderful half tints. The colors set the snow-capped jagged peaks

to advantage and the scene was unforgettable. I must revisit these mountains sometime.

In the beam sea, the motion of *Lyngen* was a slow roll, or perhaps a wallow describes it better, quite different from *Miss Mabel*'s much more jerky and erratic motion. Not surprisingly a different set of folk fell foul of it. In particular our stalwarts Mike, Stan, and Goss were all feeling pretty groggy, while Phil was there for breakfast and on deck for a short while afterwards. Then he disappeared to the saloon, where most of the others were congregated, not doing anything in particular. Stan said he felt odd not having anything to do with running the ship. Meanwhile Alan the Mate was as busy as he could be, looking disgustingly healthy and cheerful. That condition, as he said, "was only to be expected of a man who was born on a tossing deck and had spent half his life there." We passed Bear Island, the southernmost part of the Svalbard Archipelago, an inhospitable rocky protuberance halfway between the North Cape of Norway and our destination. The Norwegian Sea to port and the Barents Sea to starboard both looked equally gray, cold, and forbidding.

When we got up the next morning, August 3, the mountains of Vestspitsbergen were in sight and the sea was several degrees calmer. I joined most of the others on deck, watching the mountains grow closer. We passed a dozen or so fishing trawlers and moderate amounts of brash ice. The captain of *Lyngen* slowed the ship down and turned to avoid the bigger pieces, perhaps twenty or so feet square and sticking a few feet above the sea surface. Even so I found it disconcerting to hear ice clattering along the hull. We thought of *Miss Mabel* and her wooden construction. It would have been suicidal to venture into these seas with her!

By mid-morning the weather was sunny and the sea was millpond calm and crystal clear. Idyllic! Most of the pieces of floating ice had a few inches of snow on them, and below the waterline the ice itself showed a beautiful blue-green. On the bigger floes, those with ice showing well above water level, we could see the green shining through the snow. The patches of ice attracted myriad sea birds—gulls, guillemots, and fulmar petrels swooped down, coming within touching distance of the group. From the bows Mike saw little auks. He wrote:

They swim in front of the boat, until when nearly run down, they will either try to fly off, which involves much splattering along the water with feet well spread out aft, or alternatively they will dive, swimming down ten feet, using their wings to "fly" under water. When several of them do this at once, it is most amusing to watch them go rapidly down, quite easy to follow as they show their white behinds in the dark water.

We talked to the other passengers. Yodel was busy photographing everything in sight. A jovial old schoolmaster told Dave some interesting yarns about Spitsbergen. J. Hagerup, Jr.'s uncle, who turned out to be aboard, was too drunk to tell us anything we could understand, and an old trapper who had spent forty seasons in Spitsbergen pointed out landmarks to us. All the Norwegian crew seemed to know him. Mike was still enchanted with the scene, as indeed were the rest of us. He wrote: "The coast is grand: great steep mountains, covered with snow in places, but not as much as one might expect, as these are the western slopes, split up by mighty glaciers. These glaciers appear to be snow-covered right down to sea level, which is a bad sign, as the crevasses will be hidden."

Brash ice in Isfjorden.

Dave wrote:

By teatime we had reached Kapp Linne on the south side of the entrance to Isfjorden and could make out Alkhornet and Dead Man's Point [Daudmannsodden] on the north side. Lionel expounded on the geology of the places that he recognized and we could see the wreck of a ship on the shore of Dead Man's Plain. The place looked very barren and even a bit sinister, especially with those names in mind. We skirted the southern shore of Isfjorden and could see Barentsburg, the Russian settlement, with its huge wooden tunnel, more than a mile long, from the quay to the mine buildings. We also noticed some big cairns on local mountaintops. Later we passed Grumant City where, we were told, some eight hundred Russian women coal miners work. Didn't see any. The scenery here is fantastic with enormous cliffs of horizontal strata forming tessellated and rampart-like slopes. The incredible beauty of the place impresses us all, especially with the snow cover on the higher slopes emphasizing the relief.

At about 2 AM on August 4, *Lyngen* tied up against the jetty in Longyearbyen and we went ashore. So this was Spitsbergen! I tried to find Lionel to discover precisely what it was that we "should see." After all, we had waited a very long time to get to Sunny Svalbard.

Gordon with our Republic of Ireland flag, on board the
Miss Mabel.

Camp on St. Jonsfjorden.

Base camp near Müllerneset.

Goss at sunset.

First sight of the mountains of Spitsbergen.

Head of St. Jonsfjorden, Osbornebreen on the right, Konowbreen on the left.

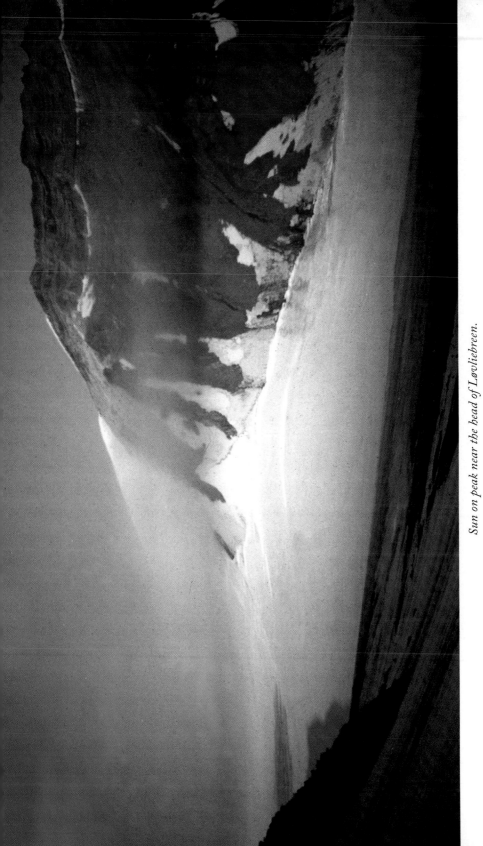

Sun on peak near the head of Løvliebreen.

Goss and Mike at a camp on a glacial moraine near the Wittenbergfjella.

Sunset over Prins Karls Forland.

Moonrise over the strandflat.

The Shambles with snow.

Beards on Sysla: *clockwise: Colin, Mike, Lionel, and Goss.*

The expedition according to Dave.

CHAPTER SIX

UP THE FJORD
WITHOUT A PADDLE

∞

Lyngen was tied up at Longyearbyen jetty; the surrounding vista enthralled us. Dave described it well:

The scene was of unbelievable chaos and shabbiness. The buildings, low sheds, looked gray and untidy. Junk, metal, wooden crates, and piles of timber lay everywhere and there was no sign of any vegetation to speak of. The sea was a pale muddy brown, like cold tea. An endless chain of coal buckets clanked its way along the shore, held up by Heath Robinson pylons. The buckets discharged at the coaling wharf, over a long ridged pile of coal. There was all manner of rubbish along the shore. The tide seemed about half in. The wooden jetty was not very wide and bore several groups of miners and officials ready to greet the ship. Many of the miners were jovially drunk. A gang on the quay enthusiastically greeted our trapper friend. We stood around, feeling rather useless, until a young man from the governor's office came to ask the expedition to come up to the governor's house, bringing our sleeping bags. We collected them and followed him in procession up the hill to the *sysselmann*'s palace, watched by all and sundry on the way.

The governor's house was new since Lionel had been there last, three years earlier. It was a wonderful wooden edifice with a palatial interior. In the main reception room were highly polished beams and four large modern pictures on the walls. Over the mantelpiece there was a polar bear skull. Very soon we were all seated in armchairs before a great window overlooking Adventfjorden. The governor's wife, Liv Balstad, a cheery, bright-eyed, brown-haired lady, greeted us with large glasses of pale somewhat watery ale. (Later she wrote an excellent book of her life as the governor's wife, entitled *North of the Desolate Sea*.) She apologized that the governor was not there: he had had to go to a party. Our accumulated mail was handed out; there was none for me. The captain and radio engineer from *Lyngen* turned up, together with the deputy governor and three Englishmen, one a mining student from Birmingham. It was obvious that there were too many of us to stay, so we made our apologies and returned to the ship. Before we left we were told that *Sysla*, the governor's motor vessel, would sail later that day, with us aboard. The captain of *Lyngen* asked us to remove our gear from the hold onto the quay. The *Lyngen* crew winched it ashore for us before an audience of drunks—it was "grog day," a monthly event. Ted and Dennis said they would stand guard over the pile of boxes. They tried in vain to get some sleep, lying on top of kitbags, while the rest of us grabbed a few hours in our bunks.

Despite the warm greetings we had received from the inhabitants, Longyearbyen was a pretty gaunt place. Nearly all the buildings were of wood and well insulated, the cavities between their double walls being packed with a fibrous material that looked rather like wood wool. In a landscape almost completely devoid of sizeable vegetation, the buildings and roads seemed dull and untidy. The roads were terrifying places. Enormous earth-moving trucks and bulldozers kept tearing along them at great speed. The backdrop of large, barren hills did nothing to brighten the scene. These were about one thousand feet high, with just a little tundra vegetation on the lower slopes. They all seemed to consist of flat-lying sandstones and shales, with some thick seams of coal. From several coal mines half-way and higher up the slopes, elaborate cable and pylon systems carried coal in buckets to the loading jetty. One of the mines was still smoking. During the war the Royal Navy had shelled the mines to prevent their use by the Germans, and later the Germans had set them on fire to prevent their use by the Allies.

At 5:30 AM, after a tedious night of conversations with very happy Norwegians, Dennis came down to the fo'c'sle to wake Goss and Gordon so that they could relieve Ted and him on the quay. Goss and Gordon were slow in moving and before they were ready to go ashore, *Lyngen* had to move away from the quay to allow *Ingeren*, a nine-thousand-ton tramp steamer, to tie up. Ted and Dennis were thus marooned, reliefless.

In *Lyngen*'s saloon Knut, the stoker, was having an early break-fast of coffee, bread and butter, and jam. He insisted we join him. Knut, a friendly type, was a natural clown, complete with goofy expression. We had got on well with him since Tromsø where he had offered Gordon two pounds for his buffalo-head pipe. Dave and I went on deck, where the towering steel sides of *Ingeren* confronted us. Eventually we climbed on the roof of *Lyngen*'s bridge and thence onto the tramp. From its huge hold, cranes were removing concrete girders, cinema chairs, bicycles, and all manner of large odds and ends. We then relieved a very tired, hungry, and fed-up Ted and Dennis and took a turn guarding our gear, talking with various still-sozzled miners in mixed Norwegian, English, and German, until Lionel called us for proper breakfast at eight o'clock. For the rest of the morning we watched *Ingeren* unloading while Lionel and Ted went off to meet the governor, Haakon Balstad. Shortly after Ted and Lionel left, a bunch of us decided to investigate the town, the main part of which lay a mile or so inland. Phil and Mike inspected the

Carrying gear through Longyearbyen.

89

bakery to buy something that would do for lunch. The man wanted five and a half kroner for it, which exceeded their wealth, so they left without anything. Meanwhile Dave and I went to the main company store, which was presided over by a short, rotund man with a beard and a woolen hat, which he took off and replaced with a cloth one as we entered. We found a few items to supplement our field rations and some other things that looked useful. We then started a weird conversation with the cloth-hatted manager. He wouldn't let us buy anything. We could acquire it by saying we wanted it, but he said he wasn't allowed to charge us for it. All of his usual customers worked for the coal company and purchases were deducted from their wages. "No," he said, "no money," adding, "it's all yours," which he pronounced as "s'all yorn." We reckoned his name must be Saul Yorn.

The governor remembered Lionel from the earlier expedition and greeted him and Ted warmly. In addition to his palatial house, he had a brand new sealer-type motor vessel of about two hundred tons and the last word in luxury, named *Sysla*. He confirmed that we could certainly use her for transport to and from our field area. *Sysla* was anchored some way off and after lunch her captain, Pete Andreassen, a very impressive type with excellent English, came on board *Lyngen* to meet us. *Sysla*, it was planned, would pick us up again from our field area on September 12 or thereabouts, perhaps as late as September 14. The *Sysla's* motor tender and crew ferried all our kit out to her. The boatmen weren't very clever about that, for they loaded the crates three high, well above the gunwale level of the tender. Outside the shelter of the jetty there was quite a good chop and the tender rolled alarmingly. Mike, who with Phil had accompanied the load, had to jerk one crate inboard to prevent it going into Adventfjorden. He was then bashed on the leg by a flying jerry can of paraffin. However, with brute strength and ignorance, the load was soon stowed on *Sysla's* deck and, after we had waved a farewell to *Lyngen*, we were all stowed in *Sysla's* saloon.

Sysla was a very sturdy craft, fitted with the best that money could buy. She had cost five hundred thousand kroner, a lot of money. The interior was spotlessly luxurious. Despite her upscale amenities, she was a practical vessel, designed for work in ice and in rough seas; even the crow's nest was radio-equipped. We were well settled in the saloon by 3 PM, although very hungry because of lack of lunch, when two daughters of *Ingeren*'s captain came on board along with the female radio operator of the ship. All three women were good looking, lively, buxom blondes. This unusual female companionship, coupled with our famished condition, made us all a little hysterical. Laughter was free and uncontrolled. Stan turned on all of his party pieces for them and kept us all in stitches. Our ancient trapper friend and a sozzled companion also found their way on board and explored everything and every part of the ship. It took them about twenty minutes to say "cheerio" to us fifty times or so before they left. At 8 PM the engines of *Sysla* were started—a very reassuring solid, slow thumping. We said our farewells to Alan the Mate, had a group photograph taken on deck, and began a gargantuan supper as we cast off for St. Jonsfjorden, closely followed by *Lyngen*. She soon overtook us, because *Sysla* was not very fast. During the evening the weather began closing in and getting wetter. As we sailed along the northern coast of Isfjorden the sea became appreciably rougher and the west wind freshened. Dave and I did the washing up for the steward, which pleased him no end, while he sat on a stool and told us tales of the war in Spitsbergen.

As we approached Daudmannsodden the weather looked so bad that Captain Andreassen was doubtful about landing the coastal plain quartet at Müllerneset. By the time we passed Farmhamna the sea had begun to die down, but it was still too rough and too foggy to land the box of food there. The captain promised to do so on his return journey. Soon we could make out a black speck south of Müllerneset, which was the hut that the coastal party was going to use as its base camp. As we got closer it appeared more and more of a shambles. Dave wondered why it had been built at that particular spot, but there it was. By 4 AM *Sysla* lay about three hundred yards off shore, just outside a line of shallow rocks. The two seamen—Dave swore their names were, or should have been, Lars Svensen and Sven Larsen—rapidly launched the tender, with half of the stores plus Lionel and Stan aboard. They rowed away very skillfully, passing between the rocks and through the breakers to the short stretch of stony beach below the hut. We could see how cold and wet the work was, as our friends waded from the boat with awkward and heavy loads, across the beach and onto dry land. Stan felt he should have had a large red L (for Learner) on his back, for he felt a complete greenhorn.

Sysla *at her dock in Longyearbyen.*

Expedition assembled on Sysla. *L to R: Mike, Dave, Gordon, Lionel, Phil, Colin, Ted, Stan, Goss and Dennis.*

Dave, Gordon, and the other half of the stores followed very shortly. They all shook hands with Sven and Lars who returned to *Sysla*, only to turn around immediately and return to shore. They had forgotten their paraffin. Ted passed the cans over, with suitable wisecracks, and delivered the captain's repeated assurances that he would deposit the precious box of supplies at Farmhamna. Leaving the four of them on the desolate foreshore, feeling cold, tired, and a bit apprehensive, but intact and definitely on their own bit of Spitsbergen, miserable though it was, *Sysla* blew them a farewell hoot, gave the cape a wide berth, and turned into St. Jonsfjorden.

In the fjord, sheltered from the westerly winds by the snow-covered mountains of Prins Karls Forland, the sea became much calmer. The quiet waters were dotted with loose ice and a few small bergs from the Osbornebreen (Osborne Glacier), which formed a three-mile-wide ice cliff at the head of the fjord. The sky was now a most glorious blue with a large sea-green streak over the foreland. Seven ducks winged their way along the fjord. The mountains were tall and majestic. It all might have been better in our own vessel, but it was pretty darned good as it was! Goss spotted two seals—we thought they might be ringed seals—lying asleep on an ice floe. They had been there long enough for their fur to dry out in the early morning sun, so that when

Farewell to Sysla *from base of the inland party, near head of St. Jonsfjorden. Gaffelbreen (glacier) in background.*

Base camp of the inland party. Phil contemplates his future.

they looked up in surprise their faces were ringed with fur, almost as though they were wearing fur-trimmed anorak hoods. In a few seconds they slithered to the edge and plunged headlong into the water. The *Sysla*'s crew tried to shoot another seal they spotted, but missed. Our destination was a stretch of gravelly beach on the south side of the fjord, between the shallow valleys of Charlesbreen (Charles Glacier) to the east and the Løvliebreen (Løvlie Glacier) to the west. We too got cold, wet feet as we carried our crates, bags, rucksacks, and paraffin cans from the boat to dry land. We had remembered the paraffin but somehow left behind the Thomas splint, and we had to keep *Sysla* waiting for another boat trip to shore. However, for us the landing exercise was much safer than it had been for our friends at the exposed location at Müllerneset. By now it was about 7 AM.

Let Goss paint the scene:

As *Sysla* moved off, giving a cheery farewell blast of her horn, we tackled the disorderly heap of possessions and began to set up base camp on some nearby flattish stony ground a few feet above high-water mark. The surroundings impressed us all: sea, glaciers, serrated peaks, and bouldery moraines filled the view all around. Nowhere, apart from our tiny camp, was there any evidence of human activity.

Birds there were in large numbers, of course, mostly gulls and other sea birds but ducks and geese too, and small birds, such as sandpipers, making a living along the beach. Most unusual to us were the lovely little black-capped arctic terns, who so resented our intrusion into their territory that they would often form a team and swoop down close to us in a great flurry of feathers and long red bills, sometimes making actual contact. Waving our arms or even an ice axe would only just hold them away when they were really angry.

We put up our two Meade tents, the ones without flysheets, and a larger store tent. The Meades were among the best mountain tents then available. The floor area was about five feet wide and seven feet long and they were almost five feet high at the ridgeline. They had sleeve doors at one end, a bit difficult for entry and egress, but very weatherproof, and a closable window at the other. The ground sheet was sewn in and extended a few inches up the walls. They were excellent two-man tents, when equipped with flysheets. But there were three of us to be fitted into each, and we had no flysheets. Still, the weather was glorious, so while Dennis and Mike made a meal, Ted went off with ice axe and shovel to construct a latrine tent, and Phil, Goss, and I wandered along the shore to collect driftwood for a recreational fire. Fifty years later, as I was writing this account, I realized that the Norwegians had named the adjacent point on the fjord shore Piriepynten, in honor of good old Roger.

∞

It was August 5, everyone was safely ashore, and we had as much food and equipment as we should ever have. It looked as though we had five or six weeks in which to do as much geological work as we possibly could. The mission of the four people at Müllerneset was fairly closely defined. Lionel was working on the Hecla Hoek rocks and Dave was mainly finding, mapping, and examining the raised beaches along the shore. Lionel's work was in two parts. First, he wanted to examine the structure of the Hecla Hoek formation and the features of its deformation and metamorphism. His detailed structural study would involve the mapping of the deformation structures (foliations, folds, lineations, and so on) formed during the initial period of tectonic activity (broadly known as the Caledonian Orogeny) that had affected the Hecla Hoek. The orientation of deformation structures visible in the field would be a guide to the broad directions of compression and extension that affected the region during the orogeny. The deformation and metamorphism of the original sedimentary and igneous rocks of the Hecla Hoek also affected the micro-structure of the rocks (the shapes and orientations of the individual crystals), so these too would be part of the study. For this procedure he needed specimens of known orientation for later laboratory study using a microscope. To collect such specimens he would mark horizontal lines on an outcrop and also the direction of magnetic north before knocking off the marked piece of rock from its outcrop with his hammer. These were "oriented" specimens. After a while, Lionel wasn't too perturbed when Stan referred to them as "oriental" specimens.

Lionel's second task was to determine the extent of the fossiliferous (mainly brachiopod, coral, and crinoid-bearing) Carboniferous rocks that Brian and he had found in 1948 near Kapp Scania, near the mouth of Isfjorden. By examining the deformation structures in these rocks, he hoped to learn something about the post-Carboniferous tectonic activity that had emplaced them in the Hecla Hoek rocks. This second deformation must also have affected the older Hecla Hoek rocks. With luck, Lionel thought, he might find traces of both deformations in the older rocks and be able to distinguish them from each other.

In order to cover as much ground as possible, he intended to make two traverses, the first one from Müllerneset eastwards along the shore of St. Jonsfjorden, at least as far as the Charlesbreen. There he would have the opportunity to meet up with the inland people if they happened to be at their base camp. The second traverse would be south from Müllerneset to the Eidembreen, where he and his crew also hoped to pick up and use the other box of food, dropped at Farmhamna from *Sysla*.

Dave and Gordon, with their two-man tent and flysheet, would be plodding along the coast, more or less in company with Lionel and Stan. The area is rich in landscape features associated with the previous covering of the land by an ice sheet and with the subsequent rise of the land from the sea, as the ice sheet receded. Dave intended to look for raised beaches—evidence of these former sea levels—to measure their elevations with an aneroid barometer. The nongeologists accused him of just making sandcastles all the way

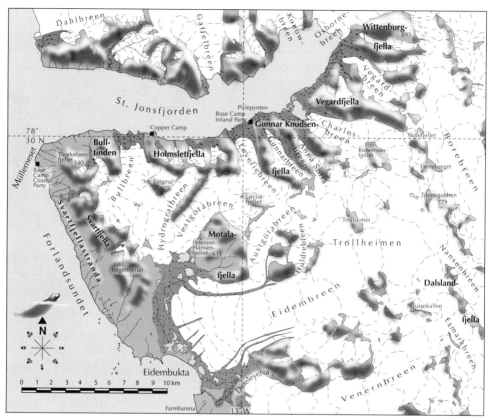

Field area and base camps of the Birmingham University Spitsbergen Expedition, 1951, based with permission on the Norsk Polarinstitutt maps A8 and B8 of the 1:100,000 series (1988). Elevations are in meters. Note: because of the thirty-seven-year difference between the dates of the expedition and of the aerial photography for this map, and the retreat of most of the glaciers since then, some of the descriptions in the text of the glacier termini differ from the map.

along the fjord, but he was looking for ancient seashells, from which he expected to establish geological ages for the beaches. In this way he could learn more about the vertical movement of the land relative to sea level, and perhaps would be able to infer something of the former extent of the glaciers covering the land.

The tasks for the inland party were not defined quite as closely. Phil and Goss intended to make a systematic investigation of the stratigraphy of the Carboniferous and Permian rocks in the area south of St. Jonsfjorden. That kind of work had been started in Vestspitsbergen during Isachsen's expedition around 1910. In the 1930s, he and Anders Orvin, a senior geologist working with the Norsk Polarinstitutt had continued with similar work at Kongsfjorden, north of St. Jonsfjorden and also south of Isfjorden. However, these rocks vary a lot between the two places and no real age correlation between the stratigraphic columns in the two areas had been made. A close examination might well allow precise correlation with the fossiliferous beds at Kapp Scania. Incidentally, it was Anders Orvin who had identified as Carboniferous the fossils found by Brian and Lionel in 1948.

To achieve these ends, Phil and Goss intended to investigate the rocks exposed in the outcrops accessible from the relatively crevasse-free Løvliebreen and Charlesbreen, which they intended to use as their main roads southwards. This really means that they would try to correlate the rock formations with the successions that had previously been recorded at Kongsfjorden to the north and Isfjorden to the south. Not having seen either locality, they would not find this an easy task. Phil, with his two rock carriers, initially Mike and me, intended to start by examining the rocks exposed on the mountain called Holmesletfjella, north of Vestgötabreen, a western tributary of Løvliebreen, and then on the ridges that formed the cirque around the head of Løvliebreen. Perhaps there would be time to venture farther south, across the cirque towards the *nunataks* around Trollheimen. Then, after a couple of weeks or so, Phil and his rock carriers would return to base, perhaps exchange the two field assistants with those who had accompanied Goss in the first fortnight, and head back to the exposures in the Trollheimen area and farther south and east. Meanwhile Goss, with Ted and Dennis, would travel across the Charlesbreen to make their first camp in the lateral moraines there and work the mountain, Vegardfjella, along the north side of Charlesbreen. Later they would make a new camp farther up Charlesbreen and examine the exposures around Robertsonfjellet. In the second half of the abbreviated season, Goss would probably work on the exposures north of Vegardfjella, perhaps reaching as far as the Wittenbergfjella (Wittenberg Mountains). In this way the geologists would be able to cover a great deal of ground and, while they might not be completely satisfied with the work they accomplished, their findings would be a new contribution to the knowledge of the local geology.

∞

Although we were very tired, our first "night's" sleep at the inland base camp (from, say, 11 AM to 4 PM) was none too restful because we were not used to the dazzling effect of the low sun on the fabric of the tents. Over "breakfast" in late afternoon on August 5—we struggled through the sleeve entrances of the tents many times, roused by huge crashes of ice from the calving Osborne and other glaciers. Very seldom did we see the falling ice; by the time the sound reached us the activity was over.

One of the six of us was a perfectionist. Phil pointed out that a neighboring spot, a few yards away, would be a much better site for the stores tent. So we moved everything, a long and tiring effort involving food crates weighing upwards of one hundred pounds each, but we finished the chore by 8 PM. There we were: six neophyte arctic explorers, on the shores of an unexplored arctic fjord. All of us were enthralled. Mike wrote:

> We have our two brown sleeping tents up, as well as the green store tent, the cooking screen, and the paraffin depot. The driftwood flag-pole is complete with Union Jack—all perched in a hollow of moraine right above the fjord. There can be few spots like this on earth. From where I sit in front of our tent I can see, across the fjord, four glaciers, all a mile or more wide, and there is a fifth just out of sight behind the moraine. Snow- and scree-covered mountains surround us in all directions. The open sea, the Greenland Sea, 20 miles away to the west, is cut off completely by the mountains of Prins Karls Forland. It is 11 PM and the sun is still above the horizon, just on the shoulder of a mountain, but it does not feel cold. There is very little wind and hardly a cloud in the sky. In the heat of the day the glaciers crash and grumble continuously and lots of small bits of glacier ice float out into the fjord.

Mike and Dennis went off with the shotgun to shoot an eider duck but came back empty-handed. They did see a small seal, however, very close inshore. Goss was the only one of us who had never fired a shotgun. We insisted that he do so, though I can't recall our reasoning. His response, on hitting an empty can, was "doesn't it make a big bang!"

The following day, August 6, was Bank Holiday Monday back at home, the day we intended to reconnoiter our routes to the first field areas. Goss, Ted, and Dennis were heading eastwards to the Charlesbreen, lightly laden but each furnished with six barley sugars, two ounces of chocolate, and five MacVita biscuits for lunch. Phil, Mike, and I were going in the other direction, towards the Løvliebreen, with lunch, climbing ropes and ice axes.

We'd had a good view of the mile-wide Løvliebreen from *Sysla* as we sailed by. At that time of year the lower half of the glacier was almost free of snow. It seemed to have very few crevasses but lots of water channels. Farther up, the glacier was snow-covered but still seemed benign, offering an easy route to the rock outcrops near its head. We had several aerial photographs that showed many places where good exposures of rock were accessible, but they were oblique rather than vertical photographs, so that many mountainsides and deep valleys could not be seen. We also had a topographic map dating from about 1920, which gave us a good picture of the coastline and the near-coastal mountains, although it was less reliable farther inland. Osbornebreen had receded perhaps three miles in the thirty years since then and Løvliebreen no longer reached the fjord. It looked as if it should be easy to get onto the glacier and follow it up to its head.

The idea was to see as much of the area as possible before returning to the base camp. We started out at about 11 AM and picked our way westwards over the moraines and alluvial sands that had been deposited by the fast-receding Gunnarbreen, now just a shadow of its former self. From the extent of the moraines it was clear that this glacier, too, had previously reached the coast of St. Jonsfjorden, but now it was tucked into the mountains to the south with only a short tongue protruding northwards. The outflow streams from the glacier remnant weren't very wide or deep but we still managed to get our nether parts quite wet, in fact sopping. However, we had good boots and socks, generously supplied by Timpsons and by Jaegers, respectively. Timpsons had let each of us have two pairs of leather boots. One pair was flat-soled, for use with skis; the other was nailed with tricounis, crescent-shaped climbing nails, fixed to the welts of the boots for use on rock and ice. The nails were excellent on rock; on ice they did much of the work of crampons, which we did not have.

Altogether our boots stood up to some very rough usage, usually in appallingly wet conditions. By the time I went on my next polar expedition, in 1952, tricounis were a thing of the past and we all had boots with tough ribbed Vibram rubber soles.

We soon reached the eastern edge of Løvliebreen and starting picking our way up the bouldery lateral moraine: not the easiest progress even when one was unladen. The route up onto the glacier was simple, but it was the first time any of us had ever stood on one. Perhaps because we had ideas of snapping crevasses or something like that, we conscientiously roped up. Then Phil proved the precautions to be worthwhile by falling through the first snow bridge, waist deep into a crack. He extricated himself without assistance—too quickly for Mike or me to take a photograph. From there it looked as though we shouldn't have too much trouble in traveling south up the glacier to the exposed rocks near its head. The glacier proved to be relatively free of dangerous crevasses, with only a few inch-wide cracks. The only hesitation we faced was with the wide and deep meltwater streams, all of which could be jumped. In most places the surface was old, compacted snow, peculiarly honeycombed, which gave a very satisfying crunch as we walked on it. Rarely did we walk on clear blue ice, free of snow.

Higher up, the snow became softer and we sank ankle deep, wishing we had brought our skis. Løvliebreen levels out into a two-branched upper valley, one on either side of the uninspiring Løvliefjellet. We went up the left side, trying to mount the ridge that joins Løvliefjellet to Knudsenfjella and forms the head of the cirque basin around Løvliebreen. We crossed the *bergschrund*, the crevasse formed where the moving glacier pulls away from the static rock, and began to climb a subsidiary ridge. There we made a mistake: the rock was too loose. After one and a half hours we gave up the attempt and headed for home. Mike had great fun glissading down a snow-and-ice gully on the end of the climbing rope; Phil and I followed a little more carefully. We walked down the glacier and over the rough but not difficult ground back to base camp. On the way we saw an occasional bright little arctic flower and clump of moss peeping through the surface gravels in sheltered spots. What is more, we had the inestimable pleasure of walking over territory that we knew had never been walked on before by any human being, a thought that greatly

Part of the front of Osbornebreen, looking from the front of Charlesbreen.

A glacier flowing into St. Jonsfjorden from the north.

raised our spirits. We arrived back at base camp in brilliant sunshine, which had given hatless Mike a headache, to find that Goss's party had been back for an hour or so. They'd had an experience equally as interesting as ours, crossing the Charlesbreen to the moraines of the eastern side. To the south they could see Robertsonfjella and many unnamed peaks, set against a wonderfully blue sky. However, by the time they had started on the return trip, herringbone clouds were spread across that sky.

Goss said:

> None of us had the slightest experience of glaciers and accordingly we took great care. [The Charlesbreen, I now realize, was receding rapidly—global warming!]. Near the snout it was still quite heavily crevassed, but a little higher up it was almost a stagnant lump of ice, nearly devoid of major crevasses. [Ted saw three, which he thought were about thirty feet deep, on that first crossing.] It was also the warmest time of the year and the snow, which in winter might have hidden crevasses, for the most part had melted. The main hazards were melt-water channels. Most were only a few feet wide, but many were quite deep and dangerous, with icy water rushing through them. All the streams were jumpable.

Nevertheless, Goss, Ted, and Dennis roped up to cross the glacier, prudent in the extreme. Most of us were fairly experienced rock climbers, used to climbing in North Wales and elsewhere with the University Mountaineering Club. We almost always climbed using hemp rope: a material that had stood the test of time and was available in different weights, the heavier the safer. It was also easy to knot, although when it was wet it became stiff as well as heavier with absorbed water and harder to untie. It was at its worst when frozen. For our expedition, however, we had the new, white, silky-looking nylon rope that had wonderful elasticity and shock-absorbing capability. It was far lighter than hemp and absorbed less water, but it was slippery, too, and the manufacturers' literature highlighted the need for more complicated knots. Moreover, we were aware that when allowed to run fast through a nylon loop, enough frictional heat could be generated to melt the loop, perhaps with disastrous results. I think I was the only member of the expedition who had his own nylon rope. Someone gave me a standard 120-foot rope for helping with some water-divining work on Bircher Common in Herefordshire, of all things. Nowadays nylon has been replaced with better man-made fibers such as Dacron. Seven years later, in New Zealand, I converted my nylon rope into a clothes line on which to hang baby's nappies.

We all slept much better that night, exhausted from our long walks. Sad to say, the following morning we were late getting up, despite our intention of having a long day depot-laying. By the time we had sorted out fourteen days of stores, waxed our skis, and actually started, it was about 5:30 PM. Goss and his two load-carriers bore packs they estimated at sixty to seventy pounds each. They later learned a valuable lesson—never trust an engineer with barley sugars! As they walked at a good slow pace through the rough, hummocky lateral and terminal moraines of Charlesbreen, mini-disaster struck. In an unguarded moment on a steep slope, the can of barley sugar sweets, which we all considered essential to our survival, escaped from Dennis' pack, crashed, and sprang open, scattering hundreds of the delectable sweets over the wet mud and gravel. They retrieved most of them and secured the can more firmly to Dennis's pack. At their chosen campsite they stacked the supplies, not forgetting to mark the spot with a line of small boulders set out on the glacier. In the days ahead, in mist and snow, sometimes it was very difficult for them to find their precious depot and they were pleased to have such clear markers.

Marker stones on the Charlesbreen.

We, the other trio, did much the same thing. Mike had the Everest pack frame onto which he had strapped a crate containing two food boxes, probably weighing more than eighty pounds. Phil and I had rucksacks, weighing perhaps a bit less, and we lugged these prodigious weights along the shore, up the dry moraine valley, and after an hour or so, onto the glacier. We put on skis, changed packs around, and continued. The change didn't make the packs any lighter but they now abraded our bodies in different places. On skis, even with ski skins, we had little control of direction and were pathetically slipping and slithering around. We were pleased that there was no one to watch us. Ski skins, I should explain, are strips, sometimes made of sealskin, sometimes of synthetic material, about five feet long and a few inches wide, with loops at each end to fit over the ends of one's skis. The nap on the skins is on the snow side and is "laid" (combed?) against the direction the ski will move. In theory, therefore, the nap does not interfere with forward progress on the flat or when headed downslope. On an upslope the nap is pulled up by any downslope movement and prevents one's skis from slipping backwards when trudging uphill. Ski skins are a thing of the past now. On most skis designed for cross-country skiing, or when haul-ing a sledge, transverse serrations are cut in the soles of the skis, with the sides of the serrations at appropriate angles. However, we had skis with skins and, as Mike noted:

> About a quarter of an hour later, there is a shout from Colin who is in the rear. He had broken a ski strap, fallen over, and pulled a muscle in his groin. A conference is held, and we decide that Phil and I will carry on with lightened loads, and Colin will putter back to camp without load. Phil and I, with half loads, will carry on to within about three-quarters of a mile of the properly ski-able snow and set up the depot. We shall then go back to the accident dump and carry a second load up. By the time we do all this it is 10 PM and we leg it for home.

They reached base at about 11 PM.

Propped up with two ski sticks I went slowly back to base, my stomach and thigh hurting like bobbsey-di, to use the correct medical expression. At the edge of the glacier the moraine was quite wet. There wasn't much free-flowing water—*that* was beneath the glacier—but lots of puddles with silt suspended in various consistencies. One deepish pool was quite solid when I trod on it, but as I stood there writhing gently, waiting for a muscle spasm to go away, the mixture slowly turned liquid and I sank. The 1948 expedition had a similar experience when Josh Nunn almost disappeared from sight and had to be pulled out on a rope by Lionel. I'd met the word *thixotropic* when stirring milk and cornflour at home, but this was the first time I'd seen it in nature.

Extricating myself, I enjoyed the distant views of the peaks and snowfields of Prins Karls Forland, out beyond the end of St. Jonsfjorden, some twenty or thirty miles to the west. Inland were clusters of sharp jagged rock peaks, alternating with smooth snow- and ice-fields into the far distance; again came that inexpressible feeling of wonderment that we were the first people ever to set foot here. The geologists, after they had done their depot-laying, reveled in thoughts of the geological feasts ahead of them and, for the moment, the rest of us allowed the same thoughts to outweigh our concerns about carrying those impossibly heavy loads. I reached base about 9 PM and was pleased to find that the doctor was in. Ted applied Sloan's liniment all over the place, strapped me up, and ordered me to stay abed until the muscles had healed. That shouldn't be more than a month or two!

We were using ex-army commando rucksacks with Bergen frames, courtesy of Messrs. Oswald Bailey, dealers in army surplus gear. These were the fashion of the times for impoverished travelers on foot. They turned out to be highly practical. Compared with more modern pack frames, they had a very low center of gravity when fully laden, which seemed to be an advantage in keeping one's balance when walking over coarse scree and boulders, especially when the boulders were snow-covered. Most of our other clothing had also previous belonged to Messrs. Oswald Bailey—ex-army trousers, camouflage anoraks, and an array of other items in khaki or air force blue. Altogether there was a vague military appearance to our turnout, although, compared with the bright reds and blues of present-day equipment, perhaps we looked more like some hastily assembled third-world militia.

The following day, our third, the others again took heavy packs over the same routes, while I stayed in bed. Goss and company re-crossed the Charlesbreen to their Camp I site. They took about one and a half hours to reach the western limit of the lateral moraine. Already, Ted was becoming disenchanted with carrying heavy loads over the boulders and rough terrain, preferring the glacier for travel. Dennis, the least experienced, was still inclined to tangle or tread on the rope and did not yet know how to handle his ice axe very well, but he was learning quickly. At the campsite, using their ice axes, they raked level a patch of small stones in the moraine and set up their Meade tent. Ted was pleased with the size of the pile of stores they had carried there but felt sure they would have no trouble in eating their way through it. The sun was due west, silhouetting the peaks of Prins Karls Forland against the sky. On the other side of the fjord the Osborne and Kunow glaciers were calving prodigiously, rumbling continuously and glinting in the evening sun. Before long the Primus stove was roaring and half an hour later they were enjoying their first meal on trek. From the steaming pans came an appetizing bowl of porridge, then pemmican soup with MacVita biscuits. Hot tea rounded off the meal as they lit their pipes and concentrated on maps and aerial photographs to work out their tactics for the following few days.

After a few hours of sleep, disturbed only by an occasional rattle as stones fell down nearby cliffs, loosened from icy gullies by the warmth of the sun, they awoke about 8 AM. Ted noted: "So three men can sleep in a Meade tent—just! Spent a fairly comfortable night, and warm!" They breakfasted and started the real work of understanding and mapping the array of geological features around them.

∞

Goss explained:

> The rocks belonged to two major subdivisions. To the west of a north-south line approximately through our Camp I site was the very thick complex of contorted and highly altered sedimentary rocks known as the Hecla Hoek group. That set of rocks was largely Lionel's concern. The rocks were certainly very ancient, but their true geological age was uncertain, as they had not yielded any fossils—possibly because intense compression and high temperatures had obliterated any organic remains they might have contained. Maybe Lionel would find that the Carboniferous fossils from Kapp Scania were part of the

Hecla Hoek, which would change all that. Perhaps those fossils and the beds in which they occurred had come to lie within the Hecla Hoek outcrop by some means that we knew nothing about. Lionel was trying to unravel all of these mysteries.

Overlying the Hecla Hoek group to the east lay the rocks that were our [Goss's and Phil's] objective. They consisted of a very thick succession of younger sedimentary strata, measurable in many thousands of feet. Their outcropping area extended eastwards much farther than we could see, but our chief interest lay nearby in the oldest formations of this great succession, the lowest few thousand feet of thickness. In terms of geological age, the strata we wanted to examine were in the range of 290 to 350 million years, that is belonging to the Carboniferous System. If they turned out to be still older, say 350 to 400 million years—part of the Devonian System—these rocks would be even more interesting.

The whole sedimentary pile, together with the underlying Hecla Hoek basement, had been subjected some time after the Carboniferous Period to large-scale compression, folding and faulting, during at least one phase. We would have to be careful in establishing the correct order of succession, from oldest to youngest, of the components of the entire rock sequence. We could see that the originally flat-lying sedimentary rocks were frequently tilted and folded, occasionally standing vertically and in some places even overturned. In addition, large fractures [faults] locally brought older rocks on top of younger ones.

Geologists faced with these types of situations will, as a rule, try first to establish mappable rock units, usually ranked as "formations." A formation will typically be an easily recognizable shale, sandstone, or limestone, from a few feet to a few hundreds of feet in thickness. A location will be sought where, if possible, both top and base of the formation can be seen and where there is a continuous exposure all through. Such places are not always easy to find; when they are found the geologist tries to measure the total formation thickness, examine and describe in detail the character of the rock, and look for fossils. He may then try to follow this defined formation across country, coloring it in on his map and looking for further illustrative exposed sections of the formations above and below. With persistence and good fortune a regional succession of formations and a map of their outcrops can be built up. The determination of the ages of the strata frequently has to come later, in the laboratory, where fossils can be carefully prepared and examined and matched against their named and dated counterparts in the scientific literature.

This summary statement was so clear, even to the nongeologists, that fifty years later some of us regretted Goss had spent nearly all of his professional years with a major oil company. Although he had excelled in this work, many of us wished he had been a teacher, at which profession he would clearly have excelled even more.

∞

That day, August 9, was their first full day of geological work. After breakfast they emerged to find that the morning mist had cleared. A bright sun was shining from a blue sky with just a few cirrus clouds scattered here and there. Dennis was the cook and had made a pemmican hoosh, which all thought delicious when piping hot. They decided to take some for lunch. When it was nearly cold, Ted wrote, "I drank it, but with disgust. It's not bad when hot, but vile when it cools." They argued about whether to take a rucksack each. Ted thought one was enough for all three, whereas Goss wanted them each to take one. Obviously he was thinking about their rock-carrying potential. They took three and set off up the lateral moraine to the rocks cropping out at the head of the glacier. While Goss examined the exposure, Ted and Dennis took a round of compass bearings onto the main peaks, using their prismatic compass; then they took a round of photographs. They walked through the moraines around Vegardfjella and noted that where the moraine piled up against the mountain the melting snow gullies above had made pools of water. In places huge landslides had calved off the moraines, probably as a result of the water, and in front of the landslides was a horrid slurry of rocks and mud, which made for disturbingly slow progress. For lunch they had the vile cold pemmican, two MacVita biscuits, and chocolate. After that they continued around the shoulder of Vegardfjella, Goss still examining the exposures and collecting occasional samples. After Dennis had taken another round of compass bearings, Ted measured everyone's pulse rate. Finally, on the north side of Vegardfjella, Ted and Dennis sat down and admired the view, while Goss continued his geology and note taking. All the glaciers had receded significantly since the date of their map, about 1920, the Osborne farthest, by perhaps three miles (because the snout was floating). Ted sketched the scene and Dennis took photographs. Then they hunted for plants. There were a few grasses and even fewer small velvety-leafed plants in sheltered spots, but mostly the place was barren.

After 5 PM Goss announced he had done enough for one day and they headed home. At one spot in a slightly sloping area facing south, clumps of small plants grew in great profusion. They crossed one landslide that was very muddy, with huge blocks rolling down intermittently, and quickly decided the glacier would make much easier going, even though the snow was slushy. It was Ted's turn to cook and, for a great treat, they opened a can of blackcurrants to have with their porridge. Pure luxury! They crawled into their sleeping bags about 10:15 PM.

Their work on the following days followed much the same routine. They went around to the east side of Vegardfjella where Goss mapped away very happily and the others took rounds of angles and so on. Goss and Ted were both pleased to find limestone with abundant fossils. Goss collected lots for his work and Ted collected a lesser number for his mother and other friends and relatives. They found fox tracks but never saw an animal, and they observed many extraordinary features on the glacier, all highly interesting to them. For example, they found rounded hollows in the ice, thirty feet or deeper, with small pools of water in the bottom—thinly ice-covered because the air temperature was below the freezing point and the sunshine did not reach to the bottoms of the hollows. In one place they found the going extremely tiresome because for a couple of steps they could walk on the frozen surface of the snow and then they would step through the surface and sink six inches or so. Not knowing on which step they would sink, and how far, was disconcerting.

Ted, and I'm sure the others too, wished they had air mattresses and they tried making additional insulation under their sleeping bags with newspaper, which they had in abundance, nominally for wrapping rock samples. It worked excellently and they agreed to try it again. Ted hated having to wash greasy dishes in cold glacial water and said he'd prefer to do all the cooking but the others felt the same way, so they continued to cook in turns.

After a few days working from Camp I, Goss decided to move the camp up to the top of the basin of *névé* (compacted granular snow), a few miles east. They agreed to take food for eight days. With the tent, paraffin (a Primus-full lasted for about three cooked meals), sleeping bags, and all their personal gear, their packs weighed about fifty-five pounds each. Roping up, they headed up the glacier, the surface of which was still frozen from the chilly night air. The slush of the previous day was frozen solid, so walking was not too difficult except for the weight of the packs. As usual they took great care in crossing the transverse crevasses but those were rather few in number and were clearly visible. Every hour or so they stopped for a rest, sitting on their packs. Around 5 PM they reached the moraine bordering the extension of Vegardfjella. They cleared a campsite among the hollows in the moraine, filling the holes with smaller pieces of moraine collected nearby. Altogether it made an excellent campsite, although a bit exposed to the wind. Somewhat unimaginatively they called it Camp II. Goss made dinner, porridge with raisins, biscuits, pemmican, and a cup of Milo. Ted was satiated, he said, and they all thought they had done a good day's work.

After dinner Goss went off fossilizing around the screes and up to the lowest exposures of rock while Dennis and Ted made a big cairn. In it they left a message in a can: "12 August 1951. Birmingham University Spitsbergen Expedition, 1951. Camped here 7 days, then off in direction of Trollheimen, compass bearing: 202 degrees Mag."

They slept well that night and decided it was a good campsite. Later, however, Goss wrote:

> Every day there would be some kind of lesson to learn, sometimes many lessons. For instance the Camp II site had been leveled originally on an innocuous-looking gravelly patch of moraine. Even the first time we used the site the tent floor did not remain level. Later on there were clearer signs of subsidence, which we remedied by filling up the depression with stones and re-raking the surface before pitching the tent for a second stay. We were lucky because by the final time we passed the site it had turned into a huge fountain-like spring of glacial meltwater, with the jet rising a meter high. We had known all along that the moraine lay on the surface of the glacier itself, but had no suspicion of the presence of meltwater streams that sometimes

flow under pressure in tunnel-like systems below the surface of the ice. It appeared that one of the small surface meltwater streams that flowed in and out of the moraine had cut down and broken into the pressured system below, causing the water to erupt in spectacular fashion. Thereafter, when possible, we liked to choose campsites well away from actual glacial ice.

The trio's confidence that they could handle their environment was growing steadily. The following day Goss felt perfectly safe in working by himself on the geology of a ridge of Vegardfjella. The other two went off on a reconnaissance of the route southwards, east of Robertsonfjella. They crossed a few crevasses, several feet wide, but the route looked easy so they decided to climb the *nunatak* to the east. It stuck up above the snowfield perhaps five hundred feet and, for the most part, was composed of frost-shattered shales and sandstones, which were snow- and ice-covered in many places. They scrambled up to the ridge, with rather precarious going, whence they had a wonderful view, including part of Isfjorden, thirty miles to the south. Ted was keen to climb to the summit, which they called "Peak Alpha," up more solid but more nearly vertical rock. Dennis thought the task beyond his abilities.

The snow on the western side of the *nunatak* they had climbed was becoming very soft from the full sun, and Ted decided to go down the eastern side, avoiding the *bergschrund*, and back round the screes to their outward route. They arrived back at their campsite at 7:30 PM to find that Goss already had most of the dinner ready. After pemmican, Dennis and Ted managed two bowls of porridge each while Goss was stumped after one. However, he did manage his full share of the "special of the day": grapes in light syrup, forty-eight each. Despite sodden boots and cold feet it had been a glorious day.

So far the weather had been quite kind. Often the sun had shone and while it was quite windy and chilly, especially at night, their sleeping bags and clothing were adequately warm. It hadn't rained or snowed significantly. That was all about to change. The next day they walked to Robertsonfjellet. It was bitterly cold, probably about fifteen or twenty degrees Fahrenheit, and snowing heavily in strong wind. The going wasn't too difficult, just miserable, and while Goss scrambled up the scree to the bedrock and started measuring and mapping, Ted and Dennis, with their feet beginning to freeze, stayed at the bottom of the slope, huddled in their gas capes. Ted had found his gas cape was too long, catching in his feet, so he had amputated it and made it too short.

The following day it was warmer and raining, so far only gently. Except for Mike (who was in the other party, with Phil and me), we all had double sleeping bags, with separate waterproof covers. If one put the waterproof covers on before crawling into the bags, perspiration condensed underneath, against the cold ground, and one woke up with the sleeping bag bottom quite wet. If one didn't put the waterproof cover on, then the rain, penetrating through the fabric of the tent as a fine spray, slowly soaked the top of the sleeping bag. We regarded this as part of our education: we learned that whatever we did, we couldn't win.

Leaving everything as shipshape as they could, they trudged through the wet snow and mist back to Robertsonfjella and climbed the scree, at its angle of repose, to the hard rock—quartzite and sandstone—where Goss started working. It started to snow in earnest and they were all pretty miserable. However, Goss insisted on measuring another long section before they quit and returned to the tent. On arrival there they found the tent nearly equally miserable. After dinner Dennis was sick. Dr. Hitchcock diagnosed a chill generated by living and especially sleeping in damp or wet conditions. He prescribed moving to a better hotel.

The following morning was wasted: it was raining and snowing and they stayed in the tent where everything slowly got wetter and wetter. Ted noted in his diary, while waiting for Dennis to feel up to the day's tasks: "We are all very affable with one another—real comradeship. Talk has ranged through sex, academic subjects, our life careers, the kind of plastic net mattresses that would make our lives more comfortable, to tramps (on which Goss is a mine of information). When will *Sysla* pick us up? Can we get *Miss Mabel* back to Cork? These musings came up, among other concerns." They debated whether they could manage to sleep *comfortably* with the rucksacks in the tent, to keep them dryer. Ted thought they could. Goss and Dennis thought they couldn't. They decided to try it for one night. Dennis, a tallish fellow, complained that he wouldn't have room for his feet. By lunchtime they had despaired of life in a wet Meade tent and went to work on the northwest ridge of Robertsonfjella.

While Goss was measuring the section and collecting rock specimens, the others spent some time watching a ptarmigan, a bird about the size of a large pigeon, and her seven or eight chicks. Their plumage blended so well with the grays and browns of the rocks around that Dennis had nearly trodden on the family before seeing them. The chicks were too small to eat and obviously they couldn't kill the mother, so they just watched and were surprised, when Ted ventured too close, that one of the chicks *flew* off.

Goss reported that:

> A disquieting moment came when the three of us came wearily down towards the base of some long scree slopes and I realized that my geology notebook was no longer inside the pocket of my map case. There was no choice other than to go back up the mountainside and try to find it. [The others offered to help but Goss turned them down.] My two colleagues strode on towards the distant tent, promising to start preparing the evening meal. After an anxious half-hour of retracing the rocky uphill route by locating our footprints in the snow of occasional hollows and gullies, suddenly I spotted the orange-colored notebook lying conspicuously on a small patch of snow. Greatly relieved I made a resolution to double check that the notebook was tightly secure in its pocket at least every five minutes in future, while we were on the move.

That same evening, only a few hundred yards from camp, Goss found the remnants of a small Russian meteorological balloon lying half-hidden in the boulders of the lateral moraine. Among the decayed batteries and recording devices was a small aluminum plate, with Cyrillic characters and the date 1939.

The weather continued intermittently poor, with lots of periods of rain in which they got wet, whether inside or outside the tent. Fortunately, the rain was often followed by windy, sunny intervals when they could dry out, to a lesser or greater extent, both their clothes and their sleeping bags. A two-day blizzard proved slightly less uncomfortable since the snow didn't penetrate the tent fabric quite so readily and the sleeve-type entrance effectively kept out the wind and powder snow. The tent canvas drummed and flapped frighteningly at times against the aluminum poles. However, the tent design and the materials were good and their fragile home remained intact. The worst moments during the blizzard came whenever someone inevitably had to go outside to answer a call of nature. Otherwise, when confined to tent, they talked and, when all subjects had been exhausted, either slept or read. In addition to a few books they had newspapers galore, generously supplied by a Birmingham dealer for safely wrapping the fossils and rock samples. The newspapers were also used for extra insulation and to mop up penetrating precipitation. When the level of water in the tent exceeded the mopping capabilities of the newspapers, the occupants encouraged the water into a sump and made a suitable drain hole in the sewn-in ground sheet. They, and we three in the other inland party, were all much disappointed to find that all of the copies of the newspaper were of the same date and the same edition. Consequently we all soon learned some of the text by heart. When Goss and I met at the base camp after the first ventures, his first words to me were, "What did Drobny say to von Cramm?" I made the correct reply: "'Too bad,' says Drobny to von Cramm" (Drobny and von Cramm were tennis players engaged in the Wimbledon Tournament that year). Fifty years later, when I met Goss again at Phil's house, he asked me the same question, so I gave him the same reply.

Goss continued to attack all of the geology accessible in this area. The party had a few minor but interesting adventures with crevasses. Ted fell through the snow bridge over a water channel carrying particularly cold water, and they all learned about step-cutting and ice-belaying techniques in a classic situation. Goss wrote:

> One day we came across a simple short ice slope, maybe thirty feet high. The slope curved upwards from a horizontal gravelly base, increasing quickly to a final six feet of vertical wall at the top. It was very safe: there would be no serious consequence if anyone should "peel off." We roped up, textbook style, cutting steps and deep slots for ice-axe belays, moving one at a time. Dennis was leading up the final vertical section, cutting out generous holds for hands and feet and sending down a tinkling cascade of ice fragments over Ted and me, in the number two and three positions. Then something went wrong. Dennis came out of his steps, hit the ice slope quite gently,

and then accelerated at an unbelievable rate on the frictionless, glassy smooth surface. Ted, very close below, could not hold him when the rope jerked taut. Ted's ice axe flew out of its belay slot and went spinning away through the air as Ted went down equally rapidly behind Dennis. As number three man on a safe stance nearer the base of the slope, I saw that nothing was going to hold me. In an instant I found myself at the bottom with my companions in a tangle of rope, ice fragments, and wet-clothed bodies. This twenty-minute exercise markedly increased our respect for ice slopes of all kinds.

By August 23 they had indeed eaten their way through most of the supplies and had porridge without milk or sugar. They made a cache of their remaining food and paraffin at the cairn near Camp II and set off down Charlesbreen in wind and rain, under low clouds. At the Camp I site they picked up the collection of rock and fossil samples, then labored westwards across the foot of the glacier. As Goss wrote:

The ice was melting rapidly, leaving the surface hummocky and criss-crossed with little streamlets. The moraine heaps around the foot of the glacier were even wetter. These mounds of stones, sand, and boulders were still frozen hard a few inches below the surface so that water could not percolate downwards. Thus it would either flow away on the surface or would accumulate as muddy pools. In the faster, larger meltwater streams, the water cut steep-sided gullies that were difficult to cross with heavy loads. Bursts of bad language filled the air as we slipped and stumbled over them.

Eventually Dennis spotted two distant tents, close to our base camp. They both bore flysheets so they knew that the coastal party from Müllerneset had arrived. "In response to our whistle blasts the four occupants struggled out and came towards us through the rain."

AROUND THE RUGGED ROCKS THE SODDEN SCOUNDRELS SCAMPERED

The trio forming the other half of the inland group consisted initially of Phil, Mike, and me. As I have said, like the rest of the inland group, we were all quite accomplished at reading about the adventures of polar explorers but we had no actual experience, so that Løvliebreen was the first glacier any of us had ever walked on. Largely as an experiment, the "Løvlie three" all had skis, on which we had a little experience but not very much.

In the first few days we (Phil and Mike mainly, because my strained groin muscles were still painful) had carried those huge loads towards the head of the glacier. While I lay in bed, on August 8, these two stalwarts carried the rest of the loads up the glacier to the ski-able snow. One of the consequences of our loss of the use of *Miss Mabel* was that we had left our sleds in Tromsø. Mike's inspiration was to convert the large food box and Sir Raymond's skis into a replacement sled. The design was simple and the materials that he needed were quite limited: skis, the box, a piece of wood a couple of feet long to keep the other ends of the skis in place, a few feet of line to lash it all together and another few feet to provide hauling lines. Mike's pleasure shows in his diary: "Rather to my surprise it actually works. The whole job is remarkably rigid and runs very well. Our sled harness consists of nylon lashing strung around the tow bar, and a sling around the waist carabinered to the nylon. On it we could carry nearly all of our combined loads. In a much more light-hearted mood we sled up the glacier."

Phil wanted to start his geological survey with the formations on Holmesletfjella, north of the western tributary of Løvliebreen, called Vestgötabreen. There we would be a few miles west of the sections being examined by Goss so there was a chance that the rocks around us would lie closer to the bottom of the sedimentary rock pile. Perhaps they might even be Devonian, though again it was unlikely that Phil could attribute an age to the strata and the fossils they contained until he was back home. He wanted also to work the semicircle of outcrops that comprised the cirque around the head of Løvliebreen. The rocks looked accessible and not too difficult to move about on, with only a few very steep slopes. Between the mountain and the glacier, around the top of the cirque, was the usual *bergschrund*. Phil and Mike, towing the sled, skied laboriously over the old snow towards the proposed position for the second camp on snow, near the ridge between Løvliefjellet and Gunnar Knudsenfjella (Mts. Løvlie and Knudsen). The surface was soft and wet so that even with skis they sank in an inch or two.

They were tired: unloading the sled to make a depot, then pulling the sled back down to the edge of the snow, had been heavy work. They turned for home, with the wind blowing up and a thin mixture of snow and rain coming down. Leaving the pegged-down sled and their skis they arrived back at base about midnight, to find that I felt much better and had prepared supper for them.

After breakfast at base camp on August 9, we did our final packing for Phil's first traverse, a fourteen-day trek around Mts. Løvlie, Motala, and Holmeslet. Mike packed more quickly than the other two of us, so, since the day was warm with brilliant sunshine and no wind, he grabbed a towel and went for a chilly swim-cum-bath in a deep fresh-water pool in the moraine. He reported a pleasant glow and tingle afterwards, but no one else followed his lead. On the previous day, before he left with Goss, Ted had written a note explaining to possible visitors where we all were, but I couldn't find the note. Probably he had forgotten to pin it up in the store tent. Consequently I wrote another note, later forgetting to pin that one up, too. By the time Phil had organized the ciné camera it was 4 PM; by the time we reached the sled, it was 7:30 PM. Rucksacks were piled high on the sled so that we had nothing to carry on our backs—thank Heaven!

Mike wrote in his diary:

> The surface is soggy and quite dreadful, so that the pulling is hard. We all get our feet stuck under the surface, with skis on. Our route is up to the right of Mt. Løvlie but we run into trouble with plenty of watercourses, right in our path. This meant long detours, which slowed us up, especially as manhandling the sled across the streams meant taking off and then putting on our skis and traces. The going gets harder and harder as we move higher up the slope, but eventually we reach our first camping site, on the shoulder of the col, with a view right down to the sea by the southern tip of the foreland. Supper is served in the tent, the usual pemmican hoosh, porridge, biscuits, and tea. The temperature is well below the freezing point, so we are camped on hard, frozen snow—drinking the stuff, too. It's 1 AM and bright sunlight. It has been lovely weather all day. Now for our first night's camp on snow!

There was no suitably level site for the tent on the moraine. Rather than camp near the foot of the glacier, with a correspondingly long walk to work each day, we pitched the tent on the snow. Mike and Phil were apprehensive about sleeping on snow but I encouraged them—based on my one night's sleep on snow, between the tracks of the railway line at the top of Snowdon one New Year's Eve. We leveled a space for the two-man tent into which all three of us moved. At ground level we laid down the two waterproof covers for the sleeping bags. It was cozy, to say the least, but not too uncomfortable. Our bodies quickly melted the underlying snow to fit their shapes and we fitted very nicely into these hollows. We added layers of newspaper underneath, for better insulation, again taking the opportunity to make sure we knew exactly what Drobny had said to von Cramm. We added such spare clothing as we had. The other two of us envied Mike, who had a sheepskin waistcoat. Why on earth we hadn't brought small air mattresses defeated our imaginations. This omission was nearly as bad as not having flysheets. We squeezed into the tent with our packs, some food, the cooking stove, and everything else. Did I say cozy? I meant cramped. Two of us slept with our heads at the back of the tent and the third, the cook for breakfast, lay the other way round, with his head to the doorway. However, the weather was reasonably fine, or at least acceptable, with low clouds and a bit of wind—until it rained! I'll return to that point soon. When we woke up next morning at 10 AM it was definitely a working day.

For our first day of geology Phil took us on foot through soft snow to the col in the Holmesletfjella, due north of our camp. From there we climbed up the ridge to the west. While Phil measured the section and wrote it all down, Mike and I messed around, photographing and looking at the plentiful flowers. The views over St. Jonsfjorden, looking right up Osbornebreen, were truly wonderful; I took a round of compass bearings onto all the identifiable peaks while Mike sketched Motalafjella, the mountain to the south, for Phil. By 4 PM we had got back to the col for lunch. We were trying to set an earlier daily routine, working from 8 AM to 10 PM instead of 10 AM to midnight. Mike suggested that while Phil and I climbed up the ridge to the east he, Mike, should return to the camp and collect all our skis, thereby making our return home easier. One of the happiest sights of our little party was seeing Mike trudging along, trailing a line of skis, each with a ski boot fitted, looking like a duck and string of ducklings. We reached home at about 8 PM after a glorious run downhill. Later we had the first disaster in the tent: I spilled the washing-up water.

My stomach and thigh muscles had been painful on the previous afternoon and when I woke next morning they were more painful than when I first hurt myself. It turned out to be a good day to stay "indoors": the weather was bad, with mist blowing in a cold north wind. Phil and Mike skied over to the south ridge of Holmesletfjella and had a miserable time. They climbed the abominable quartzite scree—one, two, or three steps laboring upwards, followed by one, two, or three steps slipping downwards—until they reached the rocks. Phil spent a great deal of time sketching, measuring, hammering, and rock collecting. Mike, wearing a balaclava, anorak with hood up, gloves, and mitts, wondered whether there might not be a better place to do these things. The wind strengthened until it was a real gale. They reached home at about 9 PM to find me holding down the tent, after re-guying it and putting snow lumps to hold down the edges. That, of course, made the interior even cozier. Mike wrote, "Colin has made a weird and wonderful hash of everything he can think of—it is not a success." I, on the other hand, thought it was pretty good. It isn't every day one gets to taste chocolate-flavored pemmican!

Next day, Sunday, August 12, while Mike and Phil prepared for work, I made breakfast again because my muscles were still very sore. I was sorry to miss that day's trip because it promised to be a long and interesting one. Equipped with extra biscuits and chocolate they set off on skis down the Vestgötabreen, round the tip of the south ridge of Holmesletfjella, and across the subsidiary glacier to the knob on the end of the west ridge of Holmesletfjella, which Phil had christened "Mt. Enigma." He stopped to study a few outcrops. They had to carry their skis across patches of blue ice and moraine, reaching the end of the south ridge at about 2 PM. There were thick patches of moss and lichens, and Mike found several new (to him) alpine plants. Phil was pleased to find a band of mica schist, full of garnets—very small ones, unfortunately. It was nearly 7 PM before they reached Mt. Enigma, after an hour or more of uphill plodding on skis with skins on. Phil found the geology to be fully worthy of the name he had given to the mountain. Mike sat in the sun, trying to keep warm and thinking about the next meal, due at 8 PM. However, at 8:30 PM Phil suggested going down Bullbreen to see the other side of Enigma. Their skis (and food) were now some distance away. They plodded down the glacier, sinking six inches at each step. Eventually Phil was satisfied. They returned to the skis and, especially, the food, by that time much needed. For Mike, lunch was an event to be prolonged as much as possible—he even sucked his pieces of chocolate, while Phil chewed his in his rush to return to work.

After lunch they climbed to the top of the ridge to see the rocks there. Mike went with Phil for the exercise—he had fallen through a snow patch and had wet feet. Down again! At about midnight they started working on tomorrow's ration of chocolate and biscuits. On skis they crossed the glacier to a low col on the south ridge. Mike wrote:

> Dreadful business cutting across the slope on hard surfaces with ski skins. You never know if you are falling forwards or backwards and balance is hypothetical. About an hour later we reached the col, having skirted two big *bergschrund*s and scrambled up and over the rocks

with skis on our backs—very hard work at the end of a day. Then came the long uphill ski back to the tent where Colin, bless him, had laid food on. We arrived at 2:15 AM and just about collapsed. Food, then sleep in a bag which Colin had aired and was less damp and much warmer. And that was Sunday! Mt. Enigma is to be remembered as a petrel nesting site and a wonderful place for alpine plants.

Everyone woke late on August 13 to a thick, clammy mist. We lay abed until 2 PM discussing our options, eventually deciding to move camp a few miles southeast, to the col between Løvliefjella and Motalafjella. We had packed by 6 PM and the other two had a very hard time pulling the sled uphill through the softened slow. I plodded along on skis, pulling very little. After a couple of hours and a couple of miles we were all pretty exhausted and, since visibility was almost zero, camped. After rewaxing the skis, having dinner and so on, we reckoned we deserved an extra cup of Milo.

The next few days were memorably miserable. It snowed several inches outside the tent and rained a comparable amount inside. Phil decided to see if he could do anything worthwhile on the near ridge of Motalafjella and he and Mike set off, leaving me with the impossible task of drying out our sleeping bags. I erected a clothesline between two skis but then the dry snow turned to wet snow and drying made no progress. The skiing surface and the weather were equally atrocious and the others soon gave up. Following their ski tracks, they returned to the tent. We tried the sleeping bags inside their nominally waterproof covers, a procedure that required the skills of a contortionist in the cramped tent and did no good anyway. We just got wetter with perspiration as well as precipitation. Mike's shoulder melted a depression that assumed the role of a sump-hole for water in the tent. Woken by the coldness, he tried to squeeze the water out of that part of his sleeping bag. All the newspaper was completely sodden. After breakfast Phil skied up to the ridge and soon returned, reporting that the slopes on the north side were reasonable but, as far as he could see in the negligible visibility, the south side was mainly scree, which, as Mike noted, "is bad for sledding." Dodging the drips, Mike trimmed his moustache and his nails, cleaned his teeth, and wrote a book on *Spitsbergen Camp Cooking for Three*. It was very short, because the evening meals were identical to the breakfast dishes, except that the breakfast meals came with vitamin tablets.

Phil wrote up his notes and I read. I had brought a couple of books with me, a battered hard-bound copy of Alex Munthe's *Story of San Michele*, which I had bought for one shilling, and the Penguin classic, Guy de Maupassant's *Boule de Suif.* I remember being annoyed when the rain drips splattered on *San Michele*. I am amused to find that I still have both books, *San Michele* with the warped cover and the dried drip marks and the Guy de Maupassant, inscribed "Colin Bull, for Birmingham University Spitsbergen Expedition, Summer 1951." I still have a copy, too, of *Hints to Travelers* (1901 edition) but I can't find in this edition the passage where I had thought it said that it never rains inland in Spitsbergen. Perhaps that quotation came from a different book or perhaps it was just a figment of our imaginations and some day we shall find that we did bring flysheets.

The next day, despairing of the mist, snow, and rain, we decided to move anyway and crossed the col to Austgötabreen, so that Phil could work on the other side of Motalafjella. After a midday meal it was still snowing quite hard, but we packed up and then, of course, found that the new snow had made sledding next to impossible. With all three of us pulling immensely hard, getting ourselves hot and sweaty, we eventually reached the ridge top. There the mist started

Mike and Phil with "sled" on inland snowfield.

to dissolve, a bit of blue sky appeared, and a reluctant sun showed itself. A breath of hope! The other side of the col was scree for a hundred feet or so, followed by very steep snow. Relaying, we carried the rucksacks, tent, and then the sled itself down to the top of the snow, before lowering the reloaded sled down on the end of the climbing rope. This worked well for two hundred feet or so, followed by the inevitable disasters. Phil couldn't hold the belaying ice axe and Mike was pulled out of his stance and down the slope, getting sopping wet. The sled got away completely. At the bottom of the steepest part of the slope the sled very adroitly jumped the *bergschrund* and careered down another quarter of a mile or so, stopping upright with no harm done. We camped where it stopped. Phil took a ciné film, which slowed us a lot and made us all very cold.

For a few hours the wind blew from the northeast, the dry quarter, and in the early morning we put everything out to dry, including the sodden newspapers. By noon thick mist came down again. Phil headed down the Eidem Glacier to work on Motalafjella while Mike and I followed a northeast course back over the ridge to collect our depot from the upper Løvlie. The food box was safe and sound and contained an unexpected number of luxuries, including one can of Mr. Smedley's unmarked goodies. Perhaps it would be yellow plums! The trip back was mainly downhill and went quickly, only an hour or so, which left us with perhaps four hours before Phil would return. Mike and I talked for a while, and then I remembered Roger Pirie's certificate about an imaginative sea-cook. I made a great delicacy out of Quaker Oats, raisins, and butter (well, margarine) pressed into a flat round cake and burned it all in the lid of one of the saucepans over a low smoky Primus. Mike noted: "Colin called it 'Kaki Wats' and reckoned it was an ancient aboriginal treat." When Phil returned we ate it anyway. The Smedley's can turned out to be peas and diced carrots, so I mixed it in with the pemmican and called it Irish Stew. Very good! I thought that dehydrated onions might have made it even better.

The next morning the weather was foul, heavy rain driving against the tent door, a boisterous southwest wind, and very low cloud. Not a working day! The bottom end of Mike's sleeping bag was wringing wet from the puddle of rain blown in through the door and the top end was equally wet from the rain coming through the tent and collecting in the sump hole caused by his shoulder melting a hole in the snow. However, Mike is a very restrained individual and wrote in his diary:

It was too wet for comfort! Thank goodness my sheepskin waistcoat has a waterproof layer that the water has not yet penetrated. How one manages to keep cheerful and without harsh words to one's companions, I do not know, but somehow we do. I am the wettest of the party, the rain having been beating worst on my side of the tent. Colin and Phil have double sleeping bags, one of which is lain on while the other is slept in. This keeps one bag fairly dry even if the other does get wet. I just have a single, thicker bag. Phil is on the opposite side of the tent and is more or less dry, lucky for him.

Everything that is still fairly dry is heaped in the one corner, at the back of the tent, where the drips are fewer, and two people sit on this. The third person squats near the door by the cooking utensils, which we keep on the lid of the sled box, our cooking board. And these positions are kept for ten hours or so, as the weather is foul all day. It is virtually impossible to straighten out one's legs—all movement must be conducted without touching the sides of the tent, if humanly possible. You stay where you are until everyone is stiff, and then you all change positions. The water drips in continually: the only hope is to get the drips to follow well-defined channels, from which they can be mopped up. Despite all our care, everything is damp, to say the very least.

After breakfast we discuss in detail the faults and the points to be remembered about our equipment and take notes for the use of future expeditions, if any. This passes most of the day. In the evening we cook, and how! Apart from the usual supper we have half a can of corned beef, mixed with egg, as an omelet, followed by half a can of gooseberries, our first fruit for some time. Then follows a painful period due to the effects of overeating.

About 10 PM we start to go to bed. Colin gives me his under bag to sleep in, and it goes down over my wet bag, placed drier side up. We have my yellow groundsheet to shower the drips to one side and retire in hopes that it will be fine in the morning.

Sunday August 19: I wake up at 6 AM feeling cold under my hips and on inspection find that the bag I am sleeping in is just about wet through and is getting wetter from my bag underneath, which is just sodden. This is the end, and I get up! One third of the tent is unusable, and the two sleeping bodies occupy the rest of the space. It is too wet outside for mopping up operations to be possible, without waking up the whole tent, undesirable in the extreme with two half-asleep boys in bed, so I get into, and for three hours stay, in the space between the legs of two bodies lying shoulder to shoulder. Talk about a squash! For two hours I read Colin's *Story of San Michele* in a sitting position, by which time my left leg has completely gone to sleep. From then until 9:15 AM I remain in a kneeling position, with the book on Colin's hips. Why it wasn't more uncomfortable I don't know, but I stayed there without undue muscular strain.

By this time I am fed up, and the boys get up while I go outside to clear up and mop up the pool of water by the door. The mist is as thick as ever, with light drizzle from the southwest. My hands have lost all feeling by the time I go in the tent again. So I put them in Phil's discarded night socks to warm them up. He has gone outside in wet ones, to keep dry things dry, or maybe he is in bare feet (on snow!), a habit we have all got into for short trips, as easier than putting wet boots on, outside in the rain. It is all right for two or three minutes; afterwards, feet warm up quite quickly, especially in my fur-lined boots.

We start our can of bacon for breakfast, and very nice too! After breakfast there is a break in the mist and the rain stops, for the first time in thirty-eight hours! Phil and Colin arrange to work on the nearby ridge. I stay behind to get things dried up as much as I can. I get the sleeping bags out in the wind and they dry a little. I also clear the dirt and loose paper out of the tent. But about 3 PM back comes the rain and mist, soon followed by Colin and Phil. You can't do outside work in such wretched mist.

My own bag is still too wet to have in the tent. It will stay that way until the wind swings back to the northeast, cold but dry. Then things will improve! We had our evening pemmican about 4 PM and have bacon and eggs, porridge, gooseberries, and biscuits for supper. Then sleep, maybe?

I slept fitfully on top of Colin's inner bag, with all the clothes I can lay my hands on—usual sweaters, plus one of Phil's, and my anorak, two pairs of trousers, and a windproof. Could have been worse!

Monday, August 20: I get up at nine, feeling tired. The mist has lifted, giving promise of a fine day. At breakfast it is arranged that I will stay in camp to dry sleeping bags in the wind while the others make the long-awaited attempt to climb Motalafjella.

Phil and I had a great day on Motalafjella, in weather that by recent standards was superb—that is, it didn't rain. The ascent comprised five hours of scree bashing, not our favorite occupation, followed by an hour or two of scrambling over rock. We did reach the top (884 meters elevation), a genuine first (and probably last) ascent. Phil worked away steadily while I engaged in the usual supernumerary activities with compass, camera, and sketchbook. I concluded that I wasn't a very good sketcher so instead I wrote an account of this notable "First Ascent" for the British Alpine Club magazine, which, of course, was never sent to them. Occasionally Phil would say, "Come and look at this, Colin," and I would show interest in his bits of limey sandstone or sandy limestone. Then came three more

Phil, prepared for the first (and last?) ascent of Motalafjella.

hours of scree bashing as we came down again to snow level. The angular blocks of frost-shattered rock would not run so we had to be careful as we came down, still in our ski boots, not to turn an ankle. From the bottom we blew whistles, by prior arrangement, in the hope that Mike would hear them and start supper, which he did. We arrived back, very tired, to a special dinner with peas in the pemmican and went to bed at about 1 AM.

The following day was almost equally good as a drying day. After a good warm-water wash Phil and Mike skied northwards to "do" the geology of the ridge between the spots where we had brought the sled over and where we had left the depot that Mike and I had collected. I stayed to supervise the drying activities. On the previous day, immediately after The Big Soak, these activities began with wringing the water out of the sleeping bags—it's really demoralizing to have to squeeze water out of the bag in which you expect to sleep the following night. The scene bore very little resemblance to my romantic picture of the activities of real polar explorers. By the end of its second drying, Mike's bag was dry enough for him to sleep in without having to wear his waterproof pants. I also had a wash, and at about 7 PM I skied to the spot where Mike and Phil had left their skis on reaching "Sled Col" and towed them, by the approved Mike Box method, to "Depot Col," which my colleagues had just reached. After supper we discussed expedition finances, concentrating on the wisdom, or otherwise, of not buying flysheets.

For the next two days it rained continuously. Mike and Phil had changed sides in the tent and we erected an internal flysheet made of two gas capes over Phil's side of the tent. The wind changed direction and Mike's bag became uninhabitable again, so he slept in one of mine. We stayed in the tent and no work was done.

For our final day, August 24, it rained but not as hard as before. Unutterably miserable, cold and wet, we packed. Every job seemed to take an interminable time. When we took down the tent we found, as suspected, that we had been living on a pedestal, nine to twelve inches high. The surrounding snow had melted that much, with all the rain, and a small crevasse had opened near the back of the tent. We stuffed our garbage into it, took a photograph of the pedestal, and set off on skis, pulling the heavy sled back over the route to Depot Col and down the "King's Highway"—the Løvliebreen. We left the sled at the old depot site, since Phil would need it again for the second trip. With rucksacks again we finished the tiring but uneventful plod in the rain back to base. Both of the other parties were there, Goss's trio and the Müllerneset quartet, and we had a great reunion with much talk about our experiences over the last two or three weeks. A comparison of beards showed Mike to be the clear winner in terms of length, strength, and blackness. Obviously beards thrive in a wet environment. Dave claimed that a family of lemmings lived in his beard, but produced no evidence. Lionel and Stan, while investigating the geology of a local mountain, had met several ptarmigan, three of which they had killed after a vigorous chase. In the pouring rain they had cleaned them and made a stew. The other seven people had eaten most of it on the previous evening but there was still enough left for the three of us to make a memorable meal, followed by a few base-camp luxuries, such as canned golden plums and a shot or two of hot whisky toddy. Over coffee we soon filled the tents with pipe and cigarette smoke as everyone settled to the serious business of smoking and talking at once.

Goss's party had returned before us and had claimed the greatest luxury of all. Two of them, Ted and Goss, moved into the flysheeted tents with the coastal party, while Dennis, who drew the short straw, and the three of us had to spend another damp night. The inland parties anticipated that it might continue to rain inland so, as the "coastal four" departed westwards, the rest of us unpicked the seams of our sleeping-bag covers and started to re-tailor them to fit over the ridges of the Meade tents. With guy lines made from bits of nylon cord, and using the ridgepole from the store tent, they seemed to fit quite nicely. They might appear improvised and gauche but they worked surprisingly well as ad-hoc flysheets. The only disconcerting aspect about them was that the rain would collect in sagging pouches, which a sudden puff of wind would noisily empty. Goss was absolutely certain it was a polar bear outside the tent, answering a call of nature. A happy although wet homecoming!

Altogether we had lost about half of our working time and had never reached Trollheimen, to which I had been looking forward. It was a nicely shaped mountain and who knows, there might still be a troll or two in residence. Obviously things could have been much, much worse. We had all survived and had been well fed, but viewed from the perspective of fifty years, that fortnight still ranks as the most uncomfortable and unpleasant time I've ever spent. However, the three of us got along with each other amazingly well. I can't remember any hard words, except a very brief one when I spilled the porridge on a sleeping bag. Mike, who kept a very full account of our lives, only once noted: "Most uncomfortable. Tempers are getting a little frayed."

In April 2002 Mike summed it all up. He wrote:

> We went on a geological expedition, not just a camping holiday. I realize it is difficult to make the collection of rock samples either interesting or exciting to a nongeologist. But the fact that we never even considered abandoning our cramped, wet, and uncomfortable tent, living on dull and monotonous food, demonstrates our dedication to the geological.

LIFE ON THE *STRANDFLAT*

Our four friends, Lionel, Dave, Gordon, and Stan, whom we had last seen on the desolate beach near Müllerneset, were already at our base camp, which they called "Reunion Camp," when we six *hommes de l'interieur* arrived. Goss and his rock carriers came from the east and, the following day, Phil with Mike and I arrived from the west. The quartet from the coast had an interesting story to tell.

I hadn't spent any time at all with the coastal party, however, and Dave, Stan, and Gordon have produced such excellent accounts of their activities that I am sure I cannot improve on them. By and large, I shall quote verbatim from their stories. Dave starts the account:

Life on the *strandflat* began for us late at night on August 5. We had made it to this almost featureless cold coastal strip and a horrible looking wreck of a hut that was to be our base for six weeks. Armed with his ice axe, Stan ventured into the place but it was free of polar bears. We recalled Captain Andreassen's words as we traveled to this spot, that one of his crew had killed a huge polar bear near Osborne Glacier, at the head of the fjord, during the previous week. As we were put ashore he hoped we had adequate firearms. The sea and land were all shades of gray and we felt that way too. The prospect was of six weeks or so of miserable weather, expedition rations, no radio, no medical officer, one rifle (a Mannlicher .300, which belonged to Lionel) to protect us from goodness knows how many polar bears, and only ourselves for company. There was no sign of any decent rock for me to play with—no Old Red Sandstone oozing with fossil fish or Carboniferous rocks crammed with crinoids, corals, cephalopods, and the like. What a prospect, only a few bits of raised beach to look at and maybe the odd whale skeleton if I were lucky! Still, that is what the Royal Geographic Society gave me all that seventy-five pounds for, so I'd better make the most of it! "It" was, as far as I could see, this flat plain, several miles wide and all beastly Hecla Hoek metamorphic rocks and scattered gravel and shingle. One could see that there was definitely not anything resembling the magnificent step-like raised beaches of the Spitsbergen fjords. The attractions of the place were rather limited, although on the landward side the mountain front did rise up steeply and suddenly from the coastal plain and promised some good views of the *strandflat* plain and the inland snowfields.

A few solitary seabirds wheeled about us while the sea lapped gently on the rocky beach. It all felt very lonely, quiet, still, and sad. The appearance of the hut told us of twenty years or so of neglect. It seemed once to have housed three men in fair comfort. The Norwegian magazine pages pasted on the walls inside the hut were from the mid-1930s, but their girlie pictures gave no indications of any clothing fashions in vogue then. They aroused our interest only momentarily; food and bed were more to the point. We wandered around kicking at rusty old cans, bottles, and other garbage, of which there was a lot in the tundra mosses and grass. Several pieces of driftwood nearby afforded a small flagpole so the expedition flag was hoisted fairly quickly, just in case anyone should sail by. A brace of duck came flying by and when a second pair appeared, heading along the shoreline, we blazed away with enough shot to sink a battle cruiser, but the ducks took no notice. Humiliation! This was a situation to be repeated fairly often, though later we were somewhat more successful.

After an hour or so *Sysla* appeared again from St. Jonsfjorden and sailed away southwards in the middle of Forlandsundet (Foreland Sound). She looked a very small boat out there as we waved farewell to her—our last connection with the outside world for six weeks or more.

Lionel's sketch of base camp. Prins Karls Forlund in background.

Honor guard at flag-raising ceremony:
Stan, Dave, and Gordon.

The hut wasn't fit to live in and we would not be using it much, so our Meade tents were soon put up on a foundation layer of dead moss and grass. Sleeping bags, other gear, and explorers were installed, Gordon and I in one tent, Lionel and Stan in the other. Two small homes, called "Chez Nous" and "Mon Repos," were thus established close to the hut. The store tent was erected nearby. Our first Spitsbergen meal was soon prepared on the little Primus stoves and we were ready to tuck into our porridge (with raisins and a little dried milk) and some of the real expedition food—pemmican hoosh with biscuits. Then we lit up our pipes and felt relaxed. Before climbing into our sleeping bags there was the ritual of the evening pee and scrutiny of the shoreline in case a bear or other unfriendly creature was around. Stan remarked how strange it was that so many of the chunks of ice drifting down the fjord resembled the head of a swimming bear. In fact, no bear ever appeared, but we observed the precaution. In the sleeping bag it was warm and pretty comfortable once one had moved the clumps of moss around under the ground sheet to the best advantage for one's hips. I did not feel drowsy, even though it was now 9:45 AM. It had been broad daylight throughout the time we had been there. However, soon, to the quiet murmuring of the waves on the beach, we drifted off into a sound sleep.

Having removed boots and outer clothing, which went to make pillows, we slept soundly until four in the afternoon, despite the bright daylight. At 2 PM Gordon had got up to slacken the guy ropes as it was pouring rain, but the flysheets worked well, and we emerged nice and dry—well, dry anyway. We gathered in the store tent to cook breakfast and stuffed ourselves on hefty helpings of porridge. It seemed a good idea to examine our locality a bit more. I found the old brazier from the hut and set it up as a more or less permanent fireplace. There was all manner of driftwood on the beach for a fuel supply, logs from Scandinavia or Siberia, as well as a great deal of flotsam and other rubbish tossed overboard from ships. Wooden boxes and fishing gear were common, all heaped up at the high tide mark, some of this material being pretty old and some very recent, all brought up by the North Atlantic Drift.

Through the field glasses Lionel spotted a flock of ducks to the north, off the headland a quarter of mile away. There were also hundreds of them sitting on the beach, presumably gathering there before

Snowfield camp with drying newspapers.

The coastal quartet enjoy a "pretend" feast of walrus.

flying off south for the winter. We set off hopefully to secure duck for supper. What happened was typical of many subsequent occasions. I took up position with the double-barreled shotgun while the others detoured inland to drive the ducks towards me. After an age I heard shots. The ducks scattered in all directions. A lone duck came towards me and I fired both barrels at twenty-five yards. Feathers flew and so did the duck—straight on! Shortly afterwards the boys returned and we all crept back to camp empty-handed. Later that day we had a go at another bunch of ducks and Lionel shot a single individual with the rifle. Fortunately, a bullet through the neck killed it, but it fell into the sea. Stan stripped off and waded in to retrieve it, a practice not to be recommended in a cold sloshing sea complete with floating pieces of ice. The duck cooked well, though there really was not much meat.

Gordon continues:

On August 9, Lionel and Stan were staying near base while Dave and I went off to investigate the raised beaches to the east. Before we set off, Lionel shot a seal through the head. It was about thirty yards out to sea and we then had to decide how to fish him out. We built a timber raft from washed-up pit props, on which Lionel volunteered to paddle out, but the waves were too powerful for us to launch the raft. In any case the water was bitingly cold, too cold to put even a foot in. We eventually secured the seal by tying a long string to a geological hammer, throwing the hammer out to sea beyond the corpse, and pulling on the string to pull him ashore. Lionel scored the winning throw. We grabbed the seal by his back flippers when he came within reach and hauled him on the beach. By this time it was 3 PM and Dave and I beetled off to do some geology. We worked south along the coast about two miles and then trekked inland. Lionel's heel was still very sore and seemed to be turning septic, so he and Stan nobly volunteered for the task of dissecting the seal. When Dave and I arrived back at camp at 9:20 PM, Lionel and Stan had certainly had a good go at the seal. The skin was off and nailed to a board for curing. Pounds of blubber (for oil) lay in an old pan, and in the hut were plates of dark colored steaks. The horrid remains of the carcass lay some distance from the camp and I gave it a wide berth. We had seal steak and peas for supper, but it was very sickly. We did not care for it and have had none today.

Fifty years later Dave revealed to me the rest of the seal story:

Seal meat was not a great success. It was oily, somehow, though I don't think it was fishy in any way. We ate fair-sized steaks of it and enjoyed the novelty as much as anything else. Then we thought that, since Eskimos prize the liver, we would try that. Cutting into the liver, we found lots of quite large worm-like parasites. That put us off, with a vengeance! We never consumed another mouthful. We did not even want to know exactly what the parasites were.

Again Dave, from his diary:

Meanwhile Gordon had been clearing out the hut—a huge pile of dirty old bedding, newspapers, rotten clothes, boots, cans, and pottery lay in front of the place. We fed it to the fire. Stan and Lionel

A chilly Stan as duck retriever.   **Seal meat tonight!**

went off to the stream twenty yards away to build a dam for our water supply. Gordon and I moved food boxes into the hut which, now swept out, was quite roomy. We patched up the holes in the windows with flat pieces of wood. All the same, we kept to the tents for sleeping. After supper of beans, sausages, and tea we turned in, despite the glorious sunshine and marvelous view across the sound to Prins Karls Forland. It was 2 AM. Throughout our weeks on the *strandflat* we seemed to go to bed progressively later and to rise correspondingly later. Somehow we never actually lost a day that way, and, in the last couple of weeks there, as the hours of darkness grew, we got back to keeping more normal hours.

Let Stan take over for a moment. He wrote:

We had a lovely little stream near the hut, by the three graves (don't ask!). Glacial water causes diarrhea, we had read, so a suitable medicine had been packed. We found, in fact, that we were all constipated. We wondered whether we would join those in the graves! I changed into pajamas at night. Food was adequate, with the midday bar of chocolate (courtesy of Cadbury's) especially welcome. Porridge with sultanas for breakfast and pemmican at night kept us going, Because it was always light, we had to get into a routine of going to bed at about the same time each day, even though at bedtime it was often sunniest.

I was "allocated" to Lionel, whose expertise (he had been to Svalbard before) was greatly appreciated by us all. I helped by carrying his geological specimens and standing by rocks to be photographed so size could be established. I always knew I would be useful!

Here's Dave again:

The crew of the *Sysla* had told us about two young Englishmen, geology students from Imperial College, London, named Atkinson and MacDonald, who were working on Prins Karls Forland. During our first days at Mülterneset, when the weather was good, the view of the foreland was always interesting. Frequently the island was under heavy cloud and, by the look of it, was being pounded with rain. We felt sorry for Atkinson and MacDonald, who indeed, were having a terribly wet time, as we learned later.

We spent this and the next day putting the hut in order as far as we could, greatly improving the waterproofing with odd bits of driftwood—even the door became closeable, more or less, although a few chinks remained through which the wind whistled impressively. We named it "The Shambles" and suspended over the doorway three metal fishing-net floats, like the three balls of a pawnbroker's shop. With the food boxes and our gear stowed away and the light and heat of our Tilley [paraffin pressure] lamp, the inside was very snug and we were proud of our restoration work. Late one evening Lionel made a crayon sketch of the scene and I took photos of our work.

The word *strandflat* is a good Norwegian name for the broad, flat low strip of land found on many arctic coastlines. It rises from the beach, or from low cliffs, to an altitude of some 150 feet at the foot of the steep mountainside inland. In width it can be up to about six miles. Such a pronounced and conspicuous land feature with its cover of gravel and raised beach deposits has always been a bit of a puzzle to geographers and geologists. It looks as though it has been produced by rapid coastal and glacial erosion at a time when sea level was 150 feet or more higher than it is today, probably during the last cold snaps in the ice age of the Pleistocene period. Here and there the *strandflat* is deeply gouged by glaciers that for the most part are in pretty rapid retreat. Each summer sees more ice melting than can be replaced by the snows of the winter. From the glaciers and melting snow on the mountains (and from the rain) pour the summer meltwaters that meander across the *strandflat* to the sea or that feed many shallow lakes. Near the sea cliffs small streams flow in the narrow clefts and gullies, slicing through the hard metamorphic rock. Almost all have deep snow patches within them throughout the summer, and in the autumn frosts they echo to the sharp reports of frost splitting the rocks.

On the landward side of the plain the mountainsides rise up quite abruptly. For the most part they were covered in scree, which was treacherous to run down as it commonly changed abruptly from fine to coarse rock fragments and one tipped forwards to nose-plough into the rubble. The high slopes were good places for a view, and apart from the noise of local rock falls or glaciers calving into the fjord, the silence was complete, utterly and eerily so.

The most peculiar features on the surface of this barren plain are perhaps the soil polygons and patterned ground. The repeated freezing and thawing of the soil has squeezed the pebbles and rock shards into ridges and stripes so that patterns of polygons up to dozens of feet across enclose centers of mud, sand, and fine rock. On sloping surfaces there may be long ridges of pebbles separated by valleys of mud and "fines." On a much larger scale, seen from the mountainside or from the air, huge areas of shingle-covered *strandflat* are cut into polygonal networks of ditches a few inches wide and deep. We concocted a theory to account for them, involving the mythical Old Man of Mount Müller and his tame trolls who dug the big polygons for a game of Svalbard Hopscotch. After a long evening in a smoke-filled tent, one could emerge into the mist and imagine them at it, not far away.

For a few days after arriving at the hut we settled in and explored the local cliffs and land. Lionel had a tender heel ["a tremendous blister," according to Gordon] and could not wear his boots—he borrowed a pair of shoes from Stan. The two of them would spend their day on the rock exposures and crags or cliffs while Gordon and I prospected for flat strips of shingle and the white shelly traces of old mussel beds. One evening Lionel and I were coming over the shingle spit at Müllerneset when we found footprints of two men headed south. They were fairly distinct but may have been very old. The site was above the reach of the waves though there was a great quantity of driftwood nearby. At the cape, Müllerneset, we climbed to the top of the cliff. There we found a grave cairn and an iron bar stuck upright in a rock; it was a similar bar to one we had found at the hut. We spent some time pondering what could explain these things and came up with several lurid theories.

To cover as much ground as possible in the limited time available, the two pairs intended to make two traverses from the hut. One traverse would be to the south to Eidembreen and Farmhamna (and the hoped-for extra box of food); the other would follow St. Jonsfjorden eastwards, at least as far as Charlesbreen, near the base camp of the inland group. They knew that the inland parties were both going to do their work in two traverses and the coastal party calculated that, if they made their fjord journey first, they would reach our camp when we should be back from our first traverses. Nowadays, of course, such reliance on casual long-range planning would never happen. We would have had regular radio schedules and possibly cell phones.

Their food supplies were adjusted to these traverses. At The Shambles they had rations to last two weeks or so. Another two weeks' food had been deposited at the inland party's base camp, near the head of St. Jonsfjorden, and another two weeks' supplies had been packed to be left by *Sysla* at Farmhamna. However, they couldn't be certain that the food box for Farmhamna had actually been put ashore, so, being prudent, they made a reserve from their supplies at the hut. This reserve left them short of food for the present.

Gordon explained it:

We now had two meals a day, breakfast and supper. Breakfast consists of porridge (two cups of oats for four people), three MacVita biscuits with margarine and marmite, and pemmican, followed by tea. Supper consists of porridge (1½ cups of oats), five biscuits, with either sausage or bacon (one can among four of us). At midday we have 1 ounce of chocolate each. Our diet is reinforced by four barley sugars a day. I feel rather empty but quite fit.

They managed to cram all the equipment and food for the trip eastwards into their rucksacks. The packs each weighed about seventy pounds—one hell of a load—and they had to struggle into their packs on the ground and then be helped up. Gordon took the precaution of writing a note about their plans for the next few days and pinning it up in the hut. They made the store tent as secure as possible and were ready to leave camp, now called "Cold Comfort Camp," at least by Gordon, at about 5 PM on August 11. After an hour or so they reached the entrance to the fjord where they voted for a rest and chocolate. Dave didn't think he was up to this trekking lark; Lionel's feet were still hurting. They considered waiting for a No. 8 Inner Circle (Birmingham) bus, but found they had left their money in the hut and hence continued to walk quite high above the fjord until they came to the slope down to the outwash delta behind Thorkelsenfjellet (we called it Mt. Müller, it being next to Müllerneset). They crossed that expanse of mud, sand flats, and small fast-running streams without actually falling in and headed for the western lateral moraine of Bullbreen, the first glacier along their route. Dumping their packs at a likely looking campsite, they plodded up the moraine for a good view of the snout of the glacier and the main outwash fan.

The glacier had retreated half a mile or so since 1936, the date of the aerial photographs they were using, and the only remaining low terminal ice cliffs were in the middle third of the glacier. In front was a lagoon and, surrounding that, a rocky moraine reaching to the shore, like two horns encircling the outwash mud and sand. The obvious question was where to cross the glacier to the eastern side, and they decided that that was a problem for tomorrow.

Cold and tired, they pitched the two tents face to face. Gordon constructed a stone fireplace close to the tents, collected wood from the beach, and cooked on the wood fire. Soon they had the standard meal ready, and the treat for the day, a small can of cherries. Relaxed in their sleeping bags they held a short singsong—something, I regret to say, that the inland groups never did. The rumblings of the calving glacier, just the other side of the moraine, and the squawking of millions of baby sea birds on the cliff, about two miles away, accompanied their efforts. Gordon regaled them by singing the Harry Pollitt saga: "Harry was a Bolshie, one of Lenin's lads, till he was foully murdered, by counter-revolutionary cads...." However, that made it rain and the flysheets flap; it became too noisy to sing so they wrote up their notes and went to sleep.

They found the coastal plain to be remarkably alive. The tundra vegetation consisted of mosses, lichens, occasional small tufts of a small short grass, and hemispherical clumps of many types of miniature rock flowers in beautiful red and yellow hues. They found a sandpiper's nest one day, a shallow hollow in the gravel with one little brown fledgling and the remains of the yellow and green speckled egg. Dave photographed the young one, much to the mother's agitation.

This was the area in which they saw four or five arctic foxes near the cliff-face bird rookery. Foxes must have been quite numerous at one time, judging from the number of ancient traps they found, and presumably this was what the trappers in their hut were after. Perhaps by the time they left, in the mid-1930s, the fox population had been nearly exterminated. There was one, a small scruffy-looking beast no bigger than a large household cat, they saw scavenging near the hut; it only understood Norwegian, they concluded, for it ignored their calls and never came close. Of other land animals they saw none: no reindeer, no lemmings, no polar bears, although they found one print of a bear-paw about the size of a soup bowl. Most important,

Gordon and Dave at a camp on a moraine.

there were no mosquitoes or other molesting insects. At sea they saw seals quite often, mainly ringed seals like the one they had shot and partly eaten near Müllerneset hut. From now on they merely threw insults at them. The seals took no notice. Dave saw one walrus in the shallows near Müllerneset, which made off noisily when it saw him; there was no sign of whales, except for whale bones, some large and ancient, scattered in the shingle of the raised beaches.

They spent three days working from this first campsite, a little spoiled by rain. Lionel (in Stan's shoes) and Stan (protecting his interests?) collected "oriental" specimens (each of which, Stan complained, was "too heavy to carry"—most being orange-sized or smaller). Lionel also measured the attitudes of all the bedding planes, fold axes, and other deformation structures found in the Hecla Hoek rocks for later statistical analysis. Stan complained about carrying specimens, but Gordon wrote, "Stan has got into specimen collecting with the enthusiasm of a professor of geology." Dave and Gordon mapped raised beach surfaces. Between Müllerneset and Bullbreen they found about eight suitable sites and dug up and collected sea-shells and also bags of silt for later microscopic examination of the foraminifera (small marine organisms with calcareous shells) they might contain. It turns out that forams (for short), at least some kinds of them, have helically coiled shells, the chirality of coiling (right or left handedness) depending on the temperature of the water in which they grew. Thus forams might be valuable indicators of past climates—and the samples were light!

The four of them were much more inventive of intellectual pursuits than either of the trios of which I was part. They read books aloud, had sing-songs (comprising rugby songs, music-hall ditties, Cornish songs from Stan—many of them exceptionally crude), and played word games (which we did play too, but not often). In bad weather, they spent time in their sleeping bags writing a four-author novel, *The Londoner*, each taking it in turn to write the next chapter. Lionel lost his pipe and they all spent an evening retracing his steps that day. Eventually Stan found it, "to the unbounded joy of its owner. It would have been a serious loss." Dave added: "Lionel, unable to concentrate or relax properly, would have slowly begun to crack up, with dire consequences for the rest of us. We would have had a zombie

Stan with stone fireplace.

or a nutter on our hands. As it was, we now had a very happy bunny and there was much relief all round." Stan reckoned that finding the pipe, by itself, justified his place on the expedition. Dave added that "Lionel, in his joy, nearly kissed him with delight. We all had pipefuls of Lionel's tobacco on the strength of the find."

Moraine bashing was not their favorite occupation. Gordon wrote,

> The moraine is an incredible mess, as if some huge superhuman force has been carrying out opencast mining. Great, elongated mounds—some hundreds of feet high—of earth-like clay, small stones, and enormous boulders are strung together at the foot of the mountains up the valley. We clambered up the valley, over boulders and patches of soft mud and little melt streams. To our left was the glacier, a mass of broken snow-covered ice, and white mist hung over the top of the valley. At the bottom, reverberating thuds shook the earth as blocks behind the ice cliffs shifted.

In the afternoon Dave and Gordon found an excellent raised beach, where they collected hundreds of *Mya truncata* shells, from the measurement of which Dave proposed to construct a frequency diagram. At the end of the day they built a cairn to mark the place where they cached the collections made by Dave and by Lionel, to be picked up on their return trip to Cold Comfort Camp. Their last night at that campsite was very rainy and the rain continued well into the next day. Stan and Lionel read alternate chapters of *The Plague Court Murders*. Gordon asked them to speak up, so that he and Dave could hear, and Stan complained that made him lose his voice. In the morning Dave got a film jammed in his camera. Lionel freed it by opening the camera while inside his sleeping bag. The bag was hot and the camera reluctant so the contortions of this cocoon were highly amusing and the language was excruciating—but the film was saved. To celebrate, they had scrambled egg for breakfast, a delicious change, Gordon thought, from porridge and pemmican.

They crossed Bullbreen (named for a famous Norwegian violinist, Ole Bull, not for me!) fairly low down, after a bit of a struggle over the moraines, to reach the ice. Just up-glacier from the frontal ice cliffs they encountered the worst crevasses. The party was in no real danger of falling in but found it was still rather frightening to hear the torrents of water at the bottom, so they roped up. Since this part of the glacier was constantly calving, Stan suggested they should rename the glacier "Cow Glacier." The others showed remarkable forbearance in not stuffing him into a crevasse. The next hazard was wading a fifteen-yard stretch of an outwash stream. They decided to go barefoot, to keep dry footwear. Through the raging muddy water they could not see where they were stepping and the weight of their rucksacks made them top-heavy and unstable. The freezing cold water came only up to their knees but there were hysterically nervous predictions of what it all might do to their virility. Gordon wrote, "I felt like bursting into tears with the pain of cold feet." It was comforting to them to survive the ordeal, even with bruised feet. Stan found his first glacier "not too bad." He wrote, "the icy blue of the crevasses was horribly fascinating. While gazing into one I found a perfectly rounded stone, created thus by glacial action. It was so good it finished up in the University Geological Department Museum, suitably acknowledged, I trust." However, he thought the moraine was "beastly, when it had to be climbed, fully laden."

Lionel had to tackle this obstacle still wearing shoes: highly unsuitable, to say the least. Gordon discovered he had lost his watch but fortunately Dave and he found it, not too far away. The pin holding the strap onto the watch had broken.

Continuing along the shore, they made Gordon walk several yards ahead of the others because he crunched his issue of boiled sweets, barley sugars, greatly annoying the others. They sucked theirs! They crossed over another moraine, and then another broad outwash plain behind a headland, with several glacial streams. Stan in particular disliked these, because of the painfully stony beds and the high probability of toppling over. Beyond the plain they saw, not far inland, a small hut, about six by eight feet—totally unexpected. It had just enough room for one man either to lie in the bunk or to stand beside it. It was in rather better condition than The Shambles. On the wall was painted OCEANA 17.8.10. They were in good time for the forty-first anniversary party (it was August 14) but they decided not to wait. There were signs of more recent visitors, too—cans and bottles, a Norwegian Teddy cigarette packet—though they could deduce no dates. One or more of the visitors must have been a trapper: they found two arctic fox skulls and several heavily rusted trappers' tools. The place was an incredible mess. On the headland was a notice on an iron stake. It read "Copper Camp. Northern Exploration Company of London, claim 1905," inscribed in English, Norwegian, and German. Gordon found a good mossy campsite about three hundred yards from the hut and two hundred yards from the fjord.

Camp at St. Jonsfjorden.

147

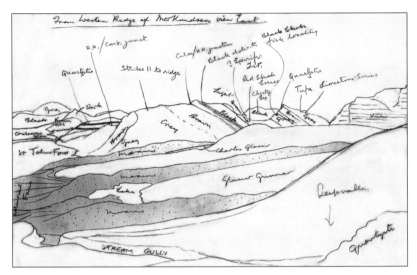

Sketch of geological features at head of St. Jonsfjorden, from Lionel's field notebook.

The view from inside the Meade tent, looking north from Copper Camp.

They spent three days there, mainly working but with one day nearly all lost to heavy rain. Dave and Gordon looked hard at one area of raised beach terracing and at the abundant signs of recent glacial retreat. Lionel, still in Stan's shoes, climbed the surrounding slopes, measuring the orientations of small-scale deformation structures in his Hecla Hoek rocks and making sketches of huge geological structures (mainly folds) exposed on the cliffs inland. He found seal and dog (?) bones close to the mountains. Gordon built another fireplace of rocks, earth, and an old bottomless pan he found in the hut, but it was of less use than he had hoped because it created such a draught that it was more like a blast furnace than a stove. So they cooked supper on their Primus stoves, but the next day heated water on the "furnace" to wash hands and faces.

Gordon and Stan inspected the medical outfit and were surprised that it contained no plain bandages, lint or gauze, no cotton wool or other wadding, no boracic ointment, no laxative, and no surgical spirit. However, they did have a hypodermic syringe and morphine. Gordon wrote, "I think Ted was a little too enthusiastic in his preparations."

Their next move along the coast on August 17 took them over some very rough ground, up and down hill, and past the foot of Løvliebreen, again much receded from its position shown on the Isachsen map. The snout just formed a dirty slope down to a large outwash fan. They had to take off their boots three times to wade the icy cold streams. From the eastern lateral moraine they could see our base camp, apparently uninhabited, and decided to celebrate the occasion immediately by eating all of the day's chocolate ration and a can of cherries, produced by Gordon, who was always ready for a party. They waded through the outflow streams of the Gunnarbreen and reached our store tent about 8 PM. Dave was very scathing about our base camp. He wrote, "the camp struck us as being awful. Muddy, unleveled, nowhere to get water and everything crammed into the badly pitched store tent. We could find no message left for us from the absentees." Gordon was even more biting:

Seldom have I seen a more desolate spot, composed almost entirely of mounds of moraine and loose piles of jagged rock fragments. There is no vegetation and the view is of various glaciers. The tent is perched on a small flat area at the side of a glacial moraine. Further, the boys seem to have been somewhat demoralized by their surroundings. Their store tent is badly set. They have opened all their crates and left the nails sticking out. The tent is split in two places. They have omitted to mount the crates on stones so that the damp from the ground can easily invade the food in the crates. They have left half-opened, half-consumed cans of food and an unwashed porridge saucepan. They have thrown kit bags, higgledy-piggledy, on the top of crates and the crates are touching the walls of the tent so that water can come through. I thought rather nostalgically of our own base at Müllerneset, with its flagpole guyed up (theirs was just stuck in the ground unsupported and has blown down) and of our crates, off the ground on rocks and covered with a rubber sheet. I pictured also the Meade tents, set square with little nameplates by them: "Mon Repos," "Chez Nous," and "Buena Vista" for the store tent.

Well, we had been delinquent in not leaving a message. Both Ted and I had written notes but somehow had forgotten to pin them up. A bit later in his diary Gordon did recognize that to find a better site for the store tent we would have had to carry our thirteen heavy crates another couple of hundred yards or more.

The quartet declined to stay at our campsite, crossing the moraine to find what they considered a much superior and more comfortable spot on a raised mossy flat area, two hundred yards to the east. It rained and blew hard from the east all day. Visibility dropped to about twenty yards and it was cold. They stayed atent until hunger forced them up for "breakfast" in midafternoon. Gordon suggested that they write a four-author story, and also a play. Then, with all of them in one tent, they played various word games, including "Famous Men," during which, Gordon complained, "We actually had to use our brains!"

During the following three days, however, the weather was not too tiresome and they all did their standard work. Gordon wrote that he and Stan spent some time

walking over to their shambolic base tent and attempting to reset it, but it is pitched right on the rocky moraine where it is quite impossible to drive in pegs. The tent, which was nearly collapsing when we commenced operations, remained a sorry sight even after our efforts.

Stan, Dave, and Gordon take five during a day of moraine bashing.

We did manage to re-erect their fallen flagpole, which is a pit prop from the beach. We fixed it with guy ropes and a rock base and hope that it may now stay up, so that the Union Jack may continue to flutter proudly in the wind, instead of lying sadly in the mud, as we found it.

One day the four of them walked across the ice of Løvliebreen, to look at the rocks on its western side. On another day Dave and Gordon walked along the coast eastwards towards the Osbornebreen, looking for raised beaches and platforms. The meltwater stream from the Gunnarbreen was thigh deep and cold, and the lateral moraine of the Charlesbreen, said Gordon, "is quite the biggest and most dangerous I have seen. It is about 200 feet high, a long steep-sided ridge of mud and jagged rocks, all resting on ice, which melts slowly and causes subsidence, mires, ice cliffs, and the occasional avalanche of scree. It is fairly safe to walk on but quite tough going."

Not having a rope with them, they declined to tackle the deep, dangerous meltwater rivers on the glacier but walked a couple of miles up the side of the glacier and then back across the lateral moraine, close to the mountain. Thus they also had to cross the Anna Sofia Glacier, about which Gordon wrote:

> [It] is a horrible little dying ice sheet that boasts neither beauty nor majesty to justify its existence. It is largely covered by bouldery moraines. We walked down to the terminal moraine to get across. The terminal moraine is a repulsive mixture of steep ice slopes, boulders, and a morass of mud patches. We were glad to be back on our own moss-covered coastal country and out of the meaningless scenery of the loose boulder moraines.

It rained vigorously all the next day, so that Stan and Lionel got thoroughly soaked while out working. However, they did some exciting geology and came back, proudly, with three ptarmigan, which they had chased and stoned to death. Gordon thought it ironic "to have killed three birds with stones and only one with two shotguns and a rifle."

Their fourth day, August 23, was "quite the most unpleasant weather we have had yet, with high wind, cold, and pelting rain." Later that afternoon, Goss, Ted, and Dennis turned up in the rain. When they were safely in camp and had removed their packs, Dave produced the whisky bottle from their food box. The effect, he thought, was splendid, a cup of the hard stuff producing friends for life! Goss also thought so, though he was sure it was rum they were drinking. The newcomers put up their wet tent but Ted and Goss moved in with the coastal four in their luxurious, that is to say, flysheeted, tents, leaving short-strawed Dennis to suffer in their wet tent. Then they all ate ptarmigan stew. Marvelous!

The following day Goss took Dave and Gordon back along the foreshore to Charlesbreen, but with so many moraines about they didn't find any beaches that looked worth excavating. In the evening Phil, Mike, and I turned up again with our sopping wet tent and clothing. We finished off the whisky bottle and the ptarmigan stew and talked a great deal. We concluded that, after all, the first half of the expedition had been pretty successful and hoped that the second half would be equally productive and a heck of a sight drier.

COME ON CHAPS, THERE'S NOT MUCH TIME!

∞

*T*hat reunion really was a great morale booster. It was particularly pleasant to have conversations with people other than our two or three companions of the last few weeks. No one had devised a method for making pemmican taste like succulent roast beef, but Stan and Lionel's ptarmigan stew was better than anything else we'd had in a long while. There was much talk about the work that had been accomplished; we began to feel that the whole expedition was not quite the foundered wreck it had appeared to be three weeks before. With an equally productive second half to the season, and better weather, we might even be able to pronounce it a success.

On this optimistic note the Müllerneset crew struck camp and, with many ribald gags and exhortations, turned west to plod off down the fjord. They were a day late, because Gordon had been *hors de combat* with a vicious migraine headache. None of Ted's tablet remedies did any good and eventually Ted gave him an injection of something, which "successfully ended everything." Dave wrote:

The return journey was accomplished without incident, overnight camps being set up again at Copper Camp hut and under Bulltinden. At the little hut we again wondered at the life of the lone prospector who had presumably wintered there before the First World War. On the slope above the plain on which the hut stood we found the beginnings of a mine shaft about ten by sixteen feet, with a few old timbers still in place. It reached about thirteen feet deep and there was a trace of copper minerals in the rubble, including azurite. Under Bulltinden the noise from the bird colony on the seaward-facing crag was as shrill and penetrating as ever. There were still several thousand birds on the cliff and wheeling around it.

The bird life, indeed, was a great fillip for all of the parties. Until the last few days of our stay, when it got very cold, the sea birds were ever-present and very numerous. Dave, Goss, and Mike all reported good viewings of glaucous and ivory gulls, as well as the more common forms such as skuas and kittiwakes. Ted, in his diary, "bemoaned my inability to follow their behavior much more closely, and also the lack of a good reference book." Petrels, auks, and guillemots soared or flittered past, singly or in small flocks. The arctic terns were our favorites, giving their famous acrobatic performances, dive bombing and pecking at heads whenever we approached too close to a nesting site. One might see a colleague in the distance suddenly break into a demented dance, with head down and arms flapping, while a semivisible tern went through the attack routine. I recall Goss quietly saying, as he was under attack in this way close to our base camp, "Oh heck, I think I'm about to have an arctic tern." The usual advice shouted to a colleague under attack was, "Throw stones at the terns!" to which the proper reply was "I'll leave no tern unstoned." Waterfowl and waders were common enough when we first arrived, but they were clearly anxious to be off south as August wore on. The coastal party did manage to shoot a few eiders and other ducks for the pot but never got a goose, which weren't common. Oystercatchers, sandpipers, and other small waders went busily along the beach, much as they do in Britain, chattering to themselves.

Dave continued with his story:

Once out onto the *strandflat* again we felt on more familiar ground—no moraines to speak of and no glacier snouts to deal with. The weather was good as we trekked past Thorkelsenfjellet, and we sang Stan's Cornish songs loudly, which the rest of us had picked up. Then there was the usual selection of rugby team ditties and other non-polite songs, all of which kept us merry. We must have gained condition since we left, for I do not recall having to stop to rest so often, despite having picked up, on the way, a good load of rock specimens for Lionel and small bags of shells and sand for me. The Müllerneset hut was soon in view but it seemed to take us an age to reach it and drop our rucksacks. It felt like home! All was well with the hut; our note had not been disturbed although the store tent, despite our reinforcements, had blown down. Our tents went up quickly, the fire was lit, and we sat by it to demolish supper. We noticed that it was now darkening quite appreciably as midnight approached. It was August 26; the season was beginning to change and there were only about twelve days in which to make the dash to Eidembreen and Farmhamna, to work out some account of the geology, and to collect at least the goodies from the food box left there.

Being back at the hut was very relaxing and comfortable. We enjoyed the calm of being indoors out of the wind. There was no flapping of tents or other noise to keep one awake or just irritated. Occasionally someone looked up and down the coast to see if an itinerant bruin might be about, but none ever was. There was much discussion as to what we should have done, had we had such a visitor. Who was the best shot? It was generally agreed that Lionel was the champion, though this was based only on the evidence of his hitting one seal, some ducks, and half a dozen cans. We always had the shotgun in reserve, loaded with solid projectile cartridges. These were probably illegal and I'm not sure how we got them, but by the time we would have had to use them our aim would have been probably a bit wobbly. In any case the guns were too heavy to carry when we left the base camp. If a bear had faced us on the trail, we would have had only our ice axes for defense. We took a day off to prepare for the work on the southern traverse and calculated that we had until about September 7 to extend our surveys as far as Eidembukta (Eidem Bay) and into Farmhamna. This would allow us to determine if the raised beach features showed anything new and if the fossil-bearing limestones found in 1948 near Kapp Scania cropped out this far north. It would also be interesting to see how far Eidembreen had retreated and changed since the aerial photos had been taken in 1936.

So we loaded up our rucksacks again with tents, sleeping bags, cooking gear, and as much food as we needed, plus a few extras. All being well there should be a wooden ration box waiting for us at

Farmhamna, with all manner of goodies to supplement the staples. In late afternoon on August 29 we set off in good weather, with a sunny sky and a tail wind from the north. Lionel's heel was sufficiently restored by now so that he wore his own boots rather than Stan's shoes. Our pace was quite brisk and we found the going good if we kept inland from the coastal cliffs with their many steep-sided gullies and walked on the drier stretches of gravel. Every so often it was time to stop and ease our loads; such an occasion was usually protracted and ended with groans and curses as we set off again. There was a deal of primitive vegetation and lichens on the rocks so that we were impressed with the general mossy cover to this low region, but all the flowers were long since over. There were a few sea birds flying up and down the coastline but far fewer than in the previous week.

Gordon noted,

Dave and I are now getting sore heels as well. The sun set in the northwest at about 9 PM, making beautiful red, purple, and mauve cloud effects. There was a new moon, and although the darkness was never more than dusk I saw the first star I have seen since we reached Svalbard. It was cold and we noticed a heavy frost. The wet sands on the beach felt crisp under foot, because the water had frozen. We crossed the outflow streams by dropping long timbers from the beach over them as bridges. Stan overbalanced from one and neatly filled his boot with icy water. We found the remains of a very old square hut, built of hewn timbers, almost rotted beyond recognition. Lionel opined that it was one of the oldest whalers' huts.

By about midnight we had reached the north side of Eidembukta, where there was a lagoon about half a mile long behind the shore, just east of a long rocky promontory and several sea stacks. The sea was running quite noisily and crashing against the headland. We decided to camp on a terrace inland of the lagoon, where a small stream broke through into it.

However, before putting up the tents they decided to walk ahead for some distance along the coast in case the men from *Sysla* had put the food depot on the northern rather than the southern side of Eidembreen. They found no sign of a cache and pitched their tents at 3 AM, half an hour after sunrise. A most impressive sunrise it was, with the glow of the rays creeping slowly down the snow-covered slope of the mountains on the foreland. Gordon thought "they looked as though they were covered in pink icing."

Dave continued:

Our tents were set up facing south across the bay to Farmhamna. It was an idyllic evening and still never got too dark to read outside the tent. We had built the usual little platform of moss and grass for each tent and felt we had a good spot, even if a bit exposed to the wind, which was still blowing from the north. The usual routine was followed, of cooking up pemmican hoosh and then porridge with a can of something extra, followed by biscuits and cheese, and then relaxing with pipes and cups of tea. Contented, we turned in, somewhat late.

They had run into a big problem. Both Lionel and Dave had found very much more interesting geology here than they had expected. They decided that time would not allow them to tackle that and the geology south of the Eidembreen. As Gordon summarized it:

The question now arises whether or not it is worth spending the time crossing the glacier, solely to obtain our food from Farmhamna. We have five days' food with us now, which will run out after breakfast on September 3. We have eight days' rations at Base Camp and *Sysla* is due to pick us up by September 15. We must budget food to last at least until 17 September and if we do not cross the Eidem will therefore have to live for a fortnight on just over half rations. Lionel, who is thinking of his geology, is all for doing this. I, thinking of the cold weather, am against it. We argued long and vigorously.

They deferred a decision until later.

Gordon wrote, "Today has been sunny, clear, and very cold. The water for our Milo froze within five minutes. Last night I slept in all my clothes except my anorak." Dave added:

It was a long workday. For Lionel it was the solid geology of the coastal cliffs and the many crags between beach and mountainsides. For me it was a quick survey of the raised marine features and collecting what shells and significant (one hoped) sediments were to be found. In fact Lionel found traces of the Carboniferous strata where he had predicted them to be and I found plenty of raised beach shells, so we were all happy! Then Gordon and I decided to look at the drainage on and around the local glaciers. However, because the weather was fine, we decided to look at the moraines and proglacial lakes first. We had a long day working in the largely dry and deserted drainage channels between the northern margin of Eidembreen and Vestgötabreen, the glacier to the north, which at that time ended perhaps three miles inland. It was peaceful out of the wind but we wondered what we would do if there were a sudden flash flood: the sides of the stream channels were steep and high. We had no such floods that day and pressed inland to the small lakes at the foot of the mountain called Petersen-Hansenfjellet. Here the lakes had once been much higher than they were on this occasion and there was no visible outflow. There was a fairly good inflow; however, despite the lateness of the season, and we concluded that any outflow must be under the ice somewhere. In spring and early summer, during a vigorous thaw, these small lakes would all merge into one big expanse of water and maybe our dry channels would become raging muddy torrents. There were no plants at all on this moraine and outwash and the whole terrain seemed new and unstable, ready to wash away in the next shower. It was really rather spooky and it kept us occupied until late evening. Back at camp it was the familiar routine of supper and putting one's feet up. It had been an interesting day.

That evening, while strolling between the crags, we came across a structure made of stout pine logs—a long narrow box, closed at one end with rocks and soil and at the other with a kind of gate. We concluded that it was probably some sort of bear trap, though exactly how it worked was not obvious. It might have been baited to set off a deadfall gate. There was not enough space to let bruin turn round in the box. The other possibility was that the bait set off a gun. It was clearly a long time since it had been operated. Did the occupants of the Müllerneset hut set it up? If so it had not been in use for nearly twenty years. Had it ever been at all successful in the quest for winter furs? We had found by now twenty or more smaller deadfall traps, set on the cliff tops and in other places where foxes might run. Several of them were in good enough condition for us to have reset them, though we didn't. They were wooden structures, rather like small garden hurdles, raised by small slivers of wood at one end and loaded with heavy rocks. As the bait was taken the supports gave way and the gate crashed down onto Foxy's head. We even found some skull bones to confirm the theory. The idea of making the rounds of these traps every few days in mid-winter gave us food for thought. Two people at the hut would have had a rough time with such a routine. We had heard that their wives accompanied some trappers. The occupants of the Müllerneset hut, however, judging by the pin-ups on the hut walls, were men who lacked connubial comforts. We wondered what had become of them, the men, that is.

Gordon thought:

This area is the most varied and pleasant part of Svalbard I have yet seen. The coast north of Eidembukta is rather like parts of the Cornish coast, with long headlands of schistose or quartzitic rock separating small coves with sandy and pebbly beaches.

The next day we [Dave and Gordon] spent at the seaside, exploring the promontory and its sea stacks, the local raised marine cliffs, and the beach deposits. Much of the time was spent sitting and searching through shell beds, making counts of the different species present, since we had already collected whatever shells seemed common. It was really rather boring but we gave the whole day to it since there was plenty of material available. To make up for the boredom I found one complete reindeer skeleton. Reindeer are now extinct in Vestspitsbergen. Stan had a slight fever and stayed in his sleeping bag, while Lionel worked locally, alone.

Stan remembered later that he had felt quite lonely all by himself. He sang himself some songs and then some hymns, including, "He who would true valor see," and felt better.

Dave continued: "Our next task (September 1) was to survey the ground in front of and south of Eidembreen, and collect the food in the depot at Farmhamna." The compromise they had reached was for Lionel to spend the day, a very long one, collecting his "oriental" samples, and making structural measurements, while the other three made the trip to Farmhamna. "The aerial photographs showed that in 1936 ice cliffs still existed at the south end of the glacier snout. In 1951 there were no ice cliffs and the edge of the ice was about 90 yards back from a low terminal moraine and beach." Gordon continued:

The first task, after a one-mile walk, was to wade the fifty-foot-wide Eidem River, which is marginal to the glacier, fast flowing and very cold. The rocky bottom was sharp and hard on the feet. We walked about two miles along a beach, which stretched the length of the snout of the glacier, only to find that a really large, deep, slow-moving river barred our way. We retraced our steps, crossed a large mud flat, and got onto the ice of the glacier itself. For some distance we followed fox tracks but the fox was obviously a visitor and didn't know where it was going, so we retreated and tried again. We crossed easily because the glacier is fast retreating and has no deep melt channels, no ice cliffs, and no wide crevasses. It is, however, a very wide glacier and was quite a long walk across.

Dave again:

South from this we could walk on towards Farmhamna. The beach itself rose to about fifteen feet above mean sea level and seemed to incorporate patches of black moraine mud. Fortunately the lagoon behind the beach seemed to drain through the pebbles, directly into the sea, so we were spared wet feet. That pleasant situation vanished at the southern end of the beach where the meltwater stream from Venernbreen, the glacier immediately south of Eidembreen, reached the sea. We crossed it by leaping from rock to rock, getting only slightly wet. Some way inland this stream flowed in a narrow gorge, perhaps fifty feet deep, making a thunderous noise. This gorge we called "Deadman's Gulch"—I suppose merely because it was at the northern end of Deadman's Plain, the open area extending south to Daudmannsodden (Deadman's Point). It was unlikely to be the only such river gorge there.

It was only a short walk, still in very pleasant weather, to the harbor-like cove of Farmhamna. Isachsen's map of this part of the coast refers to it as Port Farm, named, I think, after Farm, the Norwegian survey vessel that did much work along the coast of Vestspitsbergen around 1910. Anyway it is a splendid haven, sheltered by rocky walls to the south and west. It could perhaps have admitted the *Sysla* if the sea were calm. We were much concerned to see whether our Norwegian friends had succeeded in getting in with our food. We walked the beach almost the full length of the cove—no sign of a box. Not exactly a disaster, but a big disappointment, as we had loaded the cache with extras as well as basic rations. Then suddenly we saw it, and a large cairn to mark the spot. Three cheers! We blessed our friends. Bars of chocolate all round immediately celebrated the success of the day.

Gordon explains: "The food was quickly divided up into three loads and packed away in our rucksacks; it had survived its month on the beach without mishap. With the food we could not carry we made a large meal." Dave added:

The wooden box we left high on the beach, but the packing paper we used as kindling for a cheery driftwood fire there. The beach was cluttered with a great line of driftwood and jetsam along the high-water mark. Not only were there logs and trees but all manner of debris from shipping and civilization generally, wooden boxes, plastic items, fishing net and tackle, even perishable rarities such as oranges (none edible, we regretted) were present. We found bottles but none had messages, so we wrote a few of our own, sealed them with bits of wood and left them on the beach. None of the messages has ever been returned—just as well really, considering the nature of what we wrote.

Gordon and Dave at Farmhamna cache, inspecting the goodies.

The return to our camp was slow but happy. The day's meltwater had increased the flow in Deadman's Gulch and in the stream on the beach so that we had to wade across, with full rucksacks.

Gordon commented as he struggled through the brisk and cold water, that "the misery was only justified because our load was food. Crossing the swollen rivers was," he contended, "quite the most unpleasant part of the expedition, so far." Dave's complaints about fording cold, fast-flowing outlet rivers, especially this one, were even stronger and are unfit for quotation. As I write this, in 2003, I wonder whether his opinion about that particular river would have been any different if he had known that a decade later people at the Norsk Polarinstitutt would name it Dineleyelva in honor of Dave's geological work on his several expeditions. I suspect that his feelings would have remained the same.

Gordon continued: "At camp there was supper with extras—corned beef, canned peas, followed by a can of gooseberries and Nestles' cream—to reward us for our sixteen-mile day and Lionel for his eleven hours of work."

Stan, Dave, and Gordon wading an ice-cold outwash stream. This stream, or one just like it, was named Dineleyelva, in Dave's honor.

They spent another two days tackling the abundant local geology from Eidem camp. By this time Lionel had obtained a fairly clear picture of the extent of the Carboniferous strata emplaced in the Hecla Hoek.

∞

The weather turned vile, intensely cold with near gale-force winds and snow as hard as bullets. Working in these conditions was unpleasant and exhausting. It became so cold that they went to bed in all their clothes, even two pairs of socks. They spread newspapers between sleeping bags and ground sheets and were delighted to find they were luckier than the inland parties had been with their newspapers: the *strandflat* mob had *two* different newspapers, the *Sunday Chronicle* and the *Sunday Empire News*, although both were dated May 30, 1951. They learned the news of that day very well—rather too well, in fact.

Gordon found polar bear and reindeer skulls in a deep valley south of Petersen-Hansenfjellet. In spite of the weather, they accomplished a great amount of work. On September 4 they worked locally and then moved camp three miles north, to "Crag Camp," which they established, in pouring rain, near the foot of Peterson-Hansenfjellet. The site was more sheltered from the wind than Eidem camp but was at least one hundred yards from drinking water.

Outcrop of carboniferous rock on Svartfjella. Gordon, Dave, and Stan.

Gordon wrote:

Yesterday it rained hard in the morning, the wind blowing from the south. Dave and Lionel went off to work in their various areas while Stan and I trekked the six miles back to base (Cold Comfort) camp, to take the heavy rock specimens and collect dry socks and more film. We found the camp just as we had left it, the store tent still safely lashed on the hut roof and everything within in good order, even the sealskin, which Lionel is curing. The rain stopped in the afternoon and we returned to Crag Camp at 8:20 PM, bringing the canvas water bucket, to make less frequent our hundred-yard journeys for water. We also brought dry newspaper for the specimens and for the tent floor.

At this time they split into two pairs. Gordon and Lionel camped in the shadow of Svartfjella (Black Mountain) for a few days so that Lionel could complete his structural geology work. Dave and Stan returned to base camp. From there Dave was able to finish his work on the raised beaches near Müllerneset. The trek to the Svartfjella campsite was so warm and sunny that Gordon and Lionel walked without anoraks. After pitching the tent they climbed perhaps eight hundred feet up Svartfjella to gain a good view over the country, and then did a small and unsuccessful fossil search in the Carboniferous rocks before returning to camp, in rising wind and lowering temperature, at 8 PM.

On September 8 they "worked" the stream section down to the sea and then south to join up with the work from Crag Camp. Their search for fossils was successful. They found jasper-replaced corals similar to those at Kapp Scania. At the sea they had lunch, mainly two ounces of chocolate, and then, in short showers of snow, worked their way back up to the campsite to find their water supply had frozen up. They found another trivial source nearby, with enough for their cooking needs. They did not wash themselves.

On September 9 the weather was squally and very cold. Lionel wanted to make a final short traverse along the outcrops at the coast. That completed, they returned to their Svartfjella camp, had a meal, struck camp, and trekked back to The Shambles. Gordon wrote:

Dave and Stan had done wonders with the hut, re-blocking all the cracks with newspaper and boards. They had also windproofed the door and made a kitchen dresser, hung the cups on it, and decorated the place with antlers. They had also tidied up generally, reorganized the food, and lit the radiator. They had cooked us a meal and we had more of Dave's delightful cake. We felt thoroughly glad to be back.

Dave added:

We soon settled into our base camp and rather looked forward to the few days we had before *Sysla* arrived. Packing up should not take too long. We might wash more than our hands, and change clothes, for the first time since we left Longyearbyen. There should also be time to read, and write a few more chapters of *The Londoner*.

Lionel spent time plotting and correlating the more than one thousand structural measurements he had made in the last few weeks. By the time he was through he felt he had made progress on the problem he had set out to solve. Writing in 1952, he summarized some of his findings as follows (here shortened and simplified):

The two traverses were made, one from Müllerneset eastward along the southern shore of St. Jonsfjorden to Charlesbreen, the other

Carboniferous rocks (light color) in among
Hecla Hoek rocks (dark color) on Svartfjella.

southward along the coast of Forlandsundet to the lateral moraines on the north side of Eidembreen. Our ground surveys revealed the extent of the Carboniferous inserted slice, or inlier, and its general structural relations to the Hecla Hoek rocks on both sides of it. The Carboniferous rocks form a tectonically emplaced septum separating two different types of Hecla Hoek rocks (I called these the Eastern and Western series). This septum stretches from Müllerneset south to the north side of Eidembukta where it vanishes into the sea. It must reappear somewhere on the north end of Deadman's Plain and join up with the exposures at Kapp Scania discovered during the 1948 expedition.

The greatest width of the Carboniferous outcrop is to the north of Eidembreen, where it is wedge-shaped and about three-quarters of a mile wide near the coast. To the north it narrows until, to the west of Jørgenfjellet, it vanishes for a distance of one and three-quarters miles. Rock exposure is very poor in this area and it is possible that the Eastern and Western series of the Hecla Hoek formation are everywhere separated by a small thickness of strongly deformed Carboniferous rock. Near the southern spur of Svartfjella the Carboniferous strata appear again as a narrow band of white quartzite, exposed in a river gorge. From there the outcrop widens again rapidly as it climbs into the coastal mountains. It maintains a constant and considerable width through the length of Svartfjella and Thorkelsenfjellet and thins again slightly as it falls to the coastal plain before vanishing into the sea at Müllerneset. The Carboniferous series contains massive white, red, and buff quartzites; gray limestones; and white solidified limestones containing abundant fossils replaced by red jasper, like those at Kapp Scania. However, the fossils in the northern extension of the Carboniferous inclusion are far more strongly deformed by earth movements than are those at Kapp Scania.

Just to the north of Eidembreen, in a deep river gorge, the contact between the Carboniferous rocks and the eastern series of the Hecla Hoek is well exposed as a steeply dipping fault with a wide zone of brecciation (crushing and fracturing). The fault is parallel to the foliation (platy structure produced by deformation and metamorphism) in the Eastern series of the Hecla Hoek formation but transects bedding and other structures in the Carboniferous rocks. The contact of the Carboniferous rocks with the Western series is not as clearly exposed but seems to be more conformable than the other contact, with less discordance between the structures on either side.

Analysis of many measurements of deformation structures in the Hecla Hoek and Carboniferous rocks shows that the region had undergone two periods of deformation. The first was confined to the Hecla Hoek formation and most probably occurred during the Caledonian Orogeny in Late Ordovician to Early Silurian time, (about 440 to 435 million years ago). It was associated with metamorphism and produced folds and other structures in both the Eastern and Western series of the Hecla Hoek formation. The orientation of these structures is dominantly from west to west-southwest. The intensity of this deformation was much greater in the Eastern than in the Western series, so they may originally have been widely separated.

The second deformation affected both the Hecla Hoek and the Carboniferous rocks. It was far less intense than the first and was not accompanied by true metamorphism. It clearly occurred in post-Carboniferous time, probably in the early Tertiary. Structures formed during this deformation are oriented between northwest and north-northeast, roughly at ninety degrees to the earlier structures.

In modern geological parlance the Hecla Hoek rocks thus form a "basement" onto which younger rocks, the "cover," have been emplaced by earth movements. The structural relations between the basement and younger rocks in the Forlandsundet area are undoubtedly complex, involving large-scale folding of both basement and cover in Tertiary times. No further evidence of the true age of the Hecla Hoek rocks was found. But it seems very likely that some of them may be Precambrian (i.e., 545 million years or more old).

Before the full structural history of the Carboniferous and earlier rocks (including those to the south of Eidembreen) can be established and an accurate geological map prepared, at least another, longer, field season will be needed.

Unfortunately, Lionel was never given the opportunity to complete the work himself.

Meanwhile, at the far end of St. Jonsfjorden...

Ted wrote the best, in fact the only, account I have of Phil's second traverse to examine the rocks around Løvliebreen and the area to the south and east, so the following quotes are his unless otherwise attributed. In the evening of August 24, when I returned, wringing wet, to base camp ahead of Mike and Phil, Ted greeted me with "Why the hell didn't you leave a note?" I pointed out that he hadn't either, and we left it at that; he made the three of us a welcome brew of tea.

The next day the Müllerneset group departed, as I described earlier, carrying about seventy pounds each. Phil took miles of ciné film of their departure. Gordon didn't look well, Ted thought, and carried his pack "uneasily." I'm not surprised—it's not an easy task to carry that weight "easily." The rest of us continued to make our brand new, substitute flysheets from the sleeping bag covers. Mike dried his sleeping bag in the store tent, putting the big Primus on it, with a large plate on top, to deflect the heat downwards. It steamed away most satisfactorily. We discussed the composition of the parties for the second part of our work. Phil wanted to keep them the same, but in the end we all agreed that Mike and I should accompany Goss, while Ted and Dennis went with Phil, "to carry his rocks," as we unkindly expressed it. They set off with two weeks' food, reached the sled uneventfully and returned to base, carrying Mike's and my ski boots and Phil's specimens, which we had left with the sled. On the return trip the snow was very soft in places and they sank in up to their knees. For their supper they ate two skuas, shot by Dennis, which Ted reckoned were very nice. Finishing the sewing of the fly-sheets the following day took much, much longer than expected, so it was 8 PM before they left. Still the weather was quite good and it was light all night, so the time didn't matter. Ted noted that they were all very affable during the hard trudge up the glacier, with sixty-pound packs, as they grew to know each other better. In rolling mist they reloaded the sled, pulled it without too much strain back over the col, and set off on a compass course in the direction of Trollheimen.

In an effort to keep "regular" hours, Ted had taken an alarm clock. He set it for 2 PM; but when they awoke the visibility was almost zero, so they stayed in bed until they became very hungry, around 5:30 PM. By then the mist had lifted and they could see Knudsenfjella. After "breakfast" they skied there, so that Phil could look at the geology of the south ridge. Ted noted as they crossed the ice: "We all look quite antarctic, ploughing across snowfields, with nothing visible except your companions on skis, the driving mist, and, when it clears for an instant, a mountain top or two." While Phil dealt with the mapping of the ridge leading to "Peak B" of Trollheimen, the others tried to recognize features on Robertsonfjellet and Vegardfjella—without much success in the mist.

The tent seemed bigger with the new flysheet but was still very crowded. Dennis spilled the porridge. Ted spilled the milk. Phil was annoyed. Suddenly, as the second lot of porridge boiled, the mist cleared completely and they all trooped outside the tent to view the mountains all around. The temperature dropped very suddenly—Ted thought by ten degrees—as the wind swung round to the northeast. Soon the snow surface was very hard and slippery.

The following days were superb—clear blue skies, brilliant sunshine, and very low temperatures. After Phil had finished examining Trollheimen they moved camp southeast towards Tussekallen (Mt. Foyle), still traveling over very hard, uncrevassed snow, usually without skis. The tent was quite warm in the sun but the washing-up water froze in a minute or two when put outside. Their boots froze and were agonizing to put on in the morning until they learned to take them into their sleeping bags. Phil found very rich occurrences of fossil bryozoa and corals, which excited them all, though their hands and feet got very, very cold while they were standing around the outcrops. To the south, over Isfjorden, they could see Cathedral Rocks, nearly one hundred miles away. Esmarkbreen, the glacier flowing south down to the northern shore of Isfjorden, seemed quite heavily crevassed, and Dalslandfjella and Gestrikiandkammen, the mountain ranges to the south and east, presented an awesome spectacle. From the camp, at about two thousand feet, they could see Mts. Løvlie and Motala to the northwest, Vegardfjella to the north, and a "new" mountain east of Robertsonfjellet, which they informally named "Mt. Canning," "after one of our benefactors."

One day, while Phil went off by himself to examine the isolated peak at the north end of the Dalslandfjella range, Ted and Dennis made a plane table (the proper one was back on *Miss Mabel*) to survey and map the local mountains. They measured out twenty-foot lengths of climbing rope and established a base line 1,380 feet long. Ted wrote,

> Dennis rigged up a most ingenious plane table from two empty biscuit cans and the top of the sled box. A protractor has been made of the covering of one lid, to which is attached a piece of paper marked off in degrees. The ends of the baseline, 1,380 feet long, are each marked by a ski set upright in the snow. With this primitive equipment we set about surveying. I became progressively colder as Dennis surveyed and I assisted. Dennis appears highly delighted with his effort, remarking constantly on its accuracy. Mt. Foyle fits comfortably on Isachsen's map. We could see Phil working on his rock exposure and I could hear him quite clearly.

Dennis had not been wearing snow goggles while surveying and had a moderate case of snow blindness, so they retired to the tent when the mapping was finished and made a cup of pemmican each while awaiting Phil's return. Ted wrote, "What wouldn't I give for a mixed grill and CHIPS—or even beans on toast!"

They slept on all their spare clothes, along with layers of dry newspaper; condensation was only a small problem. Ted wrote, "Compared with nights on the first trek, this is heaven." Heading farther east, on a cloudy day, they pulled the sled north of the end of

Ski camp on inland snowfield. Note the makeshift flysheet.

the line of the Dalslandfjella chain and then northwards to the next chain, Gestrikandammer, where they camped between Mt. Canning and "Mt. Olga," named for Phil's wife, whose middle name it is. This peak is now called Tomtegubben. "The whole area is a huge snowfield, feeding the Charlesbreen, flowing north; the Eidembreen, flowing west; and the Esmarkbreen and Nansenbreen, flowing south. Dragging the sled here was very heavy work, caused by the sled box slipping off. We repacked it more securely." They pitched camp and then, before cooking supper, went over to view Mt. Olga. Climbing up to the col and then south along the ridge, they reached a high spot from which the view was "breathtakingly beautiful—peaks and ridges standing out against the snow, gaping *bergschrund*s at their feet." The rock on Mt. Olga turned out to be chert, a bedded form of silica, part of a very thick formation at the top of the local geological column and occurring in many of the mountain ridges.

For supper they had porridge, with four cubes of sugar each. Ted wished they had brought granulated sugar, which would have been easier to handle. "We all had two biscuits with honey and then Dennis had two more, unhoneyed. We are all most parsimonious about this ration business—inexcusably so—and a person who takes a heaped instead of a level teaspoon is apt to be frowned on."

Next day, with normal rock-climbing techniques, they ascended the peak of Mt. Olga. On the way up Dennis dislodged a rock—fortunately a small one—onto Phil's head, which annoyed Phil. Then, when Phil's geology work was complete, they faced a difficult ice slope and a big *bergschrund*. Ted led, choosing a route that "went beautifully." That pleased him: "Today my mountaineering experience has proved of real value."

In a near-blizzard they moved camp a few miles and found it—"*sheer hell*"—to pitch the tent. "It took three pairs of hands. The cold was intense and we were glad to get all our gear and cooking stuff inside." When they had done so, Phil cooked and added four ounces of margarine to the porridge; then they had "four biscuits, two honeyed and two unhoneyed, each."

On September 3 it was blowing force five or six but there were still many spots that Phil wished to visit, so they made an attempt to work. While filling the Primus Ted accidentally poured paraffin on his hand, which promptly lost all feeling. The temperature was well below the freezing point. They ate "a cup of pemmican, very hot, and then porridge, very claggy... egg, much appreciated, and biscuits with the last of the honey. It is thickening up outside and the wind is still powerful."

They thawed their boots over the Primus to get them on. Then they set off back towards the col north of Mt. Olga, on

a foolish quest—a fact we soon realized when we got out and made our way to the col. The blizzard was straight in our faces and cut terribly. We could see very little—nothing at all through our snow goggles, so had to slip them off for a moment every so often. On the hard ice it was difficult to stand up. We reached the col and climbed some way up the peak to the north, but had to give up and return to camp

where they spent some time building a snow wall to protect themselves from the wind.

Next day, when the wind had dropped, Phil returned to the col and mapped the ridge to the north—mainly cherty limestone, with very few fossils—while Dennis and Ted investigated a quite extensive cave in the ice, cut by meltwater. They climbed down at least sixty feet, to a cavern filled with ice stalactites and stalagmites, regretting that it was too dim for a photograph. In the cave Ted was "puzzled to hear a sound as if a church organ was playing. It lasted for about half a minute, reverberating sonorously before ceasing. No amount of my singing or ice chopping would make it recur. Ice shearing somewhere in those depths?" Returning to the surface, they waited for Phil and returned to camp.

Leaving Phil to tackle Skrivfjellet (Mt. Payne), the next *nunatak* north in the range, Dennis and Ted made a seven-hour circum-navigation of the range. They met a very wide (perhaps thirty-yard) *bergschrund* in which the snow bridge had collapsed. Wisely, they retreated to find a route around it. Back at the tent they found that two domestic disasters had occurred: somehow paraffin got into the biscuits and the strong wind tore the flysheet. In the now heavy rain, they had to emerge from the tent to fix it as best they could. Dennis's sleeping bag got quite wet.

The final few days on the icefield were long and hard. Phil wanted to accomplish as much as possible, of course, and fortunately the weather, for the most part, was fairly cooperative. They did lose their way once, when pulling the sled in very heavy mist, until they spotted their own tracks of a few days earlier to set them right again.

Suddenly, in the space of only a minute, the mist cleared and the *nunatak* came into view. It was too good an opportunity to miss, so off went Phil and Dennis to work. I felt it safer for me to stay by the sled, in case the mist should descend again. My fears and precautions were groundless. I had a fine view of Mts. Olga and Foyle while I stomped twenty times around the sled to keep warm. Then the other two returned, muffled in their gas capes, looking like Canterbury Pilgrims.

Once, when moving camp, the bag of tent pegs dropped off the sled and they had to retrace their path to find it. Before returning to the area of Trollheimen, Mts. Knudsen and Motala, they were in an area where the peaks were not named and they had fun in inventing appropriate names for many of them, most of which protruded through the ice by only a few hundred feet. The "Ice Queen" was "a beautiful white mound, with a half fold through its peak. A lovely, lovely mountain, glinting white and green in the sun." They camped to the north of Mts. "Spinnifax" and "Arrowroot," which Ted thought were "real mountains" and had a marvelous view across St. Jonsfjorden from Osbornebreen in the east to Gaffelbreen, halfway along the fjord and Dahlbreen, the glacier north of the western end.

On the morning of September 10 the sun was obscured behind the clouds and the glare off the snow was quite disturbing. They pulled the sled several miles from their last camp, up the slight slope to Depot Col, at the top of Løvliebreen and there

had lunch and inspected the slope down. It was now slippery as well as steep and at this stage we intended to be more careful than ever to get the sled down in one piece. Holding on very firmly we proceeded slowly down the slope. One pitch was ice. Dennis and I worked the sled down with ice axes. Where the slope was little more than ten degrees we were less careful and the heavy sled gathered momentum and dragged all three of us at, it seemed, tremendous speed down the slippery ice. We eventually stopped it with our ice axes and proceeded more cautiously on our way down over the icy glacier, with the slush of last week frozen into pools of thin ice, which cracked suddenly and startlingly as the sled careered across. We reached the moraine and backpacked everything to base camp at 8 PM to find that Goss and the others had arrived there but five minutes before.

The store tent had blown down and torn very badly. The biscuit can and marker pole on the beach, in which *Sysla* might have left a message, had disappeared but otherwise all seemed to be well.

∞

I was looking forward very much to the second trek. On the first, Phil, the fellow in charge because he was the only one with a purpose, was the oldest of the three of us. Our living conditions could hardly have been more unpleasant but we had been a singularly happy trio. On the second trek, Goss, equally in charge, was the youngest of the three. Would it make any difference?

It certainly made little or no difference to our method of work. We set off on August 26, carrying yet more ridiculously heavy packs, containing two weeks of food and lots of other things. Of course Goss had been along the route many times, but for Mike and me it was new. We walked across the coastal plain, over streams that could now, with luck, be crossed dry foot, up and down the moraines from the nearly extinct Anna Sofiebreen, across the mud, and then across the Charlesbreen itself. We dropped our loads at the old Camp I, had lunch, and on the way back to base camp encountered a dry stream course in the glacier, about fifteen feet deep. For practice we cut steps down one side and up the other, instead of crossing on the snow bridge a few yards away.

At base, as usual, we overslept by a couple of hours. Mike spent more time continuing to dry out his sleeping bag. We did a final sewing job on the green flysheet made from two sleeping bag covers. Mike noted, "This gives a reasonably waterproof sheet (we hope), which amply covers the tent and gives a wide eave each side for rucksacks and boots. Should improve the dryness of our Meade tent no end, if the wind doesn't rip it."

At Camp I Mike and I discovered another difference from the first trek: here we had liquid water, instead of snow and ice, for cooking, reducing the meal preparation time considerably. Shortly we discovered another difference as with very heavy packs we walked up the glacier to Camp III. We missed the sled, very much! Passing Goss's Camp II site we were all very impressed with the glacial water gusher, eight to ten feet high, and were amused at the story Goss told of camping there. It was really hard work to climb the scree slopes to the col in Vegardfjella—five minutes of stagger upwards and then ten minutes of rest—we needed it! We climbed for about an hour, with lungs, legs, back, and ankles aching fit to burst. And then we had a glorious rush down fine muddy stuff on the other side. Mike's diary continues:

> Then came an abortive effort to build a level campsite on a thirty-degree scree slope, given up when we hit water nine inches down. Across the next glacier, Vegardbreen, half a mile away to the north, is a fairly level moraine, and over to it we plod, through soggy snow, in places six inches deep. Feet wet again. On the other hand, it is a good campsite, with water nearby.
>
> August 29: Got up at 10 AM to a dry northeast wind with sun actually shining. First really fine day for seventeen days. The temperature has dropped considerably and water is hard to find and, if left for ten minutes, it freezes. Our boots, wet from yesterday and left outside, are frozen solid. We have them in the tent, by the Primus, during breakfast, and they thaw a little. Our sleeping bags, wet underneath with condensation, go outside to dry—they do.

Goss had a great long day working along the north side of the west ridge of Vegardfjella, while Mike and I took rounds of compass bearing and photographs in bright sunlight. We finished the day with a glorious long glissade down an icy snow slope. Unfortunately I fell at the end of the run and pulled my tender stomach muscle again. Altogether it was a fine day to remember, the sort of day that made the Arctic worthwhile, a day made more memorable by sausages and beans as our "luxury" at suppertime.

Mike wrote, "Colin read from Apsley Cherry-Garrard's *Worst Journey in the World*, to cheer us up with tidbits from "The Winter Journey" when the three of them sledded and camped in temperatures down to −80 degrees Fahrenheit, to show us what it is like to be really cold. The sort of trip that we are on now really shows one what absolute Hell it must have been in the Antarctic in those early days; at home it is impossible to get any real idea." That evening at about 10 PM we watched the sun set. It was a great sunset, brilliant red sky, black rocks, and white snow across St. Jonsfjorden. Our days of all-night sunlight were over and already we needed candlelight for evening chores.

The next day was even brighter than the one before, according to the exposure meter. I stayed home while Mike and Goss climbed to the col in Vegard by an easier, snowy route and thence to the highest point in the range (868 meters), whence they had a spectacular view to the south and east, to Isfjorden and beyond. At lunchtime, from the spot that Goss had reached with his mapping, they had an equally spectacular view to north and west, over Osbornebreen and Prins Karls Forland. Fluffy white clouds were forming to the west and Mike thought it wonderful to watch the cloud tops with the sun on them. As they watched, a cloud started to form at the end of Charlesbreen, spreading as it rose towards them, until they were enveloped in white mist. Goss was pleased to find lots of fossils in the last exposure he examined before returning to the tent. Mike had a good wash in glacially cold water. Goss was horrified.

Camp IV was again on a level patch of moraine, south of the Wittenberg Mountains. As we climbed up the snow and ice slopes to the top of the nearest Wittenberg peak, eight hundred feet or

Mike and Goss stop for lunch.

so above the tent, Goss was delighted to find a tufa limestone, a bit shattered from frost, as was almost every other rock we saw in Vestspitsbergen. This tufa limestone was a very distinctive bed among the Carboniferous strata and was a very good indicator of where in that thick group we were actually sampling. From the summit we could see quite easily the folding in the strata in the large faces in the peaks further north. The trip back to the tent included a highly enjoyable five-minute glissade—warm work while it lasted! Afterwards we tried obstacle races down another glissading slope. Event number three was a competition to see who could stand longest on one foot on a boulder in the middle of a small glacial stream. Finally we had a hands-and-knees race up a gentle but incredibly slippery ice slope. To reach the top was nearly impossible and quite exhausting, because we slipped downhill as much as we climbed upwards, but we all thoroughly enjoyed our version of Winter Olympics (Svalbard) 1951.

The day's work on September 1 involved the ridge northeast of Camp III. The last part of it was a forty-five-degree ice slope, up which I cut steps for a couple of hundred feet, roped up. Goss found fossils in the rocks at the top. The scree on the way down was unpleasant, as it usually was. One couldn't rely on it either to slip or to stay put. As Mike said: "Every step was an adventure!"

Crossing the glacier back to the tent we came across a moulin, the often-vertical hole in the ice where a meltwater stream has found a crack and has melted its way down. Sixteen years later on Kaskawulsh Glacier in the Yukon, my student and I spent a long time mapping the (dry) underground caverns and byways of such a moulin system. This time, in Svalbard, we merely timed the drop of pieces of ice—three and a half seconds—so that the first vertical part was about 150 to 200 feet deep. The thought of encountering such a feature hidden by a foot of snow did little for our peace of mind.

The following day Mike and I returned to the food depot at Camp I, under a cold overcast sky, to collect more supplies. Because of the recent much lower temperatures, the gusher at Camp II was little more than a bubble, six inches high. On the way back along Charlesbreen, the wind blew up. When we reached the tent we took off the flysheet, to prevent it tearing. It snowed, by morning becoming a regular blizzard. We were pleased, no end, that we had collected the week's food the day before. On this day work, and even travel, would have been close to impossible. Mike was the hero who went out, around noon, to weight down the tent with rocks on the windward side and double-up the guy lines. He also collected water for a meal from our now deeply frozen waterhole, and managed to get back to the tent with some of it still in the billycans. After struggling with the sleeve door we realized that the powdered milk was still outside; we were forced to have our porridge without milk. It became a real blizzard and the tent was moving bodily. We kept it down by stretching out in our sleeping bags until evening. It was noisy with the tent flapping. In case we should start to feel sorry for ourselves I read aloud Cherry-Garrard's description of the gale and blizzard at Cape Crozier, during *The Worst Journey in the World*, when the tent blew away and they were faced with returning to base, in darkness and with temperatures down to −80 degrees and lower, without it. (The following year, while I was preparing for my next expedition, I met Cherry-Garrard, one of the youngest men on Scott's last expedition, but by then a mature man, still kind and very helpful. When he asked me what experience I'd had of polar travel, I told him of this little incident, which amused him.) At 8 PM we made a "utility" meal, of pemmican, bacon, and Milo—those being the only items in the tent. The heat from the Primus started to melt the snow on the outside of the tent, which dripped in, so we turned the Primus out and ourselves in (to our sleeping bags).

I was on the windward side, and the tent blew against me, so that my bag was again very wet from the snow and my body heat. Mike's bag was also wet from the tent wall, so that Goss, in the middle, was the driest of the three. For a second day it was obviously not possible to work so we got dressed and lay on our wet bags for most of the day. Mike wrote:

> Phil used to keep the tent fairly tidy. Now Goss and Colin together get the place in a shambles. I lost my temper when Goss spilled the ashtray into my sleeping bag—knocked my pipe out on his head. Peace reigns again now.
>
> Wednesday, September 5, we get up at 10 am to a fine day, thank goodness! We needed one. The weather is overcast but dry with a fresh wind from the northeast. We get our sleeping bags out to dry as quickly as possible. After breakfast Goss labeled some of his

specimens, while Colin and I have a cleanliness campaign—the first thorough washing-up session for several days. We even boil the dishtowels. Then I was rash enough to wash my face and neck, with much banter from Goss, who doesn't appear to have washed since leaving Tromsø.

I, as a physicist, was also working on the steady-state principle: after a while as much dirt falls off as accumulates. Our sleeping bags weren't dry but the water in them had been moved around a bit, so we went off and studied the geology along the ridge where Goss had started work on Saturday. That project involved cutting a lot of ice steps, which was tiring. We then crossed a little glacier, roped up, and climbed "Mt. Wright," which we had taken much pleasure in naming for Billy Wright. Not only was he England's soccer captain, he was also responsible for much of our reading matter: "You can rely on Billy Wright to know what's what in soccer—just as *he* relies on Quaker Oats as his daily 'food for action,'" which appeared on every Quaker Oats package. From the top we had wonderful views to the south, down the glaciers to Isfjorden. Goss then worked his way all round the mountain. At 8 PM we turned for home, part of which was a long, exciting glissade, which resulted in wet pants again. The sunset was glorious but the wind got up sharply and we reckoned we

Crevasses on the Osbornebreen.

were in for another rough night. We were soaked again, mainly from surface water running into the tent. We were camped on moraine, only a few inches above solid ice, so a small amount of rain raised the water table to the surface.

While Mike, as a civil engineer, was left behind to remedy the hydraulic problems of our home, Goss and I returned to Mt. Wright. On coming back to the tent in the evening, we were impressed with Mike's handiwork. He had dug drainage trenches all round the tent and had partially dried out our sleeping bags, with the aid of the Primus. We needed candles to see well enough to finish cooking at 9 PM. After dinner we engaged in one of our special games, at which Goss in particular was very good—throwing stones at a target. The target was a can containing a burning candle, perched on a handy rock. Goss and Mike each won a piece of chocolate from me, three-three-two. Good fun!

We had only a couple of days left for fieldwork, and Goss was keen to visit a few places to the north and west in the Wittenbergfjella. We moved the camp to the west, onto *terra firma*—no more of this moraine-on-ice stuff for us, thank you! There were a couple of large boulders nearby with some little scrambles, which amused us for some time. In the northwest corner of the mountains Goss found bands of soft white gypsum. In later analysis he and Dave concluded that these bands, part of the "Wittenberg series," sat at the top of the column of Carboniferous and Permian rocks in our area. On another day Goss

Sunset over Prins Karls Forland.

spent a long time examining the junction between the Hecla Hoek and the Carboniferous series.

At the western end of the ridge we were only a mile from the Osbornebreen, and we were determined to set foot on it, to see if indeed it could be crossed. Mike reported on the adventure:

It is 7:15 PM when we are roped up to step onto the glacier. Goss leads, I go second, and Colin is last. The ice at the edge of the glacier is a mass of pressure ridges, about four feet high. Afterwards we meet the crevasses, great chasms up to twelve feet wide and probably 150 feet deep. We find that it is fairly easy to work along the "grain" of the crevasses, and that we can work across them slowly on ice bridges. Personally I would rather not do it again, and certainly not with a heavy pack. Still it could be done, if it had to be done, and safely, provided there was no snow to hide the snags. We take photographs to prove we have been here and beat a retreat, not before its time. It is 8:30 PM when we get off the ice, and then there follows a long struggle back to camp, first over moraine, and then over our own glacier. Getting in at ten o'clock we are very, very tired. All our tent work, cooking, and laying out beds, has to be done by candlelight: wonderful sunset tonight!

On September 10 we got up early, for us—about 9:30 AM—and, after breakfast, packed up camp for the last time. Mike wrote:

Although our packs are considerably lighter, with little food and no paraffin, the climb up the gully from camp to the first glacier is very hard work. We cross the glacier and go down a long scree slope to the coastal moraine, continually straining to keep our balance. The day is warm, with little wind, and cloudy, with a massive front moving slowly across from the northeast, leaving blue sky behind. We pass along the coastal moraine to Charlesbreen, up the ice, now very slippery, to the depot, where we brew up Milo and eat. We pick up the geological specimens and leave the twenty or thirty pounds of food to be picked up on another trip. From here on the route is well known and we get back to camp by 8:30 PM, in time to see the other party arrive ten minutes later.

All six of the inland group were safely back at base. The weather had been marginally better than during the first traverse, but not much. However, both geologists had notebooks full of good data, and were at least reasonably pleased with their accomplishments. The days to come were to prove equally trying, although in quite a different way.

CHAPTER TEN

WAITING FOR *SYSLA*

*N*ow let's see! What did Captain Andreassen actually say? It would almost certainly be September 12, I thought he'd said, when *Sysla* would return to pick us up. He'd added he might be as late as September 14. We had almost no food at base camp so Mike returned to Charlesbreen campsite with Phil, to rescue the stuff we had left there on our way back to base. They inspected the cliffs at the snout of the glaciers, photographed crevasses, and returned via the Anna Sophiebreen and Gunnarbreen. Mike noted: "Both of these are small and apparently dead glaciers; quite uninteresting."

While walking back, Phil and Mike compared their experiences. With Ted and Dennis, who both tended to be clumsy in camping, strict cooking duties were followed, in contrast to the general "give a hand" system that Phil, Mike, and I, and then Goss, Mike, and I had adopted. On Phil's second trek they only had one and a half days on skis, all the rest of their sledding being done on hard surfaces while pulling on foot.

Goss and I walked over to Løvliebreen and up to the sled depot. We collected the skis and ski boots, but left behind the box that had served both groups so well as the container on the sled. By the time we were all back in camp the weather had grown much worse, foggy over the foreland and blowing from the west. We were sure this would delay *Sysla*. A lot of ice was floating in the fjord and, stranded by the tide, on the foreshore. The seawater was obviously much colder than it had been a couple of weeks before, when the ice melted fairly quickly. Now, for the first time, we could hear from the camp waves breaking on the beach. It snowed that night, just half an inch or so, but it stuck. Ted wrote, "The scene is now truly arctic—mountain peaks covered in snow and icebergs washed up on a snowy shore."

On September 12 Mike wrote,

> The food supply is strictly limited. We are being picked up later than was expected back in Tromsø when we packed the food boxes. Sugar and chocolate are practically nonexistent. We have syrup with porridge. There are small amounts of porridge, pemmican, and margarine; there is plenty of biscuit—the only thing there is in plenty. Ted's idea is to eat fairly normal rations until after the *Sysla* is due [she was due that day, at earliest] and if she doesn't come we economize—with everything already eaten! This policy I do not agree with, but there is little to be done about it. Some people have more faith in the infallibility of the arrival of the *Sysla* than I do. I think she will come, maybe ahead of time, but I'd rather starve a little over a longer period than a lot later on.

The notable events of September 13 were that most of the ice, previously stranded on the shore, blew out into the fjord, the weather improved, and we packed a few boxes with geologic specimens and so on and carried them down to the shore. In a lengthy stone-throwing competition, our tent beat their tent by seven to two. The next day we all sat in one tent and told ghost stories. Six in a tent was a squash but at least it was warm. Ted wrote: "We're always expecting *Sysla*. Phil is worried and showing it, I think, more than I do. What a lazy day! We have very little food left."

On September 15, *Sysla* had not arrived by 7 PM. We surveyed all the remaining food and set ourselves rations that would last us for another seven days. The daily ration was four barley sugars, one quarter ounce of sugar, one and one third ounces of pemmican, one and one third ounces of margarine (reduced to half of that two days later), four ounces of biscuit, a little dried egg (enough for two dessertspoons of scrambled egg each day), an occasional cup of Milo, and tea without milk or sugar. Everything else—chocolate, porridge, and cheese—had run out.

What could have happened to *Sysla?* Dennis and Ted went off with the gun. They came back empty-handed, saying that the only birds they saw were sandpipers on the beach, cute little things about the size of a sparrow. All the rest had disappeared—those able to had flown south. The ptarmigan, which did stay over the winter, had, we presumed, put on their white winter plumage and hidden themselves.

On September 16 a high wind blew up from the west during the night, ripping our poor flysheet in two. By morning it was snowing intermittently but the wind was moderating. By evening it had backed to the north and strengthened again. Not *Sysla* weather, this! We had a long discussion about being marooned. How much sustenance can one gain from seaweed and lichen? Are there any shrimp in the fjord? How can we catch them? I remembered the account of Greely's expedition to Ft. Conger on northern Ellesmere Island, during which twenty out of twenty-eight members starved to death. I decided not to mention it.

We lay in bed till 1 PM. Mike wrote, "One's tummy feels perennially empty; though I cannot say I have felt hungry yet. That will come!" Goss found a can of sardines somewhere and we all relished our share—one sixth of a can each. What a treat! Mike wrote: "Seven ounces of food a day is enough if you spend seventeen hours in bed, and have long rests in between."

On September 17 the weather was fairly calm but the tide was definitely higher. Early in the morning we found that two crates and our last two jerry cans of paraffin had washed away. Mike wrote: "The crates are not too important, but the paraffin loss reduces our position from serious to unthinkable. Fortunately we do not have to look very far before all is found washed up along the shore. Only a warning this, but what a warning!" One of the crates, which we found about three hundred yards away along the beach, contained the spare medical stuff and Ted's extra clothing, all now soaked in seawater. In the early afternoon Mike, Ted, and I held a poetry-reading session, choosing a poem alternately. We were reading from a book Mike had brought, an anthology compiled by General Wavell, the penultimate governor-general of India, called *Other Men's Flowers*. I can still remember, word for word, one of the poems I read: "The common cormorant, or shag, / lays eggs inside a paper bag…" Mike wrote, "Later Phil, Colin, and I are in the tent together; the old intimate atmosphere is recaptured. Phil is very depressed, mainly about his wife [Joy not knowing what was happening to Phil], and who can blame him? I feel content, as yet, to lie and talk, or just lie, without undue thought about *Sysla* or the future. No good is ever done by worry, anyway."

Phil, perhaps to cheer himself up, decided to go and rewrap some of the prize rock specimens in his rucksack. After a few minutes there was a loud shout: "Boys, I've found a bar of chocolate!" Now, if I had been by myself and had found a bar of chocolate, after living on seven ounces of food a day for several days, I wonder whether I would have announced the discovery to everyone. Phil did. There were eight squares of chocolate. Phil doled out one to each of us. We voted that Phil, as the finder, should have one extra piece, leaving one square unallocated. I suggested that we have a poetry-writing contest: the author of the best poem should have the last piece. The deadline was set for four hours hence, at 8 PM—suppertime. We all sat in one tent, chewing at pencils, interminably writing and erasing words, all except Goss. He sat, cross-legged in the corner of the tent, sucking away at his pipe, just like Tweedledum (or Tweedledee) in Lewis Carroll's *Through the Looking Glass*. Then he wrote for a minute or so, put down his pencil, and continued to smoke, watching the rest of us with quiet amusement. When time was up, we read our poems in turn. Mine, I thought, was a masterpiece. It started: "I hope to heck I never see, / Another something quartzite scree" and went on, with similar lurid wording, for four or five pages. But it was clear to all that Goss was the winner. His sterling and heartfelt effort was: "Brachiopod, brachiopod! / Come out of that rock, / You recalcitrant sod!"

Goss wrote:

There were moments for reflection during those closing days in Spitsberegen. Most of us went, from time to time, a short way from the tents to be alone and absorb some of the majesty of the surrounding scene. In the fading light, during the times of cold, calm weather, it was indeed austerely beautiful. One will never forget occasions when the profound silence was broken by the rolling, thunder-like noise as masses of ice fell from the glaciers' sea-cliffs into the waters of the fjord, many miles away.

On September 18, when I went to collect water, I found that I had to stop for a little rest on the way back. One gets weak very quickly on the amount of food that we were eating. We decided that if *Sysla* had not arrived by the next day, we would walk to Müllerneset. The food reserves of the coastal four were unlikely to be more adequate than were ours, but they had a rifle and we should be able to shoot a seal. I generated a word picture of someone cooking a whole seal on a Primus, but the others didn't think it was funny. It would take us several hours to walk there, and what would happen if *Sysla* arrived while we were on the way? We were sure they would see us if we kept to the shore, but just in case, we would leave a note in the store tent, now empty except for boxes of rocks and personal things. In the meantime each tent constructed a crossword for the other tent to solve. They were hard. In the evening Dennis and Ted shot seven little sandpipers. "They are very tame," Mike wrote, "and sitting targets. It is a shame to kill them, though. However, we are glad enough to get our share and will stew them tomorrow. What one comes to! *Sysla* must come soon. It is dreadful to be completely cut off and not know whether the boat is late and is coming, or is prevented from ever coming by Russians, war, sinking, or what have you."

For the first time, on September 19, I heard someone use the word "deliverance." We really were getting worried! No one was looking forward to the trek to Müllerneset. The day was calm, perfect for us to be picked up, but it passed in the usual way. We ate our breakfast, such as it was, and in the afternoon all crowded into one tent to discuss yesterday's crossword puzzle and the sordid subject of expedition finances. We were interrupted by Dennis from the tent door, who had spotted a black spot in the distance which, although fifteen miles away, looked different from the usual bits of floating ice. Is it? Can it be? It must be? And it was! *Sysla*!

We set about our final chores: crates were nailed down and tents were packed. As soon as the vessel was positively identified we made a meal, using everything that we had left except the sandpipers. Most of us found we couldn't eat very much because our stomachs had shrunk on our limited rations. By the time Sven and Lars had the *Sysla*'s boat ashore, everything was ready for them. Phil and Mike went with the first load, to help unload the second, and the rest of us went with the third and final load. *Sysla* gave the campsite three toots on her horn; some of us gave three weak cheers. It had been an extraordinarily interesting forty-five days, but no one was sorry to leave. As we headed back down the fjord we learned that *Sysla* had been held up at Kongsfjorden for a week by bad weather of which we had been unaware. After that she had collected our London geological colleagues Atkinson and MacDonald, who had been mapping part of Prins Karls Forland.

∞

Our four colleagues at Müllerneset had arrived back from their southern journey on September 10, in good time to prepare to be picked up by *Sysla*. The hut, still loosely referred to either as The Shambles or "Our Domiciliary Unit," was still usable, even if not inhabitable. Lionel and Gordon made a short geology traverse along the coast while Dave and Stan did wonders to the hut by the time they returned, blocking all the cracks with newspaper and board and windproofing the door. They had also cooked a meal. Everyone felt thoroughly glad to be back at base.

Dave was sure that Captain Andreassen had said that *Sysla* would pick them up on September 11 or 12. They made attempts to get themselves more presentable for polite company (if they could find any) by taking what might approximate to a bath and climbing into clean clothes. After six weeks without either, they thought they might be a bit wiffy. At least they had kept their soap supply almost intact! They would be able to see *Sysla* sail by and in the time that it took her to collect the inland party from deep in the fjord, they could achieve hygienic bliss—in theory.

No sooner were they back in the hut than the weather began to deteriorate. The next day was decidedly gray and threatening. The wind was again from the north and it was cold. When they went to bed, in the dark now, there was snow in the air. Each night the dark time was appreciably longer than the previous one. Dave remarked, "It was almost sinister—how long before it would be twenty-four hours of night?"

Dave wrote,

That night it snowed, the wind blew half a gale, and we could hear the snow striking the tent. Before the night was over there was a bulge in the back wall of the tent where the snow was accumulating. Eventually Gordon got up to investigate—he was good at that sort of thing whereas I was not. About four inches of snow had fallen during the night and there had been drifting round the hut and the tents. It was decidedly colder than it had been. The wind had dropped and the entire scene now looked really arctic, though the sea was clear of any ice. After breakfast in The Shambles, with the lamp and heater on, we set off towards the cape to relish the new scene and take photographs. We wondered if the change in the weather would delay *Sysla*. There was no sign of her. After lunch, feeling lazy, we retired to our sleeping bags. I was reading *Paradise Lost* and remarked to Gordon on the lot of those poor souls in purgatory who were having a hot time of it. Did Milton know about the Arctic?

On September 12, Lionel returned to his rocks and spent the afternoon working around Müllerneset while the other three went off to Bulltinden to collect the specimens they had left there during the traverse along St. Jonsfjorden. Lionel, writing in November 1951, described the events of the next few days.

Indeed it was cold; at Longyearbyen the temperature went down to –15 degrees Fahrenheit, and it was probably colder where we were. It raged a full blizzard for several days and everything froze up. Snow continued with high wind and it became even colder. All streams and small rivers froze and became drifted over with snow. Deep drifts of dry, powdery snow also formed around the hut and tents, which froze like iron and had to be continually dug out. We had to melt snow for water, eating into our meager supply of paraffin. However, with fourteen to fifteen ounces of food per person per day we were much better off in that respect than we later learned the inland party to be.

It got so cold Gordon put on a second pullover, for the first time, and they all slept fully clothed. Dave heard sharp reports from the nearby gully. It was either the sharp change in temperature causing a rock to split or maybe the Old Man of Mt. Müller, playing tricks on them. They were frustrated that they could not go too far from the hut in case *Sysla* appeared, so they sat and froze in their tents or in the hut. Dave surprised a fox, still brown but just turning white, sniffing at the grave of the seal they had shot.

They read, played word games, and wrote further chapters of *The Londoner*. The later developments of this epic were not at all to Lionel's liking. He claimed that the others were ruining the story by introducing too many "potty" characters. On September 12 they finished their dried fruit and dried egg and on the thirteenth they ate their last can of sausages. Their remaining luxuries, as Gordon noted, were one can each of Scotch broth, corned beef, and baked beans. However, they still had porridge, milk, sugar, biscuits, margarine, pemmican, and cheese to last for seven or so more days. They were anxious days, especially for Lionel who had a passage booked on the *Mauretania* from Southampton to New York on October 9. Dave said that they contemplated huge meals and composed fanciful menus and "Babylonian entertainments." The newspapers they had were nearly all of just those two editions, but they had the opportunity to learn from Billy Wright on the Quaker Oats packages how to head the ball. Being an erudite quartet, they also learned the French version of the notice on the HP sauce bottle, which they all recited *ad nauseam* with exaggerated French accents.

When the weather began to improve again they were even more puzzled about the nonappearance of *Sysla* and grew quite pessimistic. Dave remarked, "I don't think *Sysla* will come today.... Alone and forgotten! The world is better off without us—well, without you lot!" Had the Korean War gone so far that some idiot had dropped The Bomb? Was the rest of the world still there? They shot a glaucous gull, but nothing really edible. They brought the gull carcass back to the hut and tied it to a long piece of nylon cord, threaded though a hole in the hut wall, leaving the bird as bait for a fox, in the hope that Reynard would give himself away by jerking the cord. Nothing happened. They constructed an elaborate washing place in the lee of the hut, with a large board to stand on, a log to sit on, a washstand comprising a board on top of the old iron incinerator, and a towel rail made from a rope slung between two ice axes. The hot water was in a saucepan and the washcloths froze up rather too quickly.

On September 15, Lionel spent the morning drawing and Dave carved a totem pole from a piece of driftwood while Stan and Gordon

Hunting party in search of anything edible.

played drafts, using their two kinds of vitamin tablets as playing pieces.

Gordon wrote,

Last night, when we went to bed, it was still, very clear, and very cold. The moon, which I have never seen so clearly before, was full. It looked enormous and hung just above the horizon, shining on the sea and on the snow with almost sun-like brilliance. Even the stars look much brighter than I have seen them before. The clear, dust-free atmosphere gives this effect. It must certainly be a consolation to arctic dwellers who miss the beauty of vegetation. Lionel took a color photograph of the moon above the *strandflat* and the mountains.

The next day was quite different. The weather was decidedly unpleasant, the wind blowing hard from the north. It started snowing again: fine, hard, and dry snow that continued through the afternoon and evening. The sea roughened and became quite unsuitable for any boat landing. The sky was dark gray; the sea was a lighter gray with white horses and the air was full of falling and drifting snow. They had to dig away two feet of snow from the tent entrances before they could get into them. Gordon recorded:

Winter comes. Time to leave.

To write this I am sitting in the open doorway of the hut. I have extra pullovers on, balaclava helmet, mitts, gloves, windproofs and hood, cape, three pairs of socks, army trousers, gaiters, and boots and am still damned cold. The place seems to have become genuinely arctic very quickly. There are very few birds now. We still see an occasional duck, but then it is a lone one, left behind by the large flights that have already flown south. Today we have started our last four days' rations and we are down to six pints of paraffin; we use much more per meal than before, as we have to obtain all water by melting snow. If we are still here in six days' time I don't really know what will happen. We still have some ammunition and will try to shoot another seal. In this weather, however, I doubt any success. I wish I were home!

To save their precious paraffin they modified the incinerator and cooked their meals on driftwood fires. It took an hour to cook porridge and everything tasted of wood smoke. Gordon developed a chill; he reckoned it was from having a wash a couple of days before. Stan made a pack of cards from the covers of exercise books, and they spent more and more time in bed. Lionel shot at a seal and Stan at another on the next day, but they were too far out to sea to be recovered even if they had been hit. On September 18 Gordon dreamt that he had been called up into the army again as a recruit and made the terrible mistake of saluting a sergeant major, but that made a change from his usual dreams, all of which involved large roast meals or bacon and eggs.

Dave continued with the saga:

On September 19, the weather was really good enough to raise spirits and expectations. It was quite sunny, though the wind was still from the north. At about 5 PM I went outside the hut and found myself suddenly yelling "Ship! Hey boys, it's *Sysla*." The others all dashed out and looked in the wrong direction, but there *Sysla* was, coming from the north, in the middle of the sound and making for the entrance to the fjord. We all watched until she passed the cape, and feeling very cheered, at once launched into feverish activity. We cooked an enormous meal of porridge and toasted cheese, lavishly expending the rest of the cheese. The fire was stoked and water heated for each of us to have another strip wash on the sheltered side of the hut. This amounted to not much more than a large washing-up bowl of water each, but it worked wonders. By the time we were all scrubbed and in clean clothes the wind had begun to rise and it was distinctly colder. The second wash in less than a week! Our old clothes were ceremoniously burned on the fire. The flag fluttered steadily from the flagpole and as *Sysla* emerged from the fjord there were the beginnings of white horses offshore. As we dug the tents from their snowdrifts,

Dave digging out tents.

193

closed up the remaining crates with nails we had to pull out of the hut wall, we watched the ship approaching our bit of shore very gingerly and cautiously. We brought the Tilley lamp down to the beach to guide the ship. She approached to within 150 yards or so and dropped anchor. The four of us on shore were having heart failure as we could see *Sysla* almost on top of the line of breakers marking the reef. The dusk was brightened by the moon and by the snow on the ground. Almost immediately a white and very large dinghy was lowered and our old friends Lars and Sven rowed ashore, keeping the stern to the wind all the way. Progress was very slow as she bobbed up and down on the waves. We pulled the boat onto the beach and greeted the sailors with big handshakes all round. They made it clear there was no time to lose. Lionel and Stan, with an enormous collection of boxes and gear, were loaded. The trip back to the ship, keeping the bow to the wind, looked very perilous as the sea was rising. [Lionel referred to this as "one of the most exciting experiences I have ever had."] It seemed to take forever for the boat to return for Gordon and me. We hauled the flag down and more or less shut up the hut.

When it was our turn to put out to the ship, we moved more smartly than one might imagine. We were on our way home! Meanwhile we

Cleaning up for Sysla: *Gordon, Dave, and Stan.*

had to make it out to *Sysla* through some very choppy sea. To keep up appearances, to say nothing of spirits, we sang the Eton Boating Song, to the amusement of the Norwegians. Frankly I was scared. We were unceremoniously heaved up and over the side by our colleagues, with much greeting and handshaking. Thanks were passed to Lars and Sven, who by now had the boat back on board. We gave a farewell wave to the hut and all went below. *Sysla* raised anchor and backed out into the sound, while the weather became distinctly hostile. Later Captain Andreassen confessed that he had been worried that he might have to leave us while it was such bad weather, and when he did come close there were reefs within a few inches of his keel, according to the sonar. It was a mark of his skill that he had brought us all off so successfully.

Sysla had come from Kongsfjorden, not from Longyearbyen, and had been trying to pick us up for three days already, during which time the captain had had no sleep. They'd had to make three rowing-boat journeys to take MacDonald and Atkinson off the foreland and had taken an enormous risk coming down Forlandsundet from the north, where they had to cross, at high tide, a place where the water was only one fathom deep at low tide.

Lionel, the originator of the expedition, summed it up: "We had a wonderful reunion on board after being picked up—a thrilling finish to that part of the expedition. In retrospect I would not have had it otherwise."

∞

Once we had the four of the coastal party safely on board we duly complained about the noise they had made, singing as they were rowed out. Then we all crowded into the saloon and sat around, smiling inanely and chattering away. Everything looked warm, light, and civilized except for the six of us from the fjord. We were still wearing our porridge-stained windproofs and showed a significant layer of general crud. The sea was definitely rough but when the steward called us for a meal—the six of us from the fjord first—we did our duty by the delicious white bread, butter, jam, cheeses, and meats laid out for us, along with unlimited tea. Everyone except Mike showed our full appreciation of it; he just nibbled away. If restraint is a virtue, he qualified for sainthood.

We couldn't see much of the coast, although it was moonlight. But it was interesting to glimpse the snout of Eidembreen and realize that we had been at the other end of the glacier a few weeks before. When I woke up in the middle of the night, we were calling in at Kapp Linne, the radio station at the entrance to Isfjorden. A couple of *Sysla's* female passengers were dropped there and the captain went ashore for a short social visit. He returned quite soon with a pair of radio operators due for leave. They were wonderful bearded types, in spectacles and anoraks, smoking enormous pipes. We passed a Tromsø-bound coal steamer, *Appian*, the most modern of the fleet and a comfortable and fast vessel, we were told. We had missed her by three hours or so. However, Captain Andreassen radioed to Longyearbyen for our benefit and learned that there were three coal ships in harbor at that time and there would be no difficulty in packing us off very soon for Norway. I slept on the floor of the saloon, under the table, and remember nothing more until we tied up at Longyearbyen jetty about 9 AM; nobody thought of giving us another meal. But Captain Andreassen remarked, in a most diplomatic way, that some of us might be more acceptable to conventional society if we spent some time with a bar of soap and a bucket of water.

It was a long traipse up to the governor's guesthouse, where we left our personal luggage, and then down into the valley to the miners' quarters in Nybyen. We found the bathhouse and asked for washing facilities, to the vast amusement of the attendant, a young man who was amazed at this collection of motley beings. Most of us were filthy, bearded, and disreputable, even by Longyearbyen standards. In some consternation he asked "Engelsk?" However, he supplied soap, towels, and washcloths, and we invaded the shower room. The hot water was bliss and we all did it justice. Gordon and Stan sang heartily, the sound bouncing off the concrete walls. We emerged half an hour later much, much cleaner, though Mike thought it would take several such treatments to get us properly sanitary.

Gordon wrote:

Surely Longyearbyen must be one of the bleakest and most unpleasant places of European habitation in the world. The town is situated in a deep valley, about one and a half miles wide between two long mountains, which opens onto the sea in Adventfjorden. The feature first noted is the network of overhead cable bucket-ways. The cables are supported on huge wooden pylons and they carry a constantly moving chain of buckets being drawn silently along, full ones from the pitheads and empty ones back. The bucket-ways come down from the pitheads on the hillsides and cross the valley, ending in an enormous cableway several miles long. This follows the coast from the settlement to the coal-loading quay, where there is a huge pile of coal, dug out during the winter, still to be transported back to Norway. At the quay there is always a coal ship being loaded as fast as the feed belts can work.

From the wooden pier at Longyearbyen, one road passes up a hill to the governor's house and then drops down into the valley where it forks into two. The roads are not metaled but are like farm tracks, covered in places with consolidated snow. They pass under the cableways and go about a mile inland. There are about four groups of buildings, all made of wood, set about half a mile apart. One group is the miners' mess, miners' barracks, married quarters, and the bathhouse. Another group, very well built and beautifully painted, consists of the homes of the local aristocracy, the mining engineers, medical officers, and so on. A third group has the post office and a hospital, and the fourth, some way down the hill, is the bake house. The connection between the miners' quarters and the post office is by a wooden pedestrian walk, consisting of four parallel planks to walk on and two hand railings, the whole being built on piers to form a long bridge. There are no places of amusement, only one shop, and no vegetation. It is indeed a miserable place.

Back at the pier, Phil, Lionel, and Ted went off to find the *sysselmann*, to see whether we could transfer our kit to a coal boat. The one at the coal pier, nearly fully loaded, was destined for Malmö, Sweden. Our representatives were gone for hours so we sat in the cold on the deck of *Sysla*, smelling the lunch being cooked for the crew. Famished though we were, we were not invited to join them and at 1:30 PM, a bit fed up, we started to open a crate to extract a Primus and porridge. Just then Phil, Ted, and Lionel returned. Governor Balstad was in Oslo, but his deputy had served us well. We could go on the next vessel to load, *Jakob Kjode*, a five-thousand-ton collier, with space for up to twenty-four passengers that would be loading on Sunday, September 23, and leaving for Harstad on September 24. Lionel also told us that there was an enquiry about our welfare from Roger Pirie. Small wonder, for we had expected to be back in Tromsø before September 15 and it was now September 20. We could go back to Norway on the collier and the governor would send a message to *Miss Mabel* to meet us in Harstad. In the meantime we could stay at the governor's guesthouse.

The guesthouse comprised two log cabins behind the governor's palace. The smaller and newer of the two had an electric stove and the other had beds, mattresses, and other dimly remembered luxuries. We cooked porridge at 4 PM, our first meal for eighteen hours. Several of us then retired to the other cabin, lit the stove in the room and, when the temperature soared, just lay and stewed, the warmest we had been for weeks. Somebody went to collect bread and other comestibles and at 7 PM we had another meal, cooked with great difficulty because the electricity failed. Phil, Stan, and Gordon cooked on the coal fire, using one flashlight among the three. Still the meal was most welcome: it was a large one of cabbage, chips, and revolting canned fish cakes. But the chips and cabbage were great, followed by delicious bread and cheese and jam. We listened to the radio, discovered that there was no world war, and instead heard Vic Oliver, a British comedian of those years. Then we went to bed, in *real* beds and slept until 9:30 AM. Breakfast was interrupted by the captain of *Sysla*, asking us to remove our gear, because he was leaving again.

Some of us tidied up the guesthouse while the others off-loaded the gear from *Sysla* onto the jetty and then, when *Jakob Kjode* tied up, loaded the same stuff onto her; we were grateful for the derrick that made our lives easier. We were given an enormous L-shaped cabin forward, with twenty-four metal-slatted bunks and three mattresses among the thirteen of us, for McDonald and Atkinson were also coming along, as was Jimmy Alcott, a mining student friend of Dennis's who had spent the summer in the mines at Longyearbyen. Some of us covered the slats with a layer of life jackets but they were of the cork type, very hard and knobbly. We managed.

On Saturday we all stayed on board, doing nothing except tidying up expedition business. We decided we could all keep the Jaeger sweaters—mine somehow disappeared in Greenland the following year—but the sleeping bags, anoraks, and other items were to be handed back, for use by the next expedition, if any. We had four meals daily. Goss trimmed a number of beards and made a good job of it. Mike, still the clear winner in the beard competition, refused to have his touched. In the middle of the night the vessel saw fit to up-anchor and move into the bay, very noisily. The anchor-hoisting gear, immediately above our quarters, sounded like a large steam hammer. The pipe containing the telegraph from the bridge to the engine room ran right through our cabin, and every time there was a change in engine speed the bell sounded as though it were in bed with us. At 4 AM on Sunday we moved to the coal quay and loading started straight away, continuing all day.

The coal came aboard on a conveyor belt, which directed its entire load against the steel bulkhead on which our bunks were mounted. The noise was indescribable. In compensation, however, the cook continued to feed us with enormous platefuls of freshly caught cod, tasting better than any we had ever had at home, and gradually our stomachs regained their normal proportions after their recent ill treatment.

The journey to Harstad, on the east coast of the largest of the Lofoten Islands, was pleasantly uneventful. The weather was moderate,

Our last sight of Longyearbyen.

as was the sea, and the ship was as steady as a rock. Periodically the cook's assistant poked his head into our bunk space, calling us to another meal, with the words "Spis! Spis!" Stan and I tried, not very successfully, to teach Gordon and Mike to play bridge. We talked at great length and quite soon the "hut party" knew everything about the adventures of the inland gang and vice versa. We all concluded that the coastal folk had certainly been more fortunate with the weather, with the equipment (those flysheets!), and the rations. We started to consider our scientific results and there the difference, if any, was pretty small. Both groups, at least the geologists in them, seemed much more pleased with what they had accomplished than they had any right to expect. Lionel reckoned he had done about ten times as much useful work as he had in 1948; it had been not only an exciting expedition, it had been a productive one too. On that note we cut each other's hair, had another shower, and went back on deck to watch some spectacular displays of the aurora, for now, after the equinox, the nights were really dark. To set it all off, the ship's wake was full of little sources of phosphorescent light, all very pretty.

On September 27, as we came on deck en route for the first "Spis!" of the day, land was in sight. As *Jakob Kjode* threaded her way through the forested islands towards Harstad we were delighted with the pleasing smell of pinewoods, sweet and heady, on the offshore breeze. It made a fitting end to that part of our adventure.

Before we had made fast at Harstad we sighted *Miss Mabel* giving chase, looking very trim with the deck newly painted in orange and the superstructure in cream. We waved enthusiastically and Roger replied with a flag signal: "Tell Stan to wash his handkerchief."

CHAPTER ELEVEN

RE-ENTER *MISS MABEL*

∞

*W*hile we had all been gallivanting about in Sunny Svalbard,
banging off bits of rock, wringing out our sleeping bags, and
writing breath-taking poetry, Roger and his two-man crew had spent
seven weeks trying to bring *Miss Mabel* to her best level of seaworthi-
ness for the return trip to Britain. We hoped that his supply of pink
gin had been sufficient for this undertaking. He had received our
message sent from Longyearbyen and, without trouble, had taken
Miss Mabel the one hundred miles or so from Tromsø to Harstad.
Despite his rude remarks, it was a delight to see Roger and the two
Alans on our frail but friendly craft as the *Jakob Kjode* tied up at the
quay. *Miss Mabel* was soon alongside us and very soon everyone was
working hard to transfer the expedition equipment, rock samples,
personal gear, and sundry goods and chattels from the collier back
to our own vessel. Atkinson, MacDonald, and Alcott were coming
with us as well.

Mike thought that Harstad was a dirty little town but Gordon
thought it looked much cleaner and more civilized than Tromsø, with
picturesque surroundings, gaily painted wooden houses, and particularly attractive young women—a view that may have been influenced
by the absence of similar scenes for many weeks. As soon as the customs people had dealt with us we left, ten minutes later returning to

the quay because Dennis and Jimmy Alcott were still ashore, sending telegrams home. Perhaps to make a display and certainly to make best use of the tide and to get through the islands to the open sea before dark, Roger fired up all three engines at high revs. For a while this went well, but then the ever-untrustworthy center engine broke down again. This time the engineers concluded that it simply could not be repaired. Fortunately, the port and starboard engines were roaring along fairly steadily. *Miss Mabel* must have been quite a sight, with gear strewn across the decks and everyone scampering around, stowing crates in the holds, throwing rubbish overboard, and lashing down the deck cargo. To show appreciation of our efforts the Norwegian Army started some target practice, firing shells over our heads at a target on the opposite side of the fjord.

Everyone, including Atkinson, MacDonald, and Alcott, soon seasoned members of the crew, were assigned to watches. Roger had bought some good food, so Goss and I made a special dinner, roast lamb and onion sauce and then apple pie and custard. Ted, who had been steering, didn't appear till the others had all finished, so sat down at the table alone, reading. Stan watched, stupefied, as Ted poured onion sauce over his apple pie.

We set course for Kristiansund, intending to keep well away from the dangerous Norwegian coast. Mike was on watch from 4 AM. He wrote:

> It is a lovely night, with calm sea, stars and a crescent moon. The Lofotens are nearly at an end to starboard, and land just in sight to port. Once one has woken up there is the old thrill of the early morning, with the wheel in one's hands and only the course to keep. When at sea I much prefer the night watches to the day, although the broken sleep is annoying. Gradually the eastern sky lightens, and reddens as the sun comes up behind low cloud. The stars pale and soon it is day once more.

Once we were away from the shelter of the Lofoten Islands the weather became rough enough to send many of us below to our bunks, leaving the usual hardier types to run the vessel and eat hearty meals—prepared by Goss alone, for a day or two. *Miss Mabel* ceased being friendly on the second day at lunchtime, when Goss was forced to show his mettle as a sea cook. He wrote:

The ship's motion became especially lively in the forenoon watch. The array of bubbling saucepans on the hotplates of the anthracite stove was secured as well as I knew how, and there were even lengths of wire threaded through the pot handles and then twisted around brackets and rails to keep all in place. I had slipped out of the galley on some minor errand for a couple of minutes when *Miss Mabel* encountered the "wave of the day." On my return I found that all the potatoes and some of the stew had broken loose. These mischievous vegetables were racing from side to side across the deck of the galley with the roll of the vessel, half immersed in a slurry of dirty water and gravy. As principles of economy and timeliness of meals were paramount, in a few exciting minutes I had managed to catch all the fugitive vegetables, give them a quick swill in a bucket of water and put them back in their pots to finish their allotted boiling times. From those who were still eating normally at lunch on that active day I can recall no complaints from around the dining table. What the eye does not see…

That afternoon I felt better and helped Goss clean up the galley and do the washing-up. Phil, Stan, and Gordon were on watch from midday and their story differed considerably from Mike's. Gordon wrote:

> The watch was a catastrophe. Stan and Phil were violently seasick and I was even sicker with an abominable migraine. I took the wheel first while Stan was vomiting below and Phil was on deck. Then Phil took the wheel while I vomited over the side. Phil and I continued this routine turn and turn about until Stan came and took over at 12:30 PM. I went below to lie down, my head being too bad for ought else. Phil also went below before the end of the watch, by which time Stan's seasickness was over.

When we were abeam of Kristiansund, we turned hard to port, towards the town, where we were intending to refuel. From our estimated position, we should have reached Kristiansund at 4 PM. We didn't. Instead we sailed on and on and on, seeing nothing but sea. Eventually we spotted the coast in the distance. Later Roger determined we had been over 150 miles off the coast when we turned instead of the handful of miles our navigation told us we were.

Maybe the compass was adrift again? But a nasty rumor persisted that someone had hung a pair of bicycle clips on a hook over the compass. Gordon denied it. Anyway the result was that we had lost another day and, much worse, we had to take *Miss Mabel* through the islands at night. Lionel, while on watch alone in the middle of the night, recalls hearing waves breaking on invisible rocks to either side of *Miss Mabel* as she felt her way through the narrow channels in the darkness—a most hazardous procedure. We reached Kristiansund at 8 AM.

The stopover was uneventful. We refueled, did some minor revictualing, changed the gear oil and an oil filter, and made some mechanical checks of the port and starboard engines. They had worked fairly well but the center engine, which had run a big end, had in effect become ballast. We were away again within two hours. In fair weather, with only a minor swell, we cleared Gripp Lighthouse and set a southwest course towards Inverness. On the first day all went well. At one stage Stan, the helmsman, looked up from the book he was surreptitiously reading to see a ten-thousand-ton freighter bearing down on him. He changed course rapidly. Roger, of course, noticed the change immediately and ordered Stan to resume his former heading (the marine "rules of the road" say the hold-on vessel must hold-on—whatever that means). The freighter slipped by us, too close for comfort and with no indication that they had seen us.

I made another imaginative meal with six of Smedley's unmarked cans. On the morning of the second day the note from the starboard engine suddenly rose sharply, and *Miss Mabel* began to vibrate violently and slew to port. Roger ordered us to heave-to while he and the two Alans made some tests and a diagnosis down in the engine room. The fault was traced to some problem with the propeller shaft or with the propeller itself. They didn't know which. Lionel volunteered to go over the side, swim under the stern and inspect. He stripped to his trunks, tied on a climbing rope, in case he and the vessel drifted too far apart, and dived in. Within a couple of minutes he was back on deck, explaining through chattering teeth that two blades had broken from the starboard screw (propeller). Evidently we had hit some object floating just below the surface. We were now left with only one engine, giving us a maximum speed a shade over five knots. In case anything happened to the port engine (which seemed highly likely in the circumstances) we decided to head for the nearest piece of land, the Shetland Islands, in particular for the port of Lerwick.

With fingers tightly crossed we proceeded at reduced speed. In the early light Stan, at the wheel, spotted on the horizon on the starboard bow what he at first took to be a cloud but then thought it could possibly be a mountain. To settle his doubts he called the Skipper to have a look. This was not the bearing on which we were expecting a landfall, but it eventually turned out to be Sumburgh Head, the southern extremity of the Shetland Island group. We had overshot Lerwick by fifteen miles and were heading boldly into the Atlantic Ocean! We turned north in an attempt to find the port. There followed a short but tense part of the voyage when we came uncomfortably close to some nasty-looking rocks around which there seemed to be an appreciable tidal current. With our pitiful single engine being nursed and urged to do its best, it seemed to some of us a very long time before those breakers were left behind and Lerwick came into view. Fortunately in good weather, and even more fortunately at high tide, we entered Lerwick harbor in late morning and positioned the vessel on the "hard," a concrete ramp especially designed for vessels in *Miss Mabel*'s condition. In this way I achieved another of my childhood ambitions. We had a nursery song that contained the line: "So we ran the vessel ashore, on the Rub-Dub Isles." It was Lerwick instead, but we ran the vessel ashore, bow first in early afternoon. The plan was to have the shipwrights, who serviced the fishing fleet, remove the good propeller from the useless center shaft and mount it on the starboard shaft. While we waited for low tide, when this could be accomplished, most of us went into the fascinatingly gaunt town for a large meal of fish and chips, which cost us two shillings and six pence each, and to telephone our families. Apart from a letter or two we had been out of touch for three months and we were now several weeks late. While we knew that all was well with us, our families did not.

At this stage Lionel, quite wisely, decided to leave us. Taking only a few of his most exotic rock specimens and leaving behind, among other things, the book *Poet's Pub* by Eric Linklater, which he had lent to me to read, he caught the mail steamer to Aberdeen. He finally reached home, near London, on the evening of October 6, with just enough time to set his affairs in order and catch the *Mauretania* at Southampton on October 9. I still have the book.

At low tide a pair of shipwrights came over to do the necessary work with the propellers. As ever, it was good to see competent people working and the job only took an hour or so. We gave them the discarded broken screw and then asked for it back, figuring that we might need it to show to Commander Everitt when, and if, we managed to return *Miss Mabel* to him. On the following high tide, just before midnight, *Miss Mabel* floated free and we were on our way again. Fortune smiled on her and those aboard for the remainder of the journey, first to Inverness, although the vessel rolled more vigorously than at any time since leaving Harstad.

At dead low water we crept towards the Inverness anchorage, expecting to touch bottom at any moment. We didn't and anchored outside the lock entrance well after dark to be greeted, but not boarded, by lockmen and customs, the latter telling us that "now is a good time to get anything dutiable ashore." Unfortunately we couldn't take advantage of the invitation.

Next day, October 4, we started at 4 AM but were held up at the Newtown lock "ladder" and, after refuelling, it was 11 AM before we reached Loch Ness. All day we had light rain and mist, but that seemed appropriate for Scotland in October. We saw Alan the Mate's ketch, a very trim little boat, as we passed Ft. Augustus and eventually tied up downstream of Garlocky locks.

The next morning was wonderful. We continued through the Caledonian Canal, now decked out magnificently in autumn colors, down Neptune's Staircase and on into Oban Bay. Roger went out of his way to show us all the little islands. On a fine, still autumn evening we watched the sun set in a cloud of glory. Mike noted: "As we sailed round the enclosed and sheltered bay, the wake from *Miss Mabel* spread out, seemingly to infinity, each ripple tinted yellow, red, or pink by the sunset. It was a splendidly peaceful way to mark the end of an eventful voyage."

However, *Miss Mabel* was not done with us yet! We sailed gracefully through the North Channel and the Irish Sea during the night, while the three remaining geologists, Phil, Goss, and Dave, discussed how best to record and publish the expedition's scientific results. As Goss also remarked: "The closing stages of the expedition's business

Opening lock gates by hand.

also called for careful and diplomatic management, the return of the vessel to its owner, disposal of equipment, and last but not least, the proper winding up of financial matters." To show that her spirit was still very much alive, at 6:15 PM *Miss Mabel* rammed the lock gates in Liverpool at four knots, the stern clutch again refusing to hold, just as in Kristiansund. Because of the strengthened bow section of *Miss Mabel*, the only damage was to the lock gates and our pride.

Once safely moored in the Liverpool dock there seemed to be a touch of unseemly haste in the off-loading and dispersal of most of the scientific people, myself included. A final check showed that Mike was still the clear winner in the beard competition, the bushiest, blackest, and best. Second prize would have gone to Lionel. Joy and Chris were there to greet us and we had a celebratory party, during which most of us succeeded in cleaning up our language, which had become picturesque, to say the least, while we had been in Svalbard. We spent most of Sunday, October 7, unloading and clearing up. Many of us returned to Birmingham by the afternoon train. However, the true mariners, Roger and the two Alans, aided by Gordon, Ted, Stan (to delay having to report to the army), and Phil as deck hands, still had the task of returning *Miss Mabel* to her home port, dealing with Commander Everitt, and handling other administrative matters.

The end of the story is particularly fitting, and later Phil and Gordon told it to the rest of us. They left Liverpool with the port and starboard engines apparently working properly and a forecast that the weather would be reasonably calm. No problems were anticipated in getting back to Cork. The crew should have known better. *Miss Mabel* had a last card up her sleeve and lived up to her reputation in no uncertain fashion. In the Irish Sea she ran into a southwest gale. Early in the morning, somewhere to the south of St. George's Channel, Phil, in his bunk, became aware that the engines had stopped. An engine valve had broken, fallen down into the cylinder and, when the piston came up, it shot the valve through the cylinder head. Later it was found embedded in the deck above.

Roger decided that, with one engine only, it would be now too dangerous to risk a passage around the exposed south coast of Ireland to Cork. *Miss Mabel* was conveniently close to the bay leading to Wexford where, with luck, the engine might be repaired. Fortunately the sea was now calmer, and although the tide was falling there was just enough water for them to cross the bar and enter the narrow estuary. Jagged rocks lined the southern shore, and the dangers of navigating with only one engine were all too obvious. *Miss Mabel* moved forward slowly, scarily close to the rocks. Roger was at the wheel and sent Alan the Mate, Gordon, and Phil forward to free the heavy anchor at the bow. Stan, in his pajamas, joined them. They had unlashed the anchor and were attaching it to the davit chain with which they would lower the anchor safely into the sea, when Roger dashed out of the wheelhouse and in no uncertain terms ordered them to drop the anchor immediately. The bolts connecting the port engine to its gearbox had all sheared off and *Miss Mabel* was once more without any means of propulsion.

Skipper, vessel, and crew lay to, considering what to do next in their dangerous situation. The tide was running hard and the sea was quite rough. As the anchor dragged they were moving appreciably towards the rocks on the port side. Two fishing boats offered them lines, so that they could at least have attempted to strike a bargain with one of them. However, out of ignorance and fear they missed that opportunity but, in ever-increasing danger, they became aware of another fishing boat coming down the estuary. Now there was no alternative but to accept the offer by the fishermen to tow them into Wexford Harbor, along a channel only eight feet deep and fifty feet wide. A longish argument followed as to who should throw the rope to the other. If it were thrown one way, the fishermen would be entitled to claim the full salvage value of *Miss Mabel*; if the other way, only half. I don't know what was decided, but *Miss Mabel* was towed into Wexford Harbor and suffered the ultimate disgrace of finishing her voyage as salvage. When the other members of the expedition heard about her fate, we all gave thanks again to the *skipskontrollør* in Tromsø for forbidding *Miss Mabel* to proceed into arctic waters.

St. Jonsfjorden from the air, about 1936, looking west from above Wittenbergfjella. Photo courtesy of Norsk Polarinstitut.

Soon afterwards Phil, Ted, and Gordon had to return to Birmingham, and Stan felt he could not leave the army short-handed any longer. When he finally reached the military camp near Oswestry, the recruiting sergeant said between clenched teeth: "Well, we've got you now, Professor." This left Roger and the two Alans with the task of rendering *Miss Mabel* sufficiently seaworthy to creep round the coast to Cork. This they eventually accomplished but it took several weeks, with an appreciable increase in costs to the expedition.

As might be expected, there were now financial problems to be dealt with. In our contract with Commander Everitt, he was required to extend the insurance of the vessel if she were returned late, which of course she was. Unfortunately he had forgotten to do so. He tried to claim from us, and we submitted counter-claim on him for all the deficiencies of *Miss Mabel* that we, at our own expense, had had to cope with. We received invaluable help from Mr. Summers, the university financial officer, in sorting things out, with the result that, without going to law, the parties agreed that the conflicting claims cancelled each other out—certainly the best result we could have expected. The university initially paid the rest of our outstanding debts but then asked each of the expedition members for another contribution, fifty pounds each, to cover at least part of the salvage costs. At Cambridge University, however, I had no income at all until Christmas, when I was awarded a Shell Scholarship, but Birmingham University was kind and allowed me to pay nothing till the scholarship started and then to pay off the debt at five pounds per month. Gordon was in a similar situation. Based on the somewhat flimsy evidence that he and I had managed to sell two full-page articles about the expedition to the generous editor of the *Birmingham Post* for twenty-five pounds each, Gordon decided that he could make a better career in journalism than he could in geology. The *Westminster Press* offered him a job as a cub reporter. However, *Miss Mabel* again had the last word. The salary of a cub reporter left no margin to discharge his "salvage" obligation. So Gordon joined H. J. Heinz as a trainee industrial engineer and so began a satisfying career in industry. The long-term effects of our trip to the Arctic were beginning to show!

We have no idea whether *Miss Mabel* ever put to sea again. We fervently hope that she didn't.

CHAPTER TWELVE

AFTERMATH

$\mathcal{T}$he voyage of *Miss Mabel* and the seven weeks we spent in Vestpitsbergen were unforgettable experiences and a great education for all of us on the expedition, at the beginning of our careers. Despite the many frustrations and disasters, we did reach Spitsbergen and, in the limited time we had, we did pretty well all that we had set out to do. One aspect of the situation helped greatly: unlike in Britain, the rock outcrops were not covered with soil, vegetation, or buildings. We accomplished some good scientific work and the geology of those sharp ice-bound peaks proved so interesting that Dave and Phil organized two more expeditions in 1954 and 1958, to continue and extend the work begun in 1948 and 1951. Not surprisingly, they used public sea transport, which by that time had become available. Nowadays one can fly from Norway to Longyearbyen on any one of ten flights a week and can find accommodation there in either the Radisson Hotel or the hostel, converted from one of the miners' barracks, depending on one's budget. One still has to make one's own way to the field area and, because it still rains inland in Spitsbergen, it is advisable to take a good flysheet for one's tent, and an air mattress. A few years ago Mike met a schoolgirl who was just going on a school trip to the west coast of Spitsbergen. How times have changed!

The Later Expeditions: 1954 and 1958

Dave reported on the two later expeditions, which he and Phil had led jointly:

> Looking back on the records and diaries we kept in 1951, we were struck by the large amount of information we had collected. As Lionel had felt earlier, we were keen to pursue some of the geological questions that the mountains had revealed. The 1954 expedition was a close follow-up of the 1951 trip as far as its aims and achievements were concerned. Eight men sledded and skied inland from St. Jonsfjorden and visited old and new peaks. The weather was glorious! We went quite well equipped, clothed and provisioned for life on the ice. The Meade tents all had flysheets and we took air mattresses to keep off the glacial chill. The food rations were much as in 1951 but we took a large supply of lemonade powder, which was a godsend. The Nansen sleds and our ski equipment were very serviceable, although primitive by today's standards. In short, it was as comfortable a trip as 1951's had been miserable. The biggest problems concerned sunburn, snow glare, and thirst. We got a lot of good solid geology done.
>
> The 1958 venture was rather different as we went to western Ekmanfjorden (one of the fjords on the north side of Isfjorden, about thirty miles east of the mouth of St. Jonsfjorden) and used a small boat and outboard motor. This time the eight of us did not have to carry our camps on our backs, so food rations were a bit more ample and we had the comfort of air mattresses again. Weather conditions were pretty good and the boating was excellent across and down the western side of the fjord. No seal meat was eaten but we had the occasional duck. Scientific results were good and we collected plenty of hand specimens and fossils. I published a small paper in the *Geological Magazine* on the Old Red Sandstone of eastern Ekmanfjorden. Phil and I wrote an article in *Nature* on whale remains in glacial ice there, which has attracted several letters over the years from other people who have found similar occurrences. The reports from all these expeditions have been of much use to subsequent investigators of Spitsbergen geology, both British and European.

In each of these Spitsbergen adventures the sympathetic and generous behavior of the administrators and the long-suffering geology staff of the University of Birmingham earned our heartfelt gratitude. No one could have been more supportive than our vice-chancellor, Sir Raymond Priestley. He retired in 1952 but maintained a strong interest in us, and through him we felt we had a strong connection with the long British tradition of work and exploration in high latitudes.

Summary of Scientific Results

Most of the scientific work resulting from these expeditions has been published. For completeness I've made a list of all the papers I have found and have placed it after this chapter.

In his summary paper of 1958, "A Review of the Carboniferous and Permian Rocks of the West Coast of Vestspitsbergen," Dave makes reference to the work of Phil and Goss during our inland traverses in 1951. While Lionel's main jobs were to find the extent of the Carboniferous fossils in the Hecla Hoek beds and to discover how they got there, by working out the earth movements that had affected the Carboniferous and younger strata, the inland people, Phil and Goss and their rock-carriers, crawled around the outcrops trying to find out why the Carboniferous strata showed such great changes in composition and thickness between Kongsfjorden and Isfjorden. In the pouring rain and on slippery slopes their lot was not a happy one, but from the results of that uncomfortable and short season's work, and from those of the much more relaxed efforts in 1954 and 1958, Dave was able to fill in many of the gaps that had existed in our knowledge of the Paleozoic.

In 1953, Lionel published "Tectonic Features of the Hecla Hook Formation to the South of St. Jonsfjord, Vestspitsbergen." In that paper he sorted out some of the geological problems he had formulated. I've given his summary earlier. In the paper, however, he wrote: "Another field season is required before the publication of a geological map and accompanying report will become possible." Unfortunately, Lionel was never able to return to Svalbard.

Dave's interesting paper, "Investigations in Vestspitsbergen," published in 1954 in the *Journal of Glaciology*, gives an explanation of the formation of the partly snow-filled gullies that they found all along the *strandflat*. He also gives some account of the recession and the thinning, since the 1930s, of many of the valley glaciers we found in our various traverses.

Dave reported on the raised marine features south and east of Müllerneset for the Royal Geographical Society (*Geographical Journal,* 1954) and on their shelly content for *Norsk Geologisk Tidsskrift* in 1954. It seems that the evidence from our grey fjord fits well with the picture from elsewhere in Spitsbergen that emerged over the next few years from Norwegian and Polish investigations. During recent geological times Vestspitsbergen has suffered deep burial under glacial ice; now, as the climate warms and the ice recedes, the land is slowly rising from the sea. Periodically this process is slowed or halted so that beaches form along the coast. In our area, along Forlundsundet and St. Jonsfjorden, the beaches were pretty miserable things, scattered patches of mud and gravel, occurring up to about forty-five meters above present sea level—not the spectacular step-like banks of shingle found in the central fjords of Svalbard, where they extend up to one hundred meters in elevation.

The fossils in the beach sediments that we found in St. Jonsfjorden were mostly fragments or broken white bivalve mollusks, up to about seven centimeters long. Three species were common but there were specimens of other species as well. Most are high-arctic species but in some of the lower localities rare specimens of mid-arctic types occur. In our area the elevation distribution of the species was much the same as in central Vestspitsbergen, which seems to mark what have been called the Late Glacial Cold, Post-Glacial Temperate, and Post-Glacial Warm climatic phases. Contrasting with the fossil shell populations in the central fjords, in our area *Mytilus edulis* (the "blue mussel") seems rare and *Astarte* even less common. *Mya truncata* is the most abundant by far. This probably reflects the more turbulent inshore seas of the west coast, favoring these mollusks with stout shells, living buried in the bottom sands. Dave could find no comparable communities in the very barren modern beach sands. In general, Dave concluded, the land in our area has been rising from the sea at a rate of about 1.4 cm per year for the last 2,000 years and slightly faster than that for the period back to about 8,000 or 10,000 years. We hope that the Royal Geographical Society was pleased with the dividends from their investment of seventy-five pounds. Dave's colleague at Exeter, Clive Bowen (Bowen 1954), working with the forams that Dave collected from the beach deposits, concluded that "a more genial climate than the present arctic conditions has affected these parts of the world." Dave remarked in 2003, "Just think how much more we could have done if only we had known about radiocarbon dating in 1951, but the technique hadn't been invented then!"

In the intervening years many other geologists have worked in areas adjacent to ours, and from the combined results good geological maps have now been published. They are all given in detail in W. Brian Harland's masterpiece, *The Geology of Svalbard*, a 521-page book published in 1997 by the Geological Society of London, as Memoir Seventeen. The outcrop of Carboniferous strata with its fossil corals and brachiopods, near Kapp Scania, and its continuation northwards, are illustrated in all the appropriate maps.

∞

In 2002, all the survivors except Lionel met again in Stratford, and at lunch Mike gave me the written comments from the critic friend of one of us, Anne Jones, on the first draft of this book, which I had recently sent to all the participants. Anne's review contained lots of very valuable remarks and criticisms, which I've tried to address in writing revised editions. Anne gave much emphasis to my proposed "Aftermath" chapter, pointing out the value of the participants' own assessments of the effect of the Spitsbergen experience on each of our lives. I duly asked each of them for a contribution along those lines, including John Nunn from the 1948 expedition.

Other Members of the 1948 Expedition

John Nunn, the medical officer with the 1948 quartet, wrote an excellent short summary of that expedition in "University of Birmingham Expedition to Svalbard (Spitsbergen) in the Summer of 1948," published in *Aesculapius*, the University of Birmingham Medical and Dental Graduates Society, no. 20, July 2000. From that, among many other things, I first learned of the final traverse made by Lionel and John, when they stayed awake for fifty-seven hours in order to complete the geological work. They were fortified with amphetamine tablets, which, as John pointed out, were "free from social stigma in those days." With a bachelor's thesis based on that work Lionel gained a first class honors degree.

54 Years Later: the Surviving 'Innocents' in 2005

GORDON COLIN DAVE

MIKE LIONEL

GOSS PHIL STAN

Though much is taken, much abides; and though
We are not now that strength which in old days
Moved earth and heaven; that which we are, we are;
One equal temper of heroic hearts,
Made weak by time and fate, but strong in will
To strive, to seek, to find, and not to yield.

—*Alfred Lord Tennyson,* Ulysses

John had a very successful career in medicine, which included service as the foundation professor of anesthesia at the University of Leeds from 1964 to 1968 and then as head of the Division of Anesthesia in the Medical Research Council from 1968 to 1991. However, his time with Lionel and Brian in Vestspitsbergen had stimulated his interest in the earth sciences. He said:

> My more orthodox geological interest has been the stratigraphy of the Jurassic/Cretaceous interface at the type section in Durleston Bay, Dorset, where we happen to have a cottage.
>
> I have also had a very long-standing interest in the atmosphere, which was a spin-off from my main-line interest in respiratory physiology. I gave a paper to the Geologists' Association on January 5, 1996, which was published as "Evolution of the Atmosphere" in the *Proceedings of the Geologists' Association* (1998) 109, 1–13. To my amazement it received the Richardson Award for the best paper of the year—and I was elected to Fellowship of the Geological Society, an accomplishment for a medical person of which I am quite proud.

His current interests include work on global warming.

Lionel, who had remained in touch with Brian Baker, another member of the 1948 foursome, wrote an account of Brian's career. Brian also gained a first class honors degree with a thesis based on his Spitsbergen work. After graduating in 1949 he joined the British Overseas Geological Survey to work in Kenya and remained there until he accepted a professorship of geology at the University of Oregon in Eugene in 1970. So impressive was his work in Kenya that he quickly rose in rank and geologic stature until he became chief geologist under the colonial administration and then commissioner for mines and geology under the independent government of Kenya in 1963. But he quickly became impatient with administration and moved to the University of Nairobi where he could continue his field investigations, teach, and complete his doctoral dissertation. The work he accomplished on the great African Rift during this period is of classic dimensions.

After moving to Oregon, Brian became immersed in geochemical studies and the application of computers to basic geological problems. He died in February 1986, after several strokes while on sabbatical leave in Kenya, mourned by all who knew him.

Michael Holland, the fourth member and the leader of the 1948 expedition, did not complete his geology degree at Birmingham but moved to Oxford to do so. He accompanied a Cambridge expedition to Spitsbergen a short while later but then dropped out of our lives. Nevertheless, we were saddened to hear that he had died during an expedition to Greenland a few years later.

Dave

A fascinating and accurate report on our 1951 expedition was written by David Ward, a reporter for *The Guardian*, with a great deal of help from Dave Dineley. He called it "Sailing *Miss Mabel*" and it appeared in the *Birmingham Magazine* of the University of Birmingham in November 2001. It was this article that provoked me into compiling the present, longer account. In the article Dave said, "the expedition was fun and had a pretty steep learning curve. It was a remarkable experience. The arctic bug bit several of us." I consider that an excellent summary, in twenty-five words or less, of the whole adventure.

About his work on the *strandflat* with Gordon in 1951 Dave wrote:

Gordon and I had no previous experience of raised marine landforms in the Arctic, or anywhere else for that matter. And along the coasts of Forlandsundet and St. Jonsfjorden they were not the rampart-like banks of shingle present in the central fjords of Spitsbergen. We had to learn quickly from the scattered flowerbed-sized bits of level gravel and shingle with their giveaway decorations of small white shells. We measured heights and collected samples of shells from selected square yards of terrace, together with little bags of sand for microfossils. Back home we later read about similar surveys of the spread of different shell species by a Norwegian, Rolf Feyling-Hanssen. His work helped to put our own results in perspective. I have remained interested in post-glacial land rise and changing inshore faunas ever since.

More widespread and conspicuous were the signs and processes of periglacial conditions. Patterned ground, stone stripes, solifluxion, and frost shattering of rocks were all around us, producing features many of which looked manmade. In fact we devised theories of how the Old Man of Mount Müller and his trolls constructed these patterns to while away the long, dark winter days. Soon afterwards, I was able to detect traces of many such periglacial features in southwest England, much subdued by the passage of time. When I worked in the Canadian Arctic in the 1960s and 1970s, the same features seemed like old friends.

The Hecla Hoek rocks remained metamorphic mysteries as far as I was concerned, but the Carboniferous and Permian strata we could see far off inland and could handle as debris in the glacial moraines were another matter. In the absence of any Old Red Sandstone (Devonian) rocks with fossil fish (and Vestspitsbergen is famous for them), I was happy to search these Paleozoic rock fragments for *real* fossils—and we found lots of them, big and impressive. The prospect of visiting inland outcrops of these rocks in the spectacular mountains of the west was one of the main incentives for the subsequent expeditions that Phil and I made to Vestspitsbergen. We knew that these formations were widespread and variable throughout the western half of the island, and we felt we could add to the knowledge about them. So the 1951 expedition and the two that followed let me experience strata unseen in Britain and confirmed my enthusiasm for working in northern latitudes. This enthusiasm led me to a couple of decades of fieldwork in the Canadian Arctic islands and expanded my interest in all things arctic.

Dave's career after the 1951 experience clearly demonstrates the virulent powers of the arctic bug. He returned to University College of the Southwest of England in Exeter, and jointly with Phil, still at the University of Birmingham, was co-leader of the subsequent Svalbard expeditions mentioned above. Then he moved to the University of Ottawa, in Canada's capital, where there were long-established centers of arctic interest, including the Geological Survey of Canada and the National Museum of Canada. Thus the arctic bug was kept well and truly alive, and from 1964 through 1967, Dave led annual University of Ottawa expeditions to the far north, around Lancaster Sound. There the geological attractions were many, transport was by air and the logistics were simple—relative to his experiences on the *Miss Mabel* expedition! There were also opportunities at last for Dave to engage in his first geological love, "Paleozoic fishing," not to mention other subjects such as geophysics and Inuit archaeology.

Since then his students and colleagues have continued with the work. Dave returned to England in 1968, as professor of geology at the University of Bristol. However, the bug was still in his bloodstream and he took more geological expeditions and petroleum-prospecting parties back to the Canadian Arctic and the Yukon in 1970, 1973, 1974, and 1990. He became pro-vice-chancellor at Bristol before he retired. Even then, as he says,

> Dreams and reveries of arctic days never seem very easy to dispel. People ask why those far off places exercise such an attraction; it can be bitterly cold there, even in the summer; it is terrifyingly big, barren, silent, and empty. It can be very beautiful; locally the wildlife is marvelous and strange. Was Europe like this when Cro-Magnon man and the Neanderthals roamed, as the last Ice Age drew to a close? What stout hearts were the early Inuit, Norsemen, explorers, and whalers who learned to cope—or not—at those latitudes! Many writers have mentioned the dream-like quality of arctic experience and, like many a dream, Spitsbergen 1951 left memories and an appetite that have persisted for fifty years or more.

Phil

Phil and I have been brothers-in-law since 1956, and we had been tent companions during the most difficult time in Spitsbergen, but still I learned a great deal from his contribution to this chapter. He wrote:

> That I became a member of the expedition was a matter of pure chance, as so often happens in life. My Birmingham degree (December 1943) is in oil engineering and exploration geology. I was most interested in the geological part so I would have liked any post involving geology, but C.P. Snow and his committee in charge of military placement decided I should go, when called up, to the Royal Engineers. On my second day in the army I was run over on my motorbike by a Bren Gun Carrier and broke my leg. In the end I was commissioned in late 1945 and posted to an electrical and mechanical squadron in Palestine, where I was twice nearly killed by Jewish terrorists. I was demobilized in September 1947, and having decided to pursue a geological career, I went back to the geology department at Birmingham

to start research. This is where I first met Lionel, Dave, and Colin, who helped with the work I was doing on fluorescence of minerals. I was appointed lecturer in geology in September 1948 and throughout my career taught geology to oil engineers, miners, and civil engineers. Goss was one of the first geology students I ever taught. With all the Spitsbergen talk, I very much liked the idea of taking part in the expedition and Joy, my wife, was willing to do without me for three months. With the potential costs of the expedition, I think also that the vice-chancellor was quite glad to have an employee there to keep some financial watch.

I was able to be helpful with the expedition because my great school friend Phil Cox was ex–Royal Navy and a great sailor. He looked around for suitable boats for us. The one he suggested was a stout teak-hulled gaff-rigged ketch named *Tectona*, owned by Tom Blackwell (of Crosse and Blackwell, the tinned food people) who would have skippered for us. If we had chartered her, our journey would have been quite different because *Tectona* would have been able to deal with ice. The idea did not appeal to Ted and Lionel. More important in the end, it was Philip who put us in touch with a friend of his, Roger Pirie, also ex–Royal Navy and interested in such jobs as being our skipper. The other contact was through Don Griffiths who had recently been appointed lecturer in geophysics with us in Birmingham and had come from Manchester where he had been friendly with Alan Evans who was very keen to join us.

Life in the army is one thing and lecturing at the university is another. But working with newly graduated students in close and uncomfortable conditions, cramped, cold and wet, is quite different from either. That we got on so well is a great tribute to the personalities of all involved. We remain good friends after all these years.

As far as the geology was concerned, where I worked large areas were covered in ice, but elsewhere the sharp, high rock exposures were not covered with soil, as they usually are in temperate climates. Considerable thicknesses of strata could be examined in detail over significant distances—a great advantage of arctic conditions.

When Dave suggested we return to St. Jonsfjorden to continue the work we had begun in 1951, I was in full support. So in 1954, four of us from Exeter and four from Birmingham, including a doctor, returned to Vestspitsbergen, traveling by public transport. The weather was completely different from 1951—the sun shone twenty-four hours a day for the whole time (I think!). We had learned a lot in 1951 about working in the Arctic, so now there were just two people to a tent and we had air mattresses. We took flysheets, which extended well beyond the front of the tent, where we could do the cooking. This was known as "the Garrett end." I was able to do some good mapping.

Having caught the arctic bug, we decided to return to Spitsbergen in 1958, to look at the area to the east, towards the axis of the syncline, to see the younger strata, as far up the geologic column as the Jurassic. Again there were four from Exeter and four from Birmingham, again including a doctor. We were based on the western shore of Ekmanfjorden and this time we had our own dinghy, which saved a lot of walking. The geology was fascinating and comparatively simple. Again the weather was excellent.

Since the 1930s there has been some warming of the climate, which has resulted in significant retreat of glaciers. We found the complete body of a large whale, which must have been trapped and killed under the floating ice-front of a glacier, the present position of which is a couple of miles further back. One day we went to look at the delta sediments at the head of the fjord and there found an elderly Norwegian surveyor working by himself. He insisted on brewing for us the strongest tea I have ever tasted. The spoon almost stood up in the mug! He had no English so we never discovered what aspects he was mapping. Another memory is how the Cambridge geologists and we played soccer for England against Norway, watched by the *sysselmann*, with national flags flying. The better side won.

Looking back at those three Spitsbergen seasons, my greatest regret is that I did not keep diaries (and never have done so). There is so much I cannot remember, which is why reading extracts from all the other diaries has been so marvelous. Spitsbergen was one of the great experiences of my life.

Research has never been my strong point, but I have always thoroughly enjoyed teaching. My major contribution to the university, however, has been in academic management. The most important element of this, apart from being a member of the University Senate and Council for most of my career, was being the deputy dean from 1975 to 1978 and the dean from 1978 to 1981 of the Faculty of Science and Engineering, which at that time was almost half the university. I was promoted to professor of geology in 1981 and retired in 1990, having been on the faculty for forty-two years.

I have remained happily in touch with most members of the expedition over the years. We had planned that early in 1994 Ted Hitchcock would try to remove two congenital growths from my spinal cord. He met his unexpected and tragic death just a few weeks before the date of the operation. Such is life!

Ted

All the survivors have kept in touch over the years with each other and with Jill, Ted's widow. Only Dennis Gray has disappeared from our view. We know that he completed his M.Sc. degree at Birmingham and then went to South Africa as a mining engineer. Some time later he moved to Canada, still as a mining engineer. We know also that he died in the mid 1990s, but nothing more. Our ignorance of his later life is a pity: it would have been satisfying to follow everyone's subsequent career and to hear his considered thoughts about the Spitsbergen experience.

I wish too that I had had the opportunity to ask Ted what he considered the effect of the Svalbard adventure had been on his subsequent career. Unfortunately Ted died of a heart attack in December 1993, aged sixty-four. The last time I saw him was at our fortieth anniversary reunion, held at Stratford in 1991. On that occasion Ted showed he was still an unusually profound conversationalist. At lunch he read the letters he had written to Sir Raymond Priestley from Tromsø, from Svalbard (while we were waiting for *Sysla*), and from Birmingham after our return. For the first time I realized that Ted was also aware how fortunate we had been on *Miss Mabel* not to encounter a really strong storm. In such an event the vessel would surely have sunk.

After the expedition Ted completed his medical studies. He received surgical training in Birmingham and at University College Hospital in London and neurosurgical instruction in Oxford and Manchester. From 1965 to 1978, he was at the University of Edinburgh and then he was appointed professor of neurosurgery in Birmingham. Ted's obituary notice in *The Times* called him Britain's foremost practitioner in stereotactic and functional neurosurgery, adding, "Overseas he had been dubbed the twentieth-century "Columbus of the Brain" on the basis of his multidirectional explorations of the human brain and spinal cord. He attracted wide public attention, and some criticism, by pioneering the use of fetal brain cell transplants to treat patients with Parkinson's disease."

Ted's personal energy remained enormous. He had a large practice in neurosurgery that included our Svalbard colleague Phil, who had spinal cord problems. He was president of the European Society for Stereotactic and Functional Neurosurgery and vice president of the World Society. He traveled widely, but never again to the Arctic.

Jill, Ted's widow, added the following:

> While he was still a student Ted received a promise from Sir Hugh Cairns, the founder of the neurological unit at Oxford University, that once Ted had qualified he would see him and maybe plan his future neurological training. Then alas, shortly afterwards Sir Hugh died, rather suddenly. At Ted's first Arctic Club dinner [to which he was invited because he had been to Spitsbergen] he sat next to a dentist from Oxford and regaled him with this sad story. Ted said how he would dearly like to train at the Radcliffe Infirmary of Oxford University, but the promise had been a very personal one from Sir Hugh. The consequence was that the dentist had a word with his best friend, Walpole Lewin, the younger of the two neurosurgeons at the Radcliffe, and Ted was summoned to meet him and Joe Pennybacker, the head of the department. They agreed to have Ted as a junior house officer, once he had gained his FRCS and had spent a year in some allied neurological specialty [which he did at University College Hospital, London]. Ted also had to do two years of National Service so, nine years after qualifying and thanks to having been to the Arctic, he started his neurological training. The specialty was so small at that time that these stipulations seemed reasonable, but I wonder how many young medics these days would be willing to go back to the rigors of a house officer's life, to say nothing of the kind of salary he was then receiving,
>
> Ted took enormous pleasure in the annual Arctic Club dinners, because he met so many interesting people with so many varied occupations. Most, like Ted, had never returned to the Arctic but I

suspect that only a very special type of person has the spirit to go
there, even if only in his or her youth.

Mike

At that fortieth anniversary reunion in 1991, Mike looked round the
lunch table and remarked that all of the members, except perhaps
Dennis, about whom we knew nothing, had married and had married
only once. He wondered if this was the result of the times or whether
we all had the same quirk of character, perhaps developed during
the expedition. Dave responded immediately: "Forty years with the
same woman is *nothing* compared with three months with you lot!" I
conclude that our monogamous behavior is entirely due to our arctic
experiences, although I am at a loss to offer any explanation.

Mike too never returned to the Arctic, but his interest in things
polar has continued and deepened. As far as I know, he is the only
one of our party who has read my Antarctic book, *Silas*, about Charles
Wright, the glaciologist on Scott's Last Expedition. Some time ago
Mike wrote to me:

> Reading *Silas* I was struck by the fact that Scott chartered *Terra
> Nova*. It was too small for all the people, inadequate for the amount
> of equipment and baggage, and was overloaded in New Zealand by
> three feet at the Plimsoll line before crossing the Southern Ocean.
> *Terra Nova* nearly sank when the bilge pumps blocked. If Scott, with
> all his naval and polar experience, made such a choice, what hope had
> we students in the jungle of ship chartering? Thankfully, like Scott's
> ship, *Miss Mabel* survived, just!

On another occasion Mike pointed out that Cherry-Garrard, in
The Worst Journey in the World (the book to which I had introduced
Mike and Goss, when we were having a rough time) wrote "one feels
disposed to clamor for a Polar Factory Act, making it a crime to ship
men (to) the ice in vessels more fit to ply between London Bridge and
Ramsgate."

Mike continued:

> The parallel between *Terra Nova* and *Miss Mabel* interests me. I think
> that both charters, despite the vast differences in time, size, nautical

experience and other aspects, were made under pressure as it was felt that the vessels offered the only way that the expedition transport problems could be solved. The alternative would have been abandoning the trips in the year planned. Such pressures tend to overwhelm considerations of prudence. In our case, with *Miss Mabel*, prudence was in short supply, ignorance being bliss. But that thought is clearly hindsight. I remember I was very impressed by *Miss Mabel* at first sight.

About his subsequent career Mike says:

On my return from Spitsbergen I found myself redundant. I was soon offered a job in the design office of the authority responsible for sewage treatment in Birmingham. I did not expect to stay long, but I remained with them until I retired as chief engineer, after an interesting and fulfilling career of thirty years. My career outline is brief and not at all relevant to the Arctic. It deals mainly with subjects that will stop dead any dinner party conversation in polite society, even deader than will medical student shop talk. If you imagine one million WCs flushing simultaneously, and double that output with flows from industry and other sources, you can get some idea of the problem that confronted us. The whole sewage system of Birmingham needed reconstructing and extending after neglect through many years of economic slump and warfare.

The problems facing us included scientifically and technically challenging aspects, such as activated sludge, sludge digestion, and disposal, unattractive subjects to most people, but finding solutions to them is essential to public health. Personal accomplishments include completing what was only the second large plant to burn sewage sludge in this country. It is still working after thirty years while most such plants never work at all. It has a three-hundred-foot chimney, which gives a splendid, if terrifying, view from its top. A less creditable personal highlight was my visiting a typing pool (in search of a telephone) after being sprayed from head to foot in black sewage sludge. The members of the pool had never seen the like!

My greatest reward for a lifetime of work is in the knowledge that there are now fish in the river draining Birmingham for the first time in 150 years, since the middle of the nineteenth century. An unsung environmental achievement!

I married my pre-Spitsbergen fiancée a year after my return. We both took early retirement and continue our various interests including until recently, holidaying in Scotland where we seek to combine wild places with good food and wine.

I think that the Spitsbergen trip helped me to grow up, to expect both ups and downs in life, and perhaps it has given me the confidence to seize opportunities when they arise. It also left many happy and vivid memories.

Stan

Stan had this to say:

I had very little time in 1951 to form any opinion of the importance of the adventure to Spitsbergen that I had just completed, because I was called up for my military service on November 11. However, it certainly helped me through the rigors of National Service, and memories of the days in Spitsbergen may have cooled me down when I went to serve in the heat of Egypt.

Since then I have been involved in school teaching at various levels and cannot say that what I learned in the Arctic has played a dramatic part in my labors. But I have the quiet satisfaction of having been to Spitsbergen and having survived the voyage of the temperamental *Miss Mabel* and the perils of arctic travel as well as the knowledge that I was accepted into the expedition without even applying and, indeed, without having any foreknowledge of its existence.

Then followed the tremendous disappointment we all felt in Tromsø when we thought that the whole expedition would have to be cancelled and never reach Spitsbergen. Then we were "on again" and this time I was immensely pleased to be promoted from the nebulous position of "boatman" to being a working member of the expedition. It was a fantastic opportunity that I seized with both hands. The trip was an unforgettable set of experiences, the memories of which I have treasured ever since. How else could I have swum in the Arctic Ocean, only 650 miles from the North Pole!

Gordon

When I asked Gordon the same question he produced a very interesting, indeed fascinating, reply:

The Svalbard Expedition of 1951 no doubt changed my life, but introversion does not come naturally to me and I cannot tell how different my life would have been without it. I can say with full conviction that it cemented wonderful lifelong friendships, although I suspect that most of these were well established before the event. It gave me a taste of the awesome beauty of the Arctic, about which I still dream although I have never returned, and indeed in the coastal party we saw only a very tame version of the Arctic and were not exposed to the peaks and glaciers that faced the inland party.

I was impressed with the silence, and the fact that a bird call could carry for ten or more miles. The flotsam and jetsam on the beaches are another strong memory with its indictment of our throwaway and wasteful civilization. Although I am a gregarious person, Svalbard strengthened my growing enjoyment of solitude, first explored the previous year in the Western Desert of North Africa. Deserts are profound places, a strange conclusion about an environment with no evidence of human thought. Watching seabirds in their natural home where no one disturbs or feeds them stays forever in one's memory, and becomes, I suppose, part of one's character. Then there was the journey on *Miss Mabel*, the most stimulating and ebullient fun and the most challenging experience. I know now that we did not deserve to survive. We threw down a totally irresponsible challenge to the elements and thanks largely to the wise and kindly Norwegian authorities, and partly to sheer mechanical incompetence, we survived. Indeed, except for Mike falling into the Caledonian Canal; our noble diver Lionel, who inspected the screw; and the duck retriever, Stan, we hardly got wet.

I have no reason to feel smug about the expedition: the nearest I got to geology was collecting and carrying fossils but, in preparing for the expedition, I did learn about fundraising and recruiting, and I did learn not to crunch barley sugars! Unlike my friends I did not excel in study and, together with my unruly behavior, that resulted in my undergraduate studies being rudely interrupted by military service. In this I was allowed to roam the Western Desert with a few trucks and a handful of soldiers, ostensibly to destroy Italian gun emplacements left over from the Second World War. That occupation did teach me self-reliance and desert skills but was not a good preparation for a final degree year. So the old Brace was not surprised that the young Brace, in 1951, chose an arctic expedition over serious study in what already seemed a lost cause.

When the expedition was over and the necessity to earn a living hove into view there was not a wide choice of geology jobs available to me. I had four offers. The first was to be curator at the Geology Museum in Oxford Road, Manchester. This was hardly an attractive proposition at 315 pounds per year, especially when I still owed the university fifty pounds as my share of the salvage money for the wrecked *Miss Mabel*. Next, BP (British Petroleum) said they were willing to send me to the Persian Gulf for five years, to study slides of foraminifera through a microscope, in temperatures up to 111 degrees Fahrenheit. That didn't inspire me. The National Coal Board came up trumps with an offer of seven hundred pounds per annum, but the job was to prospect for open cast mining sites. Among other natural beauty spots, Belvoir Valley was in their sights, and I shuddered at the thought of being involved in environmental rape, so I turned them down. The last offer I was tempted to take. It involved boring for water in the Punjab. However, the prospective employer thrust on me a fifty-page contract, which I was to sign and be ready to sail three days hence. Reckless though I am, I balked at that, although I sometimes wonder... I find India a most fascinating place.

These false starts left me in the hands of the long-suffering Joint Recruiting Board of the university, in the kindly care of Peter Hordern and Bill Pearson, to both of whom I owe a great debt. Subtle steering, infinite patience, and wise guidance were never more skillfully delivered. They noted I was not a loner, albeit I had learned to value solitude, and life with a geology hammer and a couple of porters would soon pall. Industry, they suggested, with its human and intellectual challenges, might be worth exploring. Although I accepted this advice I still hankered after something that I saw as more creative. The success that Colin and I had in selling two long articles about the expedition to the *Birmingham Post* convinced me that I had the makings of a journalist. (In passing I note that in the seventy-fifth year of my life I am still considering what I am going to be when I grow up.) The *Westminster Press* offered me a position as a trainee reporter, but I had already followed up some of the industrial opportunities, driven in part by my still unsettled "*Miss Mabel* debt." Industry paid better than journalism, so industry it was.

A 1951 graduate's search for an industrial job was absolutely hilarious; anyone who has seen Peter Sellers' wonderful film *I'm Alright Jack* will know exactly what it was like. The "personnel" fraternity of that era were caricatures of themselves. I had not really grown up, and when they asked me what use a degree in geology would be for their companies, I used to reply that I could tell them whether the company was on the rocks. I soon realized that jokes were not appreciated. One particularly engaging process was that by which one joined (or was rejected by) the Rootes Group of car manufacturers. I had two interviews with a Colonel Disney. He challenged me whether I would not prefer to be in "women's stockings rather than cars" and then suddenly slapped a connecting rod on the table. "What's that?" he snapped. I knew generically but could not identify the particular engine from which it came. He reported back to Bill Pearson that he "liked that fellow Brace—he fights back," before sending me to face fifteen elderly gentlemen behind a vast board room table. As a result they offered me an appointment in the personnel department of Commer Cars of Luton. The general manager there, on the following Monday, asked "What do you want?" and when I showed him my letter of appointment, "Huh," he said, "We don't have a personnel department." I stopped myself from replying "You have one now!" and went to work for H. J. Heinz and Company in Harlesden.

The Heinz Company was a remarkably advanced employer for their day. Offices were open plan; everyone, including the managing director, clocked in at 8 AM and no one was allowed on the production floor with a bandage or sticking plaster. Cleanliness was an obsession. The canteen served all, including directors. Training was well organized and universal; I thought all industry must be like this. Fifty years later much of it is. Heinz did not make the error of having a graduate-training scheme: they gave one a job. Mine was as a methods engineer. In my first week I was given a minor problem and found myself reviewing Stefan's Law of Radiation in order to calculate a probable rate of heat loss. Step by step we were given internal training and were sent to Acton Technical College (now

Brunel University) to learn the art of work study. I tried out what I had learned in my mother's kitchen but was rebuffed by operator resistance!

In August 1953 Anthea and I were married, and I felt, quite unreasonably, that my job progress was too slow. I left the positive climate of H. J. Heinz to be a "time study engineer" in an East End sweet factory for much more money. The atmosphere was appalling; the management style was brutal and the job immediately unbearable. I stood it for about eight months before deciding I needed proper qualifications for an industrial career. Returning to Birmingham's Joint Recruiting Board I found that Peter Caswell, a fellow geology graduate, had joined with Bill Pearson. Through them I met Tom Matthew, professor of production engineering, who found me a Lucas Scholarship. Anthea abandoned her London job, where I am convinced she was working for the CIA, and took a teaching position in Walsall. With my scholarship and her salary we had enough to live while I studied for my M.Sc. Production Engineering was a new and stimulating department in which for the first time I really learned how to study.

After graduation I joined the British Iron and Steel Federation, where I helped assemble management courses for managers in the industry, eventually becoming part of the directing staff of the new Steel Industry Staff College. From there I went to the Bowater Paper Corporation, as chief production engineer of their corrugated box division. It was interesting work, and I had a fine team, but I foolishly accepted promotion to deputy head of work study in Bowater House, Knightsbridge, and a really stifling bureaucracy. Fortunately a head hunter stepped in. I was offered the task of introducing an industrial engineering function to the newly assembled Watney Mann Brewing Group. That job was a really enjoyable one in a civilized company with four breweries and 8,500 pubs. It was a dream of a job, from which I became group distribution manager and later director of operations. [This was the period when "Wot we want is Watney's," displaced "What did Drobny say to Von Cramm?" as our convivial greeting on meeting other members of the expedition.] Sadly Grand Metropolitan acquired the firm and when the government arbitrarily decided that a brewer could own no more than two thousand pubs,

Grand Met. had no hesitation in keeping the pubs and selling or closing the breweries.

In a fit of pique I made a stupid move, to become general manger and chief executive officer of the National Exhibition Center in Birmingham, in its opening year, 1976. The originally recruited general manager had quit in despair and I soon discovered why! The less than a year I spent there was an intensive consultancy assignment, putting in place a management structure, a salary scale, proper agreements with trade unions and getting a handle on what was the market for exhibitions. The problem was the chairman, who thought that a chief executive should report to an "executive chairman", thereby distorting the English language and driving both incumbents insane.

I joined Automotive Products, first as an operations director and later as managing director of the Distribution Division. I worked there for seven years, very demanding years for the British motor industry, which was feeling the first thrust of Japanese competition. At the same time North Sea Oil was pushing up the value of the pound, so that to the outside world our costs had doubled. In the end I could not agree with the board's approach to the problem, nor they with mine.

By that time, 1984, I had gained much experience of logistics generally so I joined with friends to set up a consultancy, Burman Associates, of which I am still chairman. We had an enjoyable time helping Lucas Automotive with their depot network; we advised London Buses on maintaining their fleet; we helped the Nuffield Trust to evaluate a charity called Books for Development, and I earned more in my first year than ever before or since!

At the end of the year I was appointed an associate fellow of Warwick Manufacturing Group, University of Warwick, with the aim of running a Center for Manufacturing Renewal. We did research, we ran short courses, we wrote much propaganda, but eventually the paymaster withdrew funding for the center and I turned to my favorite subject, logistics, which I still study and indeed have just launched a masters' degree in the subject. Would that I had known more about it in 1951!

Lionel

Lionel's response to my invitation to comment on the effect of the Spitsbergen adventure on his life was quite surprising. He laid as much responsibility on *Miss Mabel* as on the Hecla Hoek formation and the *Caninia calophylloides* coral fossils for shaping his life. Here's what he wrote:

> Before tackling the *Miss Mabel* episode and the expedition of 1951, I'm succumbing to temptation by reminiscing about my first expedition to Svalbard in 1948. There are two main reasons. First, the 1948 trip was my baptism of ice in Svalbard. Second, the company of two of the finest friends and colleagues with whom anyone could share an adventure honored me—John F. Nunn and Brian H. Baker. Brian is sadly gone. John (or Josh, as he was usually known in those far-off days) and I remain in touch and will as long as life permits. I found I could not rake through my recollections of the 1951 expedition and the *Miss Mabel* debacle without confessing that the earlier expedition, like most first-time experiences, lives brighter in my memory. A practical explanation for the intensity of my recollections is that I didn't lose all my personal notes from the first expedition, as I did from the second. When, on my retirement in 1989, I cleared out old research and lecture notes from the office in Berkeley that I had inhabited for more than thirty years, I threw away a Svalbard file from 1951. I thought it contained only geological musings, such as fanciful and unpublishable structural cross-sections of the Forlandsundet region. Later I realized it contained also my loose-leaf personal notes from the expedition, of which only two pages have survived, one with a hastily sketched plan of *Miss Mabel*. At first I thought this a disaster, but after reading the eloquently vivid accounts written by other members of the expedition, I think it proper that my scribblings perished.
>
> Another explanation of why events of 1948 remain unusually fresh in my mind is that we were not confined by geological aims to the coastal region, as I was on the second expedition. We were free to explore far afield, trekking inland over glaciers and icefields, as did the inland party of 1951, and climbing peaks for the sheer fun of it. I concluded at the time that, under the right conditions of season and weather, Svalbard is one of the most beautiful places on Earth.

We too used Meade tents, and, in order to make the inland parties of the second expedition feel less discriminated against, I hereby reveal that our tents had no flysheets. In retrospect, I think that some of the inland party's problems with rain came as much from having three men in a tent designed for two as from the absence of flysheets. In 1948, we were only two to a tent and had no difficulty in keeping away from the walls during downpours.

Much though I would have liked to, I was unable to continue my work on the tectonics of the basement and Carboniferous rocks of the east Forlandsundet coast. A recent check of "Geology" on the current major Svalbard web page reveals a very large number of papers published over the last fifty years, some of them dealing with the tectonic evolution of Vestspitsbergen. In 1948 and 1951, we had no plate tectonic theory to hang our ideas on and, like most geologists of the time, we were unable to see tectonic patterns now obvious to almost all geologists. Nonetheless, as far as my own work was concerned, I made some progress by applying the then-new techniques of structural analysis of small-scale deformation structures measured in the field. Although I was never able to continue applying these techniques in Svalbard, I successfully used similar but more advanced techniques in studies of complexly deformed terrains in Scotland, California, Kenya, and Norway. So I didn't come away from those weeks in Svalbard geologically unprepared for the future.

Enough of that! I did abandon the crippled *Miss Mabel* and her crew on the hard in Lerwick and I boarded the steamer for Aberdeen. I did have several hectic days putting my affairs in order before I boarded the *Mauritania* in Southampton on October 9 with a few hours to spare. From the decks of the *Mauritania*, and then, after New York, from highways across the seemingly endless United States, I did watch Polaris, nearly overhead for us in Svalbard, sink nightly in the sky. By the time I reached southern California on the Mexican border, Polaris was resting on the mountaintops to the north. This celestial transition seemed to confirm my flight from the Arctic: indeed, I never really went back. The closest I got was part of one summer in the Alaska Panhandle, two summer field seasons prospecting for iron ore in subarctic Canada, and a motor trip with my wife to Kirkenes, in the far north of Norway. On that trip I crossed the Arctic Circle for the last time.

I remained on the research fellowship at the University of California, Berkeley, until it expired in late 1952, and then accepted a second research fellowship at the University of Edinburgh until 1956. During those three years I worked in the Scottish Highlands and, much too briefly, in Kenya alongside Brian Baker.

Finally I ran out of fellowships and had to work for a living. I was about to accept a lectureship at the University of Edinburgh when a telegram arrived from my old colleague and mentor in Berkeley, Francis J. Turner, offering me an assistant professorship in the Department of Geology and Geophysics. Having almost frozen to death while suffering from a permanent cold during three Edinburgh winters (and, less creditably, because the salary offered by Berkeley was four times as much as Edinburgh thought I was worth) I high-tailed it back to Berkeley. I remained there for the rest of my professional career until I took early retirement in 1989. During those thirty-three years I taught courses in many branches of geology and geophysics and traveled widely, on field and laboratory research, in Canada, Alaska, Central America, Australia, and Switzerland. My geological interests changed with time and I became involved in high pressure and temperature experiments on the deformation and flow of rocks. I also continued with work on the microstructure and texture of experimentally and naturally deformed rock, including study of those infamous "oriental" specimens.

During these years I was lucky enough to be awarded two Guggenheim Fellowships, one in 1962 and the other in 1969. The first I spent partly in Australia at the Australian National University in Canberra, working on experimental folding of rocks with Mervyn Paterson. The rest of that year was spent in a round-the-world junket. During the second fellowship, after I had married, my wife and I spent the year traveling in Europe from the North Cape of Norway to Istanbul while I took hundreds of photographs of rock structures. These were published in book form in Germany in 1972 under the title: *The Minor Structures of Deformed Rocks*.

Looking back, I have to admit that *Miss Mabel* herself played as large a part in my later life as did my geological work in Svalbard. There were two major happenings that I think had roots in the *Miss Mabel* experience. Unlike my colleagues, I did not rush headlong into matrimony after the expedition. Not until December 1964 did I succumb, to Liv, a fair Norwegian, in Norway. We are in our fortieth year together, with two grown children and three grandchildren. Did the two Svalbard expeditions and the time I spent in beautiful Norway have anything to do with this outcome? I like to think they did.

The second major event in my life, which I find hard not to link directly with *Miss Mabel*, occurred after my early retirement in 1989. To be honest it was responsible for my retirement. I have always loved the sea. I spent some of my boyhood in a fishing village in the Thames Estuary where I haunted the tiny harbor, annoying the cockle fishermen by begging to be taken on board. Even the voyage of *Miss Mabel* failed to kill my passion; instead I think it strengthened it. In the 1970s Liv and I bought our first sailboat, a thirty-eight-foot cutter, in which we sailed on San Francisco Bay and up and down the California coast. The windy bay and the hostile central California coast are not places for timorous sailors. Our experiences there, both good and bad, served to show that we didn't suffer from seasickness and that we could confidently handle a fair-sized sailboat together, whatever the conditions; we survived winds and waves that would certainly have finished off *Miss Mabel*.

In the mid-1980s we decided to retire early and try some real ocean cruising. We commissioned a new more serious boat, a forty-three-foot cutter, which we named *Goliard* after the disreputable "wandering scholars" of late medieval Europe. I had always admired goliard poetry, which served as a vital repository of secular culture in a Europe dominated by a powerful and repressive church. Because I was planning to shed my academic stability for oceanic uncertainty, the name seemed appropriate.

In October 1989, *Goliard* sailed under the Golden Gate Bridge at the start of a four-year voyage of about sixteen thousand nautical miles that took us through the Panama Canal to the Caribbean and the East Coast of the United States, to Central and South America, and back to San Francisco. I'm happy to say our experiences on *Goliard* bore no resemblance to those I'd had on *Miss Mabel*, so eloquently and vividly recounted by others in these pages. When I contrast *Goliard*'s navigational amenities (autopilot, radar, satellite navigation, depth sounder, single-sideband transceiver and the like) and her safety equipment (four-man inflatable life raft, emergency radio beacons, spare anchors and cables, and so on) to *Miss Mabel*'s total lack of equipment of any kind, my heart misses a beat. How on earth did we survive? My personal view is that expedition members were in far greater danger aboard *Miss Mabel* than they ever were ashore in Svalbard. But I'm equally of the opinion that, without having suffered that baptism of salt during the disasters aboard *Miss Mabel*, I might never have had the courage (some might say, foolhardiness) to risk my life and that of my beloved wife on such a venture as the voyage of *Goliard*. I suspect I owe my middle-aged recklessness to fragments of youthful naiveté and rashness somehow left over from the voyage of *Miss Mabel* and resurrected in me at the right time later in life. Whatever the truth of the matter, the two experiences remain closely linked in my mind. And in view of the toll that time has subsequently taken on body and mind, I am deeply grateful that life, fate, or whatever it is that decides these things, gave me both opportunities while the going was good.

Goss

In June 2002, the surviving expedition members were lucky enough to be able to meet again for lunch in Stratford-on-Avon. All the living participants came except Lionel, who was stuck in California. All the wives came too—one for each of us—except Liv Weiss and Chris Gossage. Chris had to keep a long-standing appointment with other friends, to watch the Eastbourne tennis tournament. We missed her at the lunch and were mortified to learn the following day that, after watching the tennis, Chris had gone home with her friends and that night had died in her sleep. Poor old Goss! What a blow!

Goss's contribution, as expected, was yet another gem. He wrote:

How did Spitsbergen 1951 affect my life? In an aesthetic and spiritual sense, profoundly, but as to practicalities, here goes. Shortly after returning to the U.K. from Spitsbergen I found myself doing my two years of National Service in the British Army. I wanted, if possible, to become an officer. Those who select soldiers for officer training look for several important qualities in their candidates, most of which I did not possess. No doubt two of the listed qualities are (1) willingness to accept discomfort and pain over substantial lengths of time, and (2) a relaxed attitude towards the taking of obvious risks. When, at my interview, I spoke of my recent arctic experiences, all my inadequacies were overlooked and I was sent on to officer training school.

Immediately after my time as a National Service Army officer I was taken on by Shell, the major international oil company, as an exploration geologist. Interviews took place while I was still a soldier. Most of the required qualities were the same as for the Army. When I spread out my Spitsbergen sketch maps and notebooks before the seasoned, grizzled, senior oil men, they could quickly see that I had already done a little of what they wanted me to do for my whole career—work geological sequences and structures in unexplored, uncomfortable parts of the world. The day after my army pay ceased I was on the payroll of Shell.

After a year of oil-geological training in The Netherlands and Tunisia, Shell sent me to the new exploration venture they were starting in Turkey, where Chris and I enjoyed five years of exciting expatriate life, for me, intensely interesting. I had lengthy seasons in the field and we both had hectic social activities in the brief winter periods. Over the succeeding thirty-odd years, I worked mainly in seven different countries, from Turkey to Gabon via Kuwait and Libya, and made professional visits to about twenty others, but never again set foot in the Arctic.

Abundant oil has of course been found now in arctic regions, including Alaska and areas where Dave worked on the Canadian Arctic islands. Major oil companies have carried out survey work along the coast of Vestspitsbergen, but nobody yet seems to have started drilling. As for me, I retired from my last job with Shell, in The Hague, in 1986, having spent the last five very busy years there as central office manager for Shell's exploration operations in the Far East and Australasia.

Articulating the aesthetic and spiritual experiences is a bit more difficult and would take time, lots of deep thought, and plenty of experimental writing. Before 1951, I had walked and climbed in mountainous parts of the U.K. and had developed an appreciation and great liking for natural scenery and phenomena, but there you are never far from human habitation: farms, roads, railways, and so on. Spitsbergen was quite different. It was empty, hardly trodden by man, much of it not even seen by man. This was one hundred percent nature, a remote part of the earth that inspired in me some of the same kind of awe that people sometimes feel when they gaze into deep space, whether through a telescope or simply by letting their eyes wander across the sky on a clear quiet night. The awe stayed with me, and even after retiring I have been drawn three times to the Himalayas where I could absorb still more of the magnificence of vast, remote snow- and ice-covered mountains. I had better stop. The subject is too big. I have tried to get closer to it by geological studies, photography, painting, and drawing, and incessant trips into the country, hills, mountains, and the coast. I still go on...

Colin

Our little three-month expedition to Sunny Svalbard was the first of more than twenty expeditions I have made to the polar regions over the last fifty years. In many ways our Spitsbergen adventure was for me the most trivial of them, because I did no scientific work on my own behalf. In masochistic ways and for just plain straightforward fun, it was clearly the most memorable of them all. I've been sopping wet countless times but that was the only occasion I've started the day by wringing icy cold rainwater from the sleeping bag in which I intended to sleep again the following night. I did keep my eyes open and remembered some of the things I had seen on Løvliebreen, Charlesbreen, and on the snowfields at the top of Eidembreen. Later, as I gained more experience with glaciers in other parts of the world, many of the puzzling features we had seen in Vestspitsbergen began to make sense. Løvliebreen was almost stagnant but it still had enough life in it to produce a few sets of crevasses. Why were the crevasses near the top of the glacier nearly all transverse? Why were the ones near the snout mainly longitudinal? In the end, as usual, the explanation turns out to lie in some pretty simple-minded physics. I also learned to be very careful with written accounts of climatic conditions and have never since been on an expedition, even inland in Antarctica, where it never rains, without taking a flysheet for my tent.

Shortly after completing the Svalbard trip I moved to Keith Runcorn's laboratory at the University of Cambridge. The work there was fascinating but frustrating. Soon after Christmas 1951, I heard about the British North Greenland Expedition and I volunteered on the spot. It turned out to be perhaps the last of the old-fashioned British arctic expeditions, where all the scientists wintered over, whether or not they could do any useful work during the cold, dark time. The authorities declared that the work with the expedition would count as "work of national importance," thereby allowing me to escape military National Service. I was accepted as the geophysicist although I had never done any geophysical work of any kind. But, after all, I was a member of the Department of Geophysics at Cambridge. I was accepted entirely because of the Spitsbergen experience. Thus I spent two years, June 1952 to July 1954, with a twenty-five-man group; during the second year, I was also the chief scientist and was expected to keep a distant eye on all the extensive scientific work of the expedition. I had the opportunity to undertake many interesting activities. For the first winter, not yet having the vehicles for my work on the ice sheet, I volunteered as the pastry cook at the main base, on the edge of a lake in Dronning Louise Land, northeast Greenland. I was part of the trio that set the World Record for the Slowest Crossing of Greenland, surveying surface elevations and measuring values of gravity (to estimate ice thickness) from coast to coast. I spent the second winter, eight months of it, at Northice, a three-man station, fourteen feet square, at eight thousand feet elevation on the ice sheet, more than 150 miles from the next nearest human. I was the weather observer and also worked with Hal Lister on his glaciology studies in a fifty-five-foot deep pit that we dug. The temperature outside dropped to −90 degrees Fahrenheit.

When we went to Svalbard only Phil was married. By the time I returned from Greenland, every member except Lionel, Goss, and I were married, and Goss was getting married to Chris at Christmas, 1954. Phil and Joy invited us all to Goss's prenuptial party. Lionel couldn't come so I was the only uncommitted male and Phil's younger sister, Gillian, an art school student, was the only unattached female. Joy made a cake based on a map of Vestspitsbergen, and Gillian tried her hand at the world-famous cheesey-eggy-oatey dish and Goss's bread pudding. Gillian and I were married in 1956 and moved to New Zealand.

In those days New Zealand was the finest place to live, and the worst place imaginable to try to conduct laboratory scientific research. There was scarcely any money to buy equipment so that, if you couldn't make it yourself, you did without. After two years of frustration with laboratory geophysics and solid-state physics efforts, I despaired, and decided instead to try to organize a university expedition to the Antarctic continent, the first ever, aided very considerably by Bob Clarke, the professor of geology, who had been to the Antarctic for a few days as a visitor.

Our first four-man expedition was in many ways very similar to the Svalbard one. In begging our supplies all my letters shook my memory by starting out:

> Dear Sir, [If I could not find the name of the managing director],
>
> I write on behalf of the Victoria University of Wellington Antarctic Expedition, 1958–59. This expedition intends to leave this country...

That expedition, to the Wright and Victoria Valleys in the ice-free area of south Victoria Land, was a great success. Again it gave me and, I am sure, the other members of the party the inestimable satisfaction of being the first people ever to visit the area. It was the first of a continuing series of expeditions from Victoria University of Wellington, now numbering forty or more. I organized the next one, in 1959–1960, but did not participate because Gillian and I were expecting our second baby in the middle of the field season. However, I did embark on a decade-long endeavor that has had very wide consequences. For that second expedition I reckoned we could have five field members. The first four volunteered quickly and then we waited and waited. The fifth volunteer eventually arrived and was admirable qualified in all respects except one—Dawn was female. This I regarded as a challenge. No woman scientist had ever worked in Antarctica. The other four members agreed to the idea and so did the wives of the two married members. The university felt it would be a great social leap forward. The New Zealand Navy and the government agreed. Everyone was in favor, except the U.S. Navy: we needed their help, with a one-hour helicopter ride from the New Zealand base to the field area and *that* the U.S. Navy refused to allow—adamantly. This struck me as being asinine, and for the next ten years I tried repeatedly to include women in our Antarctic field parties. In the end, for the 1968–1969 summer, the U.S. Navy relented and allowed me to send a four-woman team—as long as they all had Antarctic experience! That was a real challenge but we succeeded! Since then most other nations have followed suit, so that nowadays there are women as doctors, carpenters, radio-scientists, geologists, journalists, and even cooks in the field and at the bases. With some exaggeration I can maintain that I liberated a whole continent for women!

I took part in the next New Zealand Antarctic expedition, in 1960–1961, but not as leader, for the same reason that Lionel had declined the position in 1951. Immediately after that expedition I took up a fifteen-month visiting faculty appointment at The Ohio State University, Columbus, Ohio, to help them establish their Institute of Polar Studies. Being slow learners, perhaps, we stayed there twenty-five years. During the 1960s and early 1970s I organized another ten or so expeditions to Antarctica and a larger number to Alaska, the Yukon, Greenland, and Peru. I took part in the fieldwork of most of these. I did *not* go to Peru, where we were working on the Quelccaya Ice Cap at almost twenty thousand feet elevation. I had become dean of the College of Mathematical and Physical Sciences by then and could not take sufficient time off to acclimatize and do any useful work. However, our younger son did take part and learned the pleasures of digging infinite amounts of snow. I've never been back to Svalbard.

Committee responsibilities seemed to pile up: administrative ones in the university, scientific ones nationally and internationally. Over the years I gathered quite a number of foreign students who wished to pursue glaciological studies with me, including Olav Orheim, who wrote the foreword to this book. I became the U.S. representative on the glaciological panel of the Scientific Committee on Antarctic Research, the international group that coordinates all of the Antarctic research, and was for twelve years the chairman of the panel, I suspect largely because no-one else wanted the job. All the meetings, always in interesting places (except for Columbus), were like old home week because several of the representatives of member countries had been my students. Since retiring in 1986, after thirteen years as dean, I've been back to the Antarctic eight times, as a lecturer (in glaciology, exploration history, poetry, and cooking, among other subjects) on the semi-luxury cruise ships. I accepted these duties largely so that

I could take Gillian along to show her a little of what has fascinated me so much for all these years.

As you see I have a ready answer when people ask me what has been the Spitsbergen expedition's place in the development of my later life and why it has remained so powerfully present throughout my lifetime. I sometimes wonder how my life would have shaped if I had not been to Spitsbergen. Necessarily the experience has also had a huge aesthetic effect on my life but, unlike Goss, I'm not quite ready yet to try to articulate that.

PUBLICATIONS FROM THE 1948, 1951, 1954, AND 1958 EXPEDITIONS

1952. Baker, B. H., Forbes, C. L., and Holland, M. F. W. Fossiliferous strata at Kapp Scania, Daudmansøyra, Vest Spitsbergen. *Geological Magazine* 89: 303–304.

1953. Dineley, D. L. Notes on the genus *Corvaspis*. *Proceedings of the Royal Society of Edinburgh* 65, 166–181.

1953. Weiss, L. E. Tectonic features of the Hecla Hook formation to the south of St. Jonsfjord, Vestspitsbergen. *Geological Magazine* 90: 273–286.

1954. Bowen, R. N. C. Quaternary foraminifera from St. John's Fjord, West Spitsbergen. *Annals and Magazine of Natural History* VII: 737–752. (Studies of the foraminifera from the beach materials collected by Dave.)

1954. Dineley, D. L. Investigations in Vestspitsbergen. *Journal of Glaciology* 2: 379–383.

1954. Dineley, D. L. Quaternary faunas in the St. Jonsfjord-Eidembukta region, Vestspitsbergen. *Norsk Geologisk Tidsskrift* 34: 1–14.

1954. Dineley, D. L. Raised features on the west coast of Vestspitsbergen, *Geographical Journal* 119: 505–508.

1954. Dineley, D. L. Some Devonian fish remains from north central Vestspitsbergen. *Geological Magazine* 92: 255–260. (Dave was good enough to examine the fossils that the University of Cambridge Spitsbergen party had collected in 1951.)

1958. Dineley, D. L. A review of the Carboniferous and Permian rocks of the west coast of Vestspitsbergen. *Norsk Geologiske Tidsskrift* 38: 197–219.

1958. Weiss, L. E. The structure of the Trygghamma-Vermlandsryggen area, Isfjorden. (Appendix to Dineley, 1958, *Norsk Geologiske Tidsskriften* 38: 218–219.)

1959. Dineley, D. L., and Garrett, P. A. Whale remains in glacial ice. *Nature* 183: 272.

1960. Dineley, D. L. The Old Red Sandstone of eastern Ekmanfjorden, Vestspitsbergen. *Geological Magazine* 97: 18–32.

1960. Dineley, D. L., and Waters, R. S. Notes on the recent advance and retreat of Seftstrombreen in Ekmanfjorden, Vestspitsbergen. *Journal of Glaciology* 3: 693–697.

1961. Holland, M. W. F. The geology of certain parts of eastern Spitsbergen. *Norsk Polarinstitutt Skrifter* 122: 1–44.

2000. Nunn, J. F. University of Birmingham Expedition to Spitsbergen, 1948. *Aesculapius* 20: 10–17.

INDEX

Note: numbers in italics refer to illustrations or maps.